Answers for California Gardeners

BY ROBERT SMAUS

Los Angeles Times
B O O K S

Editor: Linda Greer Estrin
Design: Tom Trapnell
Cover and Inside Art: Catherine Deeter

ISBN 1-883792-63-0
Copyright 2002 Los Angeles Times
202 W. First St., Los Angeles, CA 90012

First printing April 2002
Printed in the U.S.A.

Los Angeles Times

Publisher: John P. Puerner
Editor: John S. Carroll
Book Development General Manager: Carla Lazzareschi

Acknowledgments

There are no answers without questions (though not always the other way around), so I must thank all the *Los Angeles Times* readers who have written me during the last 25 years. I regret that some could not be answered, but most were. Every reply was, for me, an excuse to learn more about my favorite pastime, gardening. I also thank all those gardening professionals who helped me come up with answers.

I must thank three other gardeners in particular. Linda Estrin, who also designs the occasional garden for others, carefully edited this book, making it more logical and accurate. The illustrations come from another gardener, Catherine Deeter, whose Central Coast garden has been published. And thanks to my wife, Iris, who kept my garden going while I was busy putting this book together. While it's wonderful to have an editor and an illustrator who understand what you're talking about, it's great knowing someone who can water!

Contents

The Dirt on This Book

🍃 🍃

Background, Caveats and Other Tidbits

WHERE DO YOU TURN when the leaves on your roses look like Swiss cheese, or the buds on the Iceland poppies vanish, or you can't figure out what to grow on that shady, north-facing wall?

You could call your county Master Gardeners hotline. You could peruse a garden book (or search the web), but you'd have to make sure that the information applies to Southern California's rather special climate. Or you could simply sit down and write to the *Los Angeles Times* Garden Q&A, as many have through the years.

The Times first launched the forum with a column called The Garden Doctor during World War II. To help the war effort, many Americans had taken up growing vegetables in their "Victory gardens." It was the first time many people had grown anything at all, and they needed advice. The Garden Doctor was written by a real expert, Howard Wilcomb, deputy Los Angeles County agricultural commissioner in charge of the insect control division. After the war was over, *The Times* continued to publish The Garden Doctor, and, in 1964, Paul B. Engler, the county agricultural commissioner, another expert, stepped in.

In 1972 I began writing garden articles for *The Times*. Fifteen years later I took over The Garden Doctor, renaming it Garden Q&A, since I didn't feel much like a doctor, and I wasn't an expert—just a respectably good gardener. However, I never hesitated to call on true experts—from growers to researchers to designers, noted authorities on Southern California horticulture. As much as readers wanted a real answer from a real pro, so did I.

While I was garden editor, the newspaper typically received just under 100 questions a month, though only a small portion could be answered in Garden Q&A. Maybe a question had already been answered in the column, or it was too specific. I tried to answer those with the broadest appeal, choosing common or particularly perplexing problems. But I never lacked for reader pleas for advice. Often questions in Q&A formats are made up (one of journalism's dark secrets); Garden Q&As never were.

As the years passed, the column changed. Engler once wrote about his tenure, noting that most of the early questions had to do with vegetable gardens and that the most frequently asked question was about leaf margins turning brown. On my shift, vegetables were still a popular topic, but citrus was far and away the biggest subject of interest.

Taken as a whole, the Garden Q&A column could be said to chronicle the unique concerns of Southern California gardeners in the 1980s and 1990s. Indeed, most of the answers to questions posed by *Times* readers would never be found in a typical garden book. What you find here is quite specific to Southern California's mild Mediterranean climate. Remember that we garden in a place like no other in the country, where we can grow plants that can't be grown elsewhere, on an entirely different timetable.

This book is a compilation of published *Los Angeles Times* Garden Q&As, each of which retains the question-and-answer format. Also included are the articles most frequently requested for reprint since the publication of my previous book, *52 Weeks in the California Garden* (Los Angeles Times, 1996; updated in 2000 and furnished with an index). Where material in *52 Weeks* can supplement information here, it is so noted.

Wherever appropriate, answers have been updated to reflect current research and practices. Specifically, this includes all references to chemical controls. I mention only the chemical controls that are known to work in the case at hand and that are registered by the state for that use. However, I give preference to nonchemical means of dealing with gardening problems, sometimes even suggesting that no problem exists. I can vouch for most of the nonchemical alternative controls because I use or have tried them in my own garden, which is none the worse for wear.

The answers to some questions in this book may seem a bit obvious. But there are all levels of gardeners, from novice to sage. I can still remember some of my early questions—they must have caused many sly smiles among more advanced gardeners. And we can only thank the beginners who pose the questions we are afraid to ask, for fear of looking foolish—like "Can I pour salt on snails to kill them?"

In gardening there are no dumb questions.

How Should I Do This?

🍃 🍃

Proper Garden Techniques

G OOD GARDENS ARE BUILT from the ground up. The soil in which a garden grows is so important that gardeners are reluctant to call it dirt, which, of course, it is. But *dirt* implies nothing has been done. Avid gardeners spend hours working on and improving their generic dirt until it becomes their soil.

Some of my most enjoyable moments in the garden have been spent playing in the dirt. Think me odd if you will, but I vividly remember the first bed I improved many years ago with thoroughly decayed mushroom compost. I had discovered the compost at an abandoned mushroom farm and brought it home in a beat-up old Volvo wagon. I remember how the earth felt between my fingers when I was done, how it smelled (talk about "bouquet") and how rich and fluffy the bed looked—like a big, brown feather coverlet.

I can remember the sweat and hours spent digging and turning the soil so all of that compost was thoroughly mixed in. But who said raising a garden was supposed to be easy? And the flowers, the vegetables that resulted! Good soils truly do make great gardens.

I still have the garden spade I used. Every time I get it out, I remember all the beds prepared and all the soil turned. Soil tends to separate the men from the boys in the world of gardening. How much time and effort you are willing to spend on your dirt relates directly to how well your garden grows. Instead of looking for green thumbs on good gardeners, look for dirt packed in the cracked, chapped skin of palms and fingers. Some do wear gloves, but most like the feel of dirt between their fingers, mixing and planting with bare hands and small hand tools.

Don't think those who garden in containers somehow escape all this work. Good container gardens also require lots of work on the soil, even if it is an artificial medium that came out of a sack. Avid gardeners add to it, change it frequently and spend hours evaluating and looking for superior mixes.

Time after time, while visiting gorgeous gardens for television or the newspa-

3

per, I have been impressed by the dirt-cracked hands of the gardeners and the work they spent on improving the soil, whether in the ground or containers. Driving up to the elegant Pasadena arroyo garden of Amanda Goodan, I found her dragging off huge, immensely heavy bags of granite turkey grit, which she adds to her potting mixes to speed drainage in the containers where she grows lots of tricky plants. In the garden beds she doesn't simply scatter fertilizer everywhere; she religiously and laboriously spreads a two-inch layer of compost on the soil twice a year, tucking it among all the deliriously happy plants.

Across town, in Pacific Palisades, Lew Whitney (of Roger's Garden in Corona del Mar) turned an unbelievably bad clay into a truly amazing soil by adding a combination of things that would seem to defy logic, such as pea gravel. He clearly knows his soil and how to deal with it.

On the ancient sand dunes of Manhattan Beach, Susan Rudnicki had the opposite problem—too sandy a soil. In her lovely, plant-packed garden, everything from fallen leaves to orange peels goes into the compost piles or the worm bins, which her young son gleefully helps tend. The first time I visited, I found them with their arms up to the elbows in the piles. They were fishing out worms from the bins and making sure that everything was simmering properly. When Rudnicki first started on this sandy plot, she had brought in truckloads, not bags full, of a commercially available homemade compost.

Catherine Ratner struck rock about two inches under the sloping surface of her Palos Verdes property. Upon my arrival, she had "before" photos of the white shale (called Palos Verdes stone when it is used to pave patios) spread out on her breakfast table. "These are my excuse," she said, but she needed none. Her garden is one of the most floriferous in Southern California. It occurred to me that the best gardeners seem to get the worst dirt, but that maybe it's the dirt that forces them to garden greatness.

Notions about what constitutes a good soil have changed since I began gardening. Now it is thought that soils outside of intensely cultivated garden beds should perhaps be left alone, that trees and large shrubs do better in undisturbed, unimproved native soils. Of course, that's assuming you *have* a native soil, since many new homes carved from hillsides have nothing even resembling soil.

Purely chemical fertilizers have also become suspect, as well they should, since the consequences of adding anything unnatural to a garden should always be scrutinized, though nearly all kinds of fertilizers have their uses. In an ideal garden, litter would accumulate as it does on a forest floor or under the dry chaparral until it decays and adds its substance to the soil. Wherever possible, this is how nutrients (what people call fertilizers) should be returned to the soil. When a natural accumulation isn't appropriate or possible, compost piles and mulches can do the job. A compost pile continually stews in one corner of my garden, with only the thorniest or heftiest of branches ending up on the curb in the green waste–recycling barrel.

Do not believe those ads in magazines and on television that suggest fertilizer is the secret to gardening. Baloney! Fertilizers can help, but in my own garden, I have used very little fertilizer in the last 25 or so years. Even then, I have had minor problems with *too much* fertilizer in the soil, never too little.

Good Soil, Great Garden

WHAT A TEST WILL TELL

Why were my friend's tomatoes so small? 'Early Girl' is not a large tomato, but those from his north Orange County garden were not much bigger than cherry tomatoes. Another friend in Culver City decided to put in a new vegetable garden. She and her husband laboriously broke up a concrete slab behind the garage, under which they found bricklike clay. But what was the black-and-red stuff on top of the soil? Was it something that might be harmful?

I couldn't answer these questions, but an analysis of the soil probably could. I decided to have my friends scoop up soil for me to take to a test facility. While I was at it, I would gather a little soil from my own West Los Angeles garden, from one of the older flower beds where the soil looked great but had been in use for more than 10 years. Back then, I had had it tested by Soil and Plant Laboratory in Santa Ana. The report determined it was a good sandy clay loam that needed additional organic matter and nitrogen, the main ingredient in fertilizers. I'd been adding these ever since. Had it made a difference?

Few gardeners have their soil tested—though farmers frequently do, as do some landscape contractors. However, because so much depends on the soil, from plant growth to disease resistance, it's a good idea to find out as much as you can about your soil. A printed report gives you a little science to go with your gardening hunches. To find one of the several soil laboratories in Southern California, look in the telephone book under Soil Testing.

Soil scientist Garn Wallace of Wallace Laboratories, a soil consulting and testing firm in El Segundo, would do the testing this time. At the lab, the soil samples were sifted through a fine screen and made into a slurry to test different contents and characteristics. A sophisticated $150,000 spectrometer examined 30 elements, including mercury and lead. The lab then made recommendations on how to improve the soil.

My Culver City friend was relieved to find she did not have an inordinate amount of toxic chemicals in her prospective vegetable bed, though she and I had noticeable amounts of lead and arsenic. Although the levels were well below those considered safe for leaf and root crops, this news was unsettling nonetheless because we are both careful, mostly organic gardeners.

Wallace wasn't surprised, though, noting that soils in all the older parts of town, from Santa Monica to East Los Angeles, contain some lead and arsenic. Lead has built up through the years—from leaded gasoline fumes, house paints, fertilizers, herbicides and soil amendments. My garden and the Culver City garden had about 8 parts per million of lead, while the newer Orange County garden had only .42. "We flag lead at 30 parts per million for being excessive for edible root, stem and leaf crops," Wallace says.

Equally surprising, my Orange County friend and I discovered that we had slightly acidic soils, right here in the alkaline West. Dead neutral is 7. Mine had a pH of 6.28, while his was 5.63. (Note that the pH scale is logarithmic, so a 5.6 is 10 times more acidic than a 6.6.) Running from an acid 0 to an alkaline 14, 6.5 is often given as ideal for soils, though Wallace says this actually depends on soil type. A level of 7.5 might be ideal in a clay soil, 5.5 ideal in sandy soil. My friend in Orange County, by using complete fertilizers and fertilizing about four or five times a year, had made the soil acidic.

The Orange County garden report also found the soil too high in fertilizer elements and too salty. Most Western soils are already high in two fertilizer elements, phosphorus and potassium, so California gardeners seldom need to add either, yet both come packaged in many fertilizers. To give an example of how excesses can build up: The phosphorus level in my garden was 71 parts per million, and in the newly uncovered Culver City garden, 36 parts per million. Optimum is 4 to 7, so there was already plenty of phosphorus even in the Culver City ground. The overfed Orange County garden had 127 parts per million. Ditto with potassium. We had 142 and 92, respectively—with 60 to 120 being optimum—while he had 642!

Each fertilizer source brings with it a little mineral salt. For instance, potassium from muriate of potash, cheap and common in fertilizers, is saltier than potassium derived from potassium nitrate or potassium sulfate (look on the fertilizer package label). Measured as a value called ECe, the two West Los Angeles gardens had little salt, .81 and 1.05, but the Orange County garden had an ECe of 4.65. According to Wallace, an ECe over 4 affects many plants and probably was the reason for the small tomatoes. At this level, he says, the salinity alone would decrease the size and quantity by about 25 percent.

Many packages of fertilizer also contain trace elements, such as iron, boron and zinc. My Orange County friend and I had a little more boron than is deemed desirable.

Over-fertilizing is very common in Southern California. People fertilize plants "as they would feed a baby," Wallace says, thinking that the more they fertilize, the better things grow. But these fertilizer elements build up quickly and can become toxic to plants, actually inhibiting growth. Indeed, fertilizing is often not the cure but the cause of a problem.

Fortunately, salts and some of the excessive fertilizer can be leached from the soil. A good rainy year helps, as will putting about six inches of water on the garden inside of about a week, which is what Wallace recommends. That amount will push salts below the level of most roots, removing about 90 percent. This should be a job seldom done; otherwise all the fertilizer elements are washed out.

Unfortunately, lead, arsenic and other heavy metals cannot be leached. The only way to get rid of heavy metals is to remove the soil—another good reason always to check fertilizer labels carefully and not add any more than necessary. Organic matter incorporated into the soil binds with heavy metals so they don't get absorbed by most vegetables, although they remain when the organic matter decomposes.

Wallace recommended that the Orange County gardener back off on the fertilizing, leach the soil and then amend it to increase aeration and drainage. He suggested that my friend with the new vegetable garden add gypsum and then leach to remove sodium, which was a little high in her plot. The suggestion for my old garden bed was to stay away from fertilizers with trace elements, even organic kinds, and aim for a more neutral pH. I actually had to add lime or calcium carbonate (in very small amounts—two or three pounds per 1,000 square feet) to the soil, just as an East Coast gardener would.

Though the science behind soils is very complicated, all of Wallace's suggestions for the three gardens mentioned here were specific and easy to follow. Your soil needs would probably be quite different. Most soils need at least some fine-tuning, and a test can tell you exactly the reasons why and how to proceed.

SOIL BUILDERS: CAN I ADD SAND?

Q: Can I add sand to the soil if I have a heavy clay with poor drainage?
—M.K., LAGUNA NIGUEL

A: Adding sand to a clay soil is similar to adding sand to cement, a combination that makes concrete. Clay is made up of tiny soil particles that cling together much as cement does. Concrete is about four or five parts sand to one part cement. To keep a clay soil from turning into cement, you would need to add a lot of sand

and then thoroughly mix everything together. "The soil would have to be 80 percent to 90 percent sand to do any good," says soil scientist Garn Wallace.

According to Wallace, the easiest and best means for a gardener to improve a soil's tilth and drainage is to add homemade compost, which is why everyone should have a compost pile cooking in the back yard. (The very best method, he says, is to grow a special kind of plant, or green manure, that is then tilled into the soil, although this is not a terribly practical, or speedy, approach in garden beds where space is at a premium.) Other amendments are peat moss, mushroom compost and any of the various products made of ground bark and wood products sold by the bag at nurseries. Unfortunately, according to Wallace, "These are almost like adding sand" because you need to use a lot and they decompose so slowly.

Adding gypsum (found at nurseries) is a good idea because it replaces sodium in the soil with calcium and helps the soil "flocculate," says Wallace, meaning that it binds the tiny cementlike clay particles into larger particles so the soil becomes more porous.

To improve clay soil, then, Wallace says: Till in gypsum and compost (or the next-best material), then begin growing plants (any kind), which will improve the soil as they grow. Do not rake up leaves and other debris, but let them form a mulch. As the leaves decay, earthworms will slowly drag additional humus down into the soil. It may take a few years, but the soil will become more manageable.

See Week 46 in 52 Weeks in the California Garden.

IS STEER MANURE AN AMENDMENT?

Q: I cannot get a straight answer from any nurseryperson as to the value of composted steer manure as a mulch or soil amendment. Aware of its high salt content, I have soaked it in a bottomless trash can before use, or rototilled it directly into the soil. Am I inviting eventual problems?

—J.L., ORANGE

A: You are right about the high salt content of steer manure. According to soil scientist Garn Wallace, on a salinity scale, 1 would be a good amount for the garden and 25 would be the amount found in steer manure—it is full of mineral salts, even common table salt (because of salt licks in the feed lots).

Leaching, by soaking or running water through the manure, does remove salts, but it also removes nitrogen, potassium and other nutrients. And you don't want that salt-laden water running into the garden. Mushroom compost, incidentally, contains leached steer manure and hay, among other things.

For building a better soil, use only small amounts of steer manure. According

Steer (and cow) manure is potent stuff, often full of harmful salts.
Use very little in the garden.

to Wallace, you can safely use three cubic feet of steer manure, right out of the bag, per 100 square feet once or twice a year. In other words, you can spread a one-third-inch layer on the soil, till it in and not have to worry—rains and watering will carry the salts away. As a mulch, spread a thin layer of steer manure over the soil, as is commonly done over grass seed. Using any more is inviting problems.

Straight steer manure does add some organic matter and potassium to the soil but little else. For a better range of nutrients, Wallace says, mix it with either chicken manure, which is high in all-important nitrogen, or a sewage sludge–based product (such as Kellogg's Nitrohumus).

But why use steer manure at all? There are much better soil amendments. In Wallace's book, homemade compost is best, especially if nutrient-rich grass clippings are added in the composting process. Next best is alfalfa meal, or alfalfa hay that has been ground into inch-long pieces by running a lawn mower over it. Working like a green manure, it adds texture and nutrients. Then come bagged amendments sold at nurseries; here his favorite is medium-grade peat moss.

And there are better products than steer manure for covering lawn seed, such as Kellogg's Topper, which don't smell nearly as bad.

USING SAWDUST

Q: Is there any way in which sawdust can be used in the garden, or is it detrimental to the plants? Much of my husband's collection comes from plywood, and we hate to throw it out.

—N.B., THOUSAND OAKS

A: That's a logical question, since sawdust is used in some soil amendments and planting mixes, but only after it is thoroughly rotted and composted. Even then, it is not considered as beneficial as other kinds of amendments. Raw sawdust is a nitrogen thief and will steal this all-important nutrient from plants, harming the garden.

I get rid of the small amounts from my table saw by tossing it in the compost pile, adding some powerful, fast-acting source of nitrogen (such as ammonium or calcium nitrate) to help with its decomposition. Many recommend that you add nitrogen even to treated and composted sawdust, in case it's not completely "cooked." Because it sounds as though your husband is generating lots of the stuff, more than you can compost, you'll have to find some other way to use it—but not in the garden.

WHAT ABOUT ASHES?

Q: Are ashes from the fireplace useful in the garden?

—J.B., Lake Forest

A: Wood ashes can be used as a kind of fertilizer, high in potassium (as much as 7 percent), with some phosphorus and lots of calcium. But they can also be toxic to soil microorganisms, so use the ashes with restraint. A light sprinkling (no more than a quarter pound per 100 square feet) can be worked into the soil with a cultivator.

LIME FOR ACIDIC SOIL

Q: Believe it or not, I've been told that my soil is too acidic. It has been suggested I add lime, but what kind? There are several at nurseries.

—B.S., Los Angeles

A: That is surprising—most soils in California are alkaline. On the East Coast, where soils are almost always acidic, adding lime is common, but gardeners here should never add lime unless a soil test has shown that their soil is acidic.

If you do have an acidic soil, you want to add what is often sold as agricultural lime, which contains calcium carbonate from ground oyster shells. I'm sure you were directed to add very little. Don't add dolomite lime because it contains magnesium, which the soil in Southern California already has in abundance.

TOTAL SOIL OVERHAUL

Q: In a 1x20-foot area next to my garage I have planted annuals recommended by the nursery 10 or so times, but they promptly die. Every time I planted new flowers, I changed the soil around each plant. I water frequently but not so the soil is mushy. What am I doing wrong?

—R.W., LA MIRADA

A: I would guess that the soil needs improving—all of it. If you replace the soil only around the new plants, they are still growing in small containers of sorts—the roots stay in those little pockets of soil and do not venture out into the garden soil. Without even the drainage a container and potting soil would provide, they are susceptible to remaining too wet and dying of rots. If your watering misses them, they may dry out. The problems are worse if the bed faces south or west and gets a lot of reflected sunlight and heat.

At the very least, the whole area needs to be dug and the soil—the good amendments and the bad dirt—mixed so it is uniform in texture and content. However, the best thing to do is to improve all the soil. For your 1x20-foot bed, add two 2.5-cubic-foot bags of amendments. Spread out, that should make a three-inch-deep layer. Spade and respade this into the soil until it is thoroughly mixed to a depth of a foot. Do this job when the soil is moist and crumbles easily, not when it is dry or wet.

If yours is a clay soil, sprinkle on gypsum (found at nurseries), and work that into the soil along with the amendments. It's also a good idea, in any soil, to mix in a general-purpose fertilizer. Organic fertilizers are your best bet at planting time.

Close to the foundation of a building, there is the chance that when it was built, painted or stuccoed, something was left over in the soil that could affect plant growth. If in doubt, have the soil tested by a soil-testing laboratory.

When planting annuals, make sure that the base of each plant is not covered by soil. I've seen lots of annuals die because just a little extra soil had been pushed up against their stems. After planting, over the next couple of weeks, carefully water every plant. Do not let them dry out for even a minute. Once the roots are out into the soil, water less frequently, but apply enough each time to wet the soil to a depth of at least a foot. Watering often and to a depth of only an inch or so increases the likelihood of rotting.

See Week 38 in 52 Weeks in the California Garden.

THERE IS SUCH A THING AS A FREE MULCH

Q: I plan to use the shredded wood that city workers collect after they trim city trees. It's free! I have read, though, that putting untreated wood products on the ground attracts termites and other pests. Do you have any advice on treating wood used as a mulch, and do you feel using it is a risk?

—D.H., MORENO VALLEY

A: The benefits of using organic mulches far outweigh any problems. Organic mulches inhibit weeds, conserve moisture, moderate soil temperatures, reduce erosion from irrigation and rain, improve soil structure and, as they decompose, add nutrients. You have access to the best kind of organic mulch—shredded tree trimmings. The source of the wood mulch is of minor importance—even eucalyptus works fine, according to the Ventura County UC Cooperative Extension, which has done considerable research on mulches.

However, mulches do attract bugs. "They're broiling with them," says Ben Faber, a Cooperative Extension specialist who participated in the research. This is not a bad thing—it's necessary, in fact, for the mulch to break down.

What you want to do is mulch around permanent plants, such as perennials, shrubs and trees, not near temporary plants, such as lettuce. Little creatures such as slugs, pill bugs and earwigs eat only soft-leaved or decaying plants, doing little or nothing to permanent garden fixtures.

In my own mulched garden, only tiny slugs are any problem and only on certain vegetables that happen to be in raised beds surrounded by mulched paths. The UC Cooperative Extension research found that rough mulches actually discourage snails.

As for termites, I have never heard of mulches attracting them.

The word *untreated* here means that wood products have had no nitrogen added to them; this is perhaps what you read about. Incorporated into beds, wood products tend to steal nitrogen from the soil to use in the decomposition process, unless they have been treated with added nitrogen. If mulch is lying on the surface, though, it won't steal much. You can easily compensate for this by sprinkling a little inexpensive, all-purpose granular fertilizer on top.

❀ ❀ ❀

Tools: A Primer

SPADES AND SHOVELS

A shovel is not a spade, and a spade is not a shovel. Gardeners frequently confuse the two, trying to prepare soil with a shovel or dig a big hole with a spade. In the process, they make things tougher for themselves than need be.

A shovel is for lifting and moving heavy quantities of soil, especially if dirt is to be flung overhead. A shovel has sloping sides that keep the dirt from falling out, and the curved leading edge is easier to push into the ground. (Another kind of shovel, with turned-up sides but a flat bottom and straight edge, is for scooping—not digging.) A shovel can be used to mix or move potting soil or cement, but it does a sloppy job of soil preparation.

A spade, on the other hand, is a gardener's best friend. With an almost-flat face, it has a leading edge that is straight or slightly rounded, not sharply curved. Every Southern California gardener should have one—do not make do with only the lowly shovel. A spade can shovel in a pinch, but it has more important tasks. First, it does a precise, neat job of soil preparation (breaking up and turning the soil). And it is the tool of choice for digging up and dividing perennials and other clump-forming plants.

A spade has a close cousin in the spading fork. While the spade can be used to cut and smash dirt clods, the fork is used to mix in soil amendments. Spading forks have sturdy square or flattened tines, not rounded tines like those of pitchforks. Lean back on a pitchfork, and it bends; do the same with a square-tined spading fork, and it resists. You can work in garden beds using only a spading fork, turning the soil and adding compost each time you replant.

English gardeners would never be without their spades close at hand because they grow so many clumping plants in their spectacular perennial borders—from asters to zephyr flowers. As such, the English also make the sturdiest spades and spading forks. Forged from solid planks of steel, these tools are almost impossible to bend or break because there are no welds or rivets and the steel is so thick.

These may be a little heavy for some gardeners. If so, look for the so-called border spades and forks, which are smaller and easier to manage. American-made spades, usually lighter than the English-made, have rather short blades and do not

THE RIGHT TOOL FOR THE JOB			
	Shovel	**Spade**	**Spading Fork**
Appearance	Face has sloping sides; leading edge is curved	Face is almost flat; leading edge is straight or slightly rounded	Tines are sturdy and square or flattened
Uses	Lifting and moving heavier quantities of soil; mixing potting soil or cement	Breaking up and turning soil; digging up and dividing perennials	Mixing in soil amendments and compost

take an edge as well. My own spade is American-made (though I use an English border fork). Seldom out of reach, my spade is so used and worn that the blade is nearly two inches shorter than when I bought it 35 years ago.

Lots of gardeners don't realize that the leading edge of a newly purchased spade may not have been sharpened (for safety reasons in shipping and handling). A sharp edge is important. To sharpen it, hold the blade steady—stand on it if you must. Using a rough bastard file (any hardware store should have them), file away until the edge is slightly sharp, like an ax blade. If you can't do it yourself, get someone to do it for you.

To use a spade to prepare soil for planting, push the tool down, lean back on the handle, and flip the soil onto its side. The sharpened edge cuts into the soil, slicing small roots that are in the way. Smash clods with the spade's flat back side, or slice them with the sharp edge.

To use a spade for digging and dividing perennial and other clump-forming plants, loosen and leverage the plant out of the ground with the spade's flat blade, then plunge its sharp edge through the clump, splitting it cleanly into smaller parts. Sometimes you can pry apart roots, but more often it's easier to cut them apart. You could divide perennial plants with a shovel, digging up the plant, then cutting up the clump with a serrated kitchen knife. But using a sharpened spade is much faster.

The second half of November and all of December are the perfect time to split apart overly large clumping plants. Many clumping plants, such as agapanthus or fortnight lilies (*Dietes*), should be divided every few years. Even bird of paradise benefits from division, though this can be an arduous job because of its massive ball of roots.

Spades and spading forks can be difficult to find at garden centers—you might have to buy through the web or a catalog. Choose the handle that will feel most comfortable; it has a lot to do with your height. Short D-handles may be easier to use; long straight handles may give more leverage.

TOOL MAINTENANCE

Once, while turning new soil, I leaned back into my favorite spading fork and snapped the handle right at the ferrule. I searched for a replacement at my neighborhood Orchard Supply Hardware, which normally has an unusually large selection, but couldn't find one. So I took it to Bob Denman down in the city of Orange.

Denman loves tools, and he's an expert on the subject—he's a real tool man. A consultant for Corona, which makes tough pruning tools here in Southern California, he also has his own garden tool company. Denman & Co. specializes in sturdy or unusual garden tools, with more than 500 different kinds. The company makes some, including a beautiful old-fashioned push mower with an oak T-handle and a rugged wheel hoe called the Red Pig No. 1. They also repair and sharpen garden tools.

My fork came back looking brand new, and I had to check for the bent tine to make sure it really was mine—he had cleaned and painted it besides replacing the handle. It was almost too pretty to take out of the garage.

I suspected the handle had snapped because I hadn't properly cared for this trusty old fork, so I decided to ask the tool man for some tips on tool maintenance.

Digging Tools

Spades, forks, hoes, rakes and other big garden tools are the easiest to care for, the handles requiring the most attention. After a tool is a year or so old, the varnish begins to wear off. At that time, Denman says, sand the handle and protect it with a finish of boiled linseed oil, available at any hardware or paint store. This will keep it from drying out and splitting.

Wipe the linseed oil over the handle with a rag and let it soak in. If the handle is old and dried-out, apply several coats, waiting for each one to soak in. Wipe off any excess, then let the tool sit overnight and dry.

Once a year—usually in winter when the tools aren't being used that much (except for planting roses)—lightly sand and reapply linseed oil to every wood handle. While you're at it, thoroughly clean the blades or tines with steel wool. Tools used frequently may stay shiny clean, but seldom-used tools rust. To bring them back to new, clean and then paint them.

Paint is the best protection against rust and doesn't attract dirt, as oil does—WD-40 lasts only a few days. Denman uses Rustoleum rustproof primer, followed by a coat of Rustoleum green or red.

Then sharpen the bottom edges of spades and hoes. If they're dull, use a bastard file. Only file the inside of the edge. If you're always digging through tree roots or in rocky soil, a steep bevel (about 40 degrees) will hold up. A shallow bevel (about 20 degrees) makes digging easy, but the tool will need sharpening more often in root-filled or rocky soil. (A bevel is the angle formed by the sides that meet to form the edge, with a shallow bevel shaped like a razor blade and a steep bevel more like the edge of an ax.)

Always file by pushing away from yourself and the blade, so you don't get cut.

Keep the bottom edges of your tools sharp with a small coarse- or medium-grit diamond file. These files, Denman warns, are "very aggressive" and remove material quickly, so take only a few swipes to hone the edges at the end of each workday.

Pruners

For pruning tools the maintenance is a little move involved; there's sharpening, tightening the bolts, cleaning and lubricating. Sharpening is most important, though, because a neat, clean cut that doesn't tear bark heals quickly. For this job, Denman suggests using a diamond file with a fine grit. With a tiny file that fits in your pruning-shear holster, he says, you'll be able to take a few swipes on the blade at the end of every workday, so the shears are always sharp.

Small flat diamond files work fine, but tapered round ones are even better, especially on shears that have a narrow opening at their base. Just be careful not to file circular grooves into the blade edge. If you're new to filing, stick with a small flat file. Denman favors one just a few inches long that costs about $8.

For a bypass pruner, file only the existing bevel on the one slicing blade. Try to match the bevel put on by the manufacturer (it varies from shear to shear). For instance, Felcos have a shallow bevel (about 22 degrees), because the very edge of the blade is extra hard (at some point you will file through this hardened edge into softer metal and will have to replace the blade, but they are available separately). Coronas have a steeper bevel, about 30 degrees (though newer Coronas have 26-degree bevels).

Never sharpen the flat back side of the cutting blade. Also, never sharpen the hook, or opposing blade. Simply clean it thoroughly. It very important to keep clean the parts of the blade that pass by each other.

An anvil pruner is much more difficult to sharpen because the blade must end up not only sharp but very straight. Usually these tools must be taken apart completely for sharpening. This is one reason serious gardeners seldom use them.

On a bypass pruner, always keep the bolt that holds the blades together tight so there is no space between them. Tighten the bolt all the way, then back off a bit so the pruner closes smoothly. Each shear is adjusted differently, though. Denman says the new Coronas are designed to be easy to tighten. Felcos and older Coronas are more difficult, but it's still a step you can't skip.

Finally, thoroughly clean and lubricate the blades. Denman suggests a "miracle juice" developed in Southern California for the military called Break Free CLP, if you buy it at a gun or hardware store, or Corona CLP, if you find it at a nursery. It contains a solvent that cleans sap and rust from the blades, lubricates them and leaves a light film of protective grease to guard against rust. It uses a synthetic oil that does not attract dirt as regular oil does, but actually repels it.

With shears clean, tight and sharp, you're ready to prune the roses, and with your spiffed-up spade to dig in the flower bed.

Denman & Co., 401 West Chapman Avenue, Orange, CA 92866-1307; telephone 714.639.8106.

❦ ❦ ❦

Planting Tips

STARTING SEED—AN INSIDE JOB?

Q: In one of your columns you suggested starting seeds in flats, then moving them to larger containers before planting. Can't I start seeds right in the ground?

—S.S., GRANADA HILLS

A: Most certainly. In fact, a case could be made that all plants grow stronger when sown where they are to grow, even trees. Revegetation projects increasingly employ the direct seeding of trees, shrubs and perennials—a particularly valuable technique in arid climates such as ours. Unhampered by a container, tap roots quickly dive deep in search of water, firmly anchoring and establishing the plant.

However, for a gardener's purposes, sowing in the ground or in containers is really determined by the situation. Often it's easier to start seed in containers, and there are other advantages as well. If you have a small garden (as I do), you can begin one crop before the other is finished, before there is room in the garden. For instance, I may have winter vegetables waiting in their small containers while summer's stragglers are finishing up.

If you are plagued by slugs or snails, starting seeds in containers keeps seedlings up out of harm's way. Many people complain that their garden-planted seed didn't germinate when, in fact, seedlings were simply munched overnight. You can give seeds in flats or other containers a better soil, and they're easier to keep watered. And you can better control their environment by moving them to warmer or cooler places or giving them more or less shade.

Most flowers transplant easily, but some grow so readily from seed sown in the ground that transplanting makes little sense. In the fall, sweet alyssum, red flax, crimson Flanders poppy and larkspur are several best sown in the ground. In summer, marigold, nasturtium, nicotiana and zinnia are especially easy.

California wildflowers, which are planted in October and November, are best sown directly in the ground, though the seed must be protected with bird netting propped up on short twigs or stakes (remove after seedlings are several inches tall). Few transplant well; plants bought at nurseries usually don't take.

Some vegetables must be started in the ground because they transplant poorly—carrots, beets and cucumbers, for instance. On the other hand, broccoli and cauliflower tend to lean if they are not transplanted, placed a little deeper than they were in the pot so they stand straight.

See Week 32 in 52 Weeks in the California Garden.

SOWING MINUSCULE SEED

Q: Do you have any tips on planting small seeds, as in turnips?
—D.H., TORRANCE

A: Many gadgets are sold for planting small seeds, but I have yet to find one that works as well as simply mixing the seed with sand. The seed is easier to handle this way and much more visible, whether you are planting in rows in trays or pots, or are scattering seed over the ground. Thoroughly mix the seed with a small amount of fine-grained, even sand, such as the white silica sand sold for children's sandboxes.

PLANT HIGH, OR IT'S THE DEEP SIX

Q: Don't trees in the forest get buried by leaf litter? I'm moving a potted Japanese maple into a deeper container; can I plant it deeper?
—R.P., BEVERLY HILLS

A: Actually, trees in the forest tend to push themselves out of the soil, their bases, or crowns, remaining above ground.

A basic rule of gardening is: When planting or replanting anything, never bury the base. Doing so is sure death for even a pansy, and trees are far more susceptible to the rots and other diseases that attack the bases of plants. Always plant so that the base ends up slightly above ground level (a quarter inch or so for bedding plants, an inch for plants in gallon cans), never below. The only exceptions I know of are tomatoes and cole crops (members of the cabbage family, such as broccoli and cauliflower). Buried a little deeper, seedlings of these annual vegetables will root along their stems and stand straighter.

Having been planted too deep was found to be one of the leading causes of death for camellias and azaleas, citrus and even the tough plants used to landscape our freeways. This is the reason that, a decade ago, the planting-hole depth recommendations were changed. Now it is suggested that a hole be dug only as deep as the root ball of the plant. If the soil beneath the plant is not disturbed, it is less likely to compact or settle, and the crown will not sink with time.

In a container, the crown of a plant may also eventually end up deeper than before. When this happens, take the plant out and add soil to the bottom of pot. Do not add to the surface soil unless roots are actually exposed. Even then, cover the roots barely, or not at all if you might also cover the base of the trunk.

❦ ❦ ❦

Watering: Getting It Right

BRAND-NEW PLANTS

Q: I planted three bougainvillea and several salvias, then watered with B_{12}. A week later, the leaves were drooping and the soil still seemed wet. What's wrong?
—N.O., WOODLAND HILLS

A: The efficacy of vitamin B_{12} is a myth that dies hard. Decades ago it was shown to have no effect on the establishment of plants, though it does force gardeners to water new plantings thoroughly, which is a good thing.

Your plants have simply dried out. Even though the soil around the new plants may be wet, the potting mix in the root ball is dry. This is a common problem in winter when natural soils may take weeks to dry, but potting soils can dry in days (especially during Santa Ana winds). To check the root ball, push your finger inside. Use this as a guide to tell you when to water.

When getting ready to put new plants in the ground, here are some tips for getting them off to a good start:

• Several days in advance, water the ground, so it is moist, not bone dry, at planting time.

• The day before planting, thoroughly water new plants in their containers, so plants are well hydrated.

• After planting, mound up little watering basins around plants to help funnel water to their root balls. Break these down during rainy weather so plants don't drown.

• To gauge when new plants need watering, always check the root balls, not the surrounding soil.

Although over-watering may be the number-one killer of plants in California, it is almost impossible to over-water brand-new plantings for the first few days or weeks (as long as your soil has decent drainage and planting holes don't hold water like a bathtub). Remember that at first the roots are confined in that tiny, fast-draining root ball, and they need several weeks or more to grow out into the soil.

HOW TO IRRIGATE HILLSIDES

Q: What's the best way to water a small but heavily planted hillside? Right now I'm doing the whole job by hand, although I did find an old Rainbird sprinkler in a corner.

—C.Z., SILVER LAKE

A: That old pulsating sprinkler may certainly be the easiest way to water the hillside, but the newer low-gallonage versions put water on so slowly that it soaks in rather than running down the hill. Space them up to 50 feet apart—one in each corner of the hillside should cover the area. Put them on top of staked risers (use pipes) tall enough so they spray above the shrubbery, and water when there's no wind.

The best way to water hillsides, though, is with drip irrigation, which produces no runoff. Lay out parallel lines "that look like sheet music," says irrigation expert Robert Kourik, author of "Drip Irrigation" (Metamorphic Press), with a single supply line going up one side of the yard. On heavy soils, space the tubing up to 24 inches apart; on sandy soils, they must be 12 inches apart. Use pressure-compensating emitters, which even out the flow between the top and bottom of the hill. Kourik recommends in-line emitters, which are built into the tubing. Several good books, including the one by Kourik, detail how to install drip systems.

Drip Irrigation, *by Robert Kourik, is available through Metamorphic Press, PO Box 1841, Santa Rosa, CA 95402; telephone 707.874.2606.*

GRAY WATER IS SAFE, IF ...

Q: I propose supplementing the watering of my citrus trees with gray water, which will come from the shower and bathroom sink. Is there any downside to this proposal, and can you suggest a disinfectant I should add to the holding tank?

—R.W., LOS ANGELES

A: Though technically governed by what many consider burdensome, expensive and questionable codes, gray-water use from the shower and bathroom sink shouldn't pose any problems, according to Kourik, author also of *Gray Water Use in the Landscape* (Metamorphic Press).

He cautions, however, against holding tanks, which often become "smelly and septic." Rather, let the gray water run straight into the garden and keep moving the hose around so it can't puddle. There is no such thing as a disinfectant for gray water, and it's not needed as long as the water soaks quickly into the ground.

Water from the shower and sink is slightly alkaline, but a good soaking every few years from rains or municipal water should flush out excess alkalinity. Kourik suggests keeping a three- to five-inch-thick mulch on areas being irrigated with gray water.

Gray Water Use in the Landscape, *by Robert Kourik, is available through Metamorphic Press, PO Box 1841, Santa Rosa, CA 95402; telephone 707.874.2606.*

GREEN WITH ALGAE

Q: What can I do about the green color showing up on my soil? It is quite pervasive. Is there anything I can do to help the soil? Also, my yard is quite shady, so how much should I water?

—E.C., ENCINO

A: You have almost answered your first question by mentioning how shady your garden is. The green color on your soil is an algae—microscopic organisms lacking roots, stems or leaves—similar to the algae that grow on the sides of trees and flowerpots.

In the shady glades at Descanso Gardens, in La Cañada Flintridge, sand is thrown down to keep algae-covered paths from becoming slippery. Otherwise, says director Richard Schulhof, "Consider it a beautiful part of a cool, moist garden." It certainly won't hurt the soil or the bark of trees.

Though it is said that wettable sulfur or copper fungicides will control algae on trees and soil, I am unaware of any product being labeled for that use, and treatments would have only temporary results.

Two conditions bring on the algae: frequent, shallow watering (or winter rain) that wets only the soil surface, and too much shade. So to get rid of algae on soil, you must make the area brighter and drier. Prune and thin the vegetation overhead to let in more light; break up and loosen the soil with a long-handled, pronged cultivator to help dry it out.

Irrigate less often, but perhaps for longer intervals, to help keep the soil surface dry. Shaded areas generally need less water, unless the shade is being cast by a tree with shallow roots. Tree roots are greedy, and other plants get very little. Watering for longer periods of time ensures that both trees and plants get enough.

I can't give specific information on watering, since it varies so much from area to area, from soil type to soil type, and even within a garden. To develop a better feel for your garden's water needs, check the soil frequently with a spade or trowel. When it is almost dry, it needs irrigation.

PREPARE FOR RAIN

Q: My lemon tree is getting some yellow leaves, and I know it would appreciate something to nosh on. However, when it is raining, when do I feed my plants?

—S.S., GRANADA HILLS

A: Yellow leaves are not a positive sign that the lemon needs fertilizer; the soil
could also be waterlogged from the rain. However, says soil scientist Garn Wallace
at Wallace Laboratories in El Segundo, "It's hard to differentiate between waterlogged plants and ones that need nitrogen." Both can be problems during rainy
times.

Other than having a lab do a leaf analysis to pinpoint the ailment, you'll have
to simply look at the tree and hazard a guess. If the younger, newer growth is green-
er than the rest of the tree, Wallace says, it probably needs nitrogen. Waterlogged
plants tend to turn yellow all over. Before you do anything, check the base of the
tree, and make sure that rainwater is draining away from the trunk.

When it rains heavily, elements are washed from the soil, nitrogen and calcium being the first to go. So these are the two that should be added. Most of the
other elements in common fertilizers are already abundant in Southern California
soils—if you think you may need to add other kinds of fertilizer, have your soil tested by a soil laboratory.

To replenish nitrogen, Wallace says, use plain ammonium nitrate (sold in bags
at nurseries). It's inexpensive, works quickly, is pH neutral and isn't easily washed
out of the soil. Simply scatter it around plants. Don't overdo it, though, it's strong:
Add no more than three pounds of ammonium nitrate per 1,000 square feet, and
wash it off foliage.

To replace calcium, an important buffering agent, add five to 10 pounds of
gypsum per 1,000 square feet.

Gardeners can also use a slower-acting but longer-lasting organic fertilizer,
such as blood meal or the faster bat guano. Lightly cultivate these into the soil,
which means barely scratching them into the surface with a cultivating fork. Even
with the organics, don't use as much as the package recommends unless you are
really trying to get some growth out of new plants.

The best time to apply fertilizers is just before a spring rain. Try to scatter it
just before a storm is predicted. If the storm fails to show, water it into the soil with
a sprinkler. A few minutes should do it.

There is a silver lining in all this rainy weather news: Growth inhibitors, such
as sodium, are also washed out of the soil, making nutrients more available to
plants.

❉ ❉ ❉

Cutting Back, Dividing and Pruning

CALIFORNIA PERENNIALS

A gardener from Venice once said to me, "I can find plenty of information on perennials that require division for refreshing, but how do I treat nepeta? It looks so shaggy right now." She added: "How about santolina, helichrysum and artemisia?"

It's a good question. Here in California, these popular plants are sold as perennials, but open a typical garden book (for the most part written for gardeners in harsher climates), and you'll realize that a lot of our perennials don't die back the way herbaceous perennials described in those books do. Yet they obviously need some kind of winter pruning.

Of these, catmint (*Nepeta*) gets the scraggliest. I myself have often wondered what to do with the tangled catmints in my garden. Mary Lou Heard, of Heard's Country Gardens in Westminster, a nursery that specializes in perennials, carefully thins it a little every few months to keep it neat. Once a year, in winter, she cuts it back to within an inch of the ground, and it comes back fresh as a daisy.

Santolinas are another story. If the bare, woody growth below the leaves is cut, the plants will most likely not recover. They certainly will never look the same and will probably die. The solution is to prune santolinas lightly throughout the year so they never get too scruffy. You can try cutting back overgrown santolinas, but it is probably better to replace them with new ones and begin anew. In my garden, I've had to do this every five years or so.

Helichrysums—such as the popular chartreuse 'Limelight'—are tricky. Sneeze on one, and the whole plant falls apart, or so it seems, the stems unraveling like a ball of soft yellow-green yarn. This plant is tough and beautiful until you try to prune it. Whack it back, and you will destroy the look of the plant. Just prune the tips constantly so they don't get too big or lanky. Never try to pull off dead stems; they must be cut. Most gardeners, having found helichrysums difficult plants to keep looking good, simply replace them every three to five years. The other helichrysum, commonly called licorice plant, is like santolina. Prune it lightly but not hard; it will never recover properly.

Artemisias are tougher plants. According to Heard, cut back to foot-tall bushes, they'll most likely bounce back, though I've never had the guts to try.

When you're not certain how a plant will respond to cutting back, Heard says, lightly prune it back in fall, then let it go through winter. In early spring, if it is sprouting near the base, you can safely cut it back to those sprouts; if not, leave well enough alone.

This is how I discovered how to cut back Santa Barbara daisy. I trimmed it into a tidy little bush shape in late fall, waited, then saw that there were far more sprouts at ground level than on the cut stems. So I cut it back all the way. In the spring it was a much tidier, and fuller, plant.

There are few hard-and-fast rules for cutting back plants. Careful observation will teach you generally how to prune and cut back. At worst, you'll have some great stories to share with other gardeners—like the time I was pruning a climbing rose up on the roof and got trapped until my kids came home and rescued me from the thorns.

CUTTING BACK ORNAMENTAL GRASSES

Q: I planted a few fountain grass (*Pennisetum setaceum*) specimens in my front yard. I was told they are deciduous and need cutting, but they looked fine all winter. Do I need to cut them down to keep them looking good?

—E.M., LAKEWOOD

A: In mild climates, fountain grass does not die back. Every now and then you may want to cut it completely to the ground to let it start fresh. Otherwise, dead leaves will build up inside the clumps.

I know at least one gardener who cuts all his ornamental grasses right down to the ground each winter, usually around the holidays. But this isn't necessary in Southern California. Watch to see which go dormant, and cut those down after they brown. Otherwise wait until the clumps begin to look ratty, and either thin out the dead leaves or cut to the ground in winter. Don't jump the gun and cut them in late summer; this is when most grasses begin to make their often dramatic seed heads.

I hope you planted *Pennisetum setaceum* 'Rubrum', the purple-leaved variety. Plain *Pennisetum setaceum* seeds all over the place and has become a major pest in wild areas and along roadways.

PRUNING ABUTILON AND HELIOTROPE

Q: How does one go about pruning a flowering maple without killing it?

—R.W., LOS ANGELES

A: According to Lew Whitney of Roger's Gardens in Corona del Mar, you can safely cut back an abutilon, or flowering maple, by evenly removing as much as two-thirds of the growth. Then clean out any spindly twigs that remain. A month or so after this harsh pruning—as new growth begins—do some light trimming to reshape the plant.

Ideally, it's best to prune regularly—say, about every two months—so plants don't get too leggy. Most of us wait too long and then must whack them back, which means they won't bloom for three to six months while recovering.

Abutilons are almost always in flower, so there is no ideal time to prune—early March or early October is probably the best time. The common, fragrant, old-fashioned heliotrope (*Heliotrope arborescens*) grows in a similar fashion and must be treated much the same way.

DIVIDING AGAPANTHUS

Q: Can I divide agapanthus in spring, or is there a better time?
—L.F., LOS ANGELES

A: Divide fast-growing agapanthus in the fall so that it can become well established by June, when it flowers. It isn't necessary to divide agapanthus every year—as it is with many other clumping perennials—because it blooms best in large clumps. Although dividing does set it back temporarily, it's an economical way to get more plants.

Agapanthus clumps in the ground weigh a lot, and digging them up is a major chore. After digging out the whole clump, there are two ways to go. One is to use a sharpened, flat-bladed spade (spades can, and should, be sharpened with a bastard file, available at hardware stores). Plunge the blade into the clump and jump on it with both feet to sever the fleshy roots. Or, using a long, serrated knife, slowly cut your way through. This method works great on agapanthus in containers.

RENEWING BIRD OF PARADISE

Q: I have been trying to find out how to prune my bird of paradise. It's 20 years old and gets about 15 flowers a season. When the flowers die, they look ratty. Can they be cut off? If so, near the top or the bottom?
—B.F., WEST HILLS

A: The official city flower of Los Angeles, bird of paradise blooms better if regularly fertilized, though it can get by on next to no care. As soon as a flower fades, cut off the flowering stem as close to the ground as possible.

When clumps get old and big (as many are in Los Angeles) and if blooming slows down, the plant may need to be dug up and divided. This is a huge job, and you won't believe the thick mass of roots under the plants. But digging them out and splitting up the root ball with an old serrated knife or a very sharp spade—into chunks about a foot across—then replanting the best of these will dramatically rejuvenate old plants.

Bird of paradise also does well in large containers, so pot up the extra divisions and grow them on a patio, or supply the whole neighborhood.

REVIVING IRISES

Q: After Japanese iris and bearded iris have finished blooming, what should I do about the tall stalks and leaves? Do I need to lift the Japanese iris bulbs? Also, what should I do about the bearded iris that didn't bloom this year? Should I yank them out?

—T.D., CAMARILLO

A: Once an iris has bloomed, cut off the stalk and the attached leaf. Both kinds are perennials, so don't dig up or disturb the rhizomes.

Japanese iris need plenty of moisture (many people grow them with their roots submerged in a pond), so keep them moist in summer and fall.

Bearded iris like a little late-summer drought, so after July, water less often or not at all, then begin watering again in early fall.

Don't pull out those rhizomes that didn't flower; they will make next year's flowers. After about three years, in August, dig up the rhizomes. Save only the healthiest, and discard the old, rotted ones. Cut back the roots and the leaves so they each are about six inches long. Replant the rhizomes in clumps of three, about four to six inches apart; clumps should be about 12 to 18 inches apart. Don't bury them too deep; the tops of the rhizomes should be at or just below soil level. Most iris fanciers cover the tubers with only a quarter inch of soil.

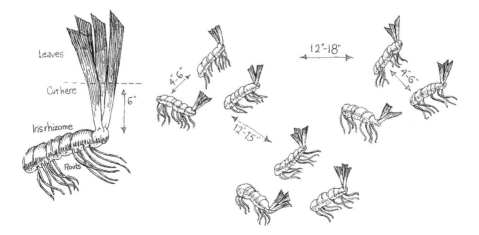

After cutting iris leaves and roots so each is about six inches long, plant rhizomes four to six inches apart, in clumps spaced 12 to 18 inches apart.

DIGGING UP DAHLIAS

Q: Can I leave dahlia bulbs in the ground instead of lifting and dividing them every year?

—J.S., ANAHEIM

A: Although the job is tedious, it's best to dig up and store the dense clumps of sweet potato–like tubers every year, according to Dick Kohlschreiber, a member of the South Coast Dahlia Society. Left in the ground, the roots may rot during winter's wet weather. And if you don't divide them, the flowers the following season will be much smaller. You want to start fresh each spring with only one big tuber per planting hole.

Dig clumps of tubers after the stems and leaves have dried in the fall. Cut stalks to within six inches of the ground, and loosen and lift the clumps with a garden fork, digging all around the plant about a foot away from the stalk. Wash the soil from the roots and put them in boxes, covered with vermiculite, so they do not get too dry in winter. Label the boxes so you do not confuse the varieties. Store in a cool, dry place, such as a garage or in the crawl space under the house.

Divide the tubers right after digging, or wait until you see sprouts in spring.

Between late March and early June, plant one tuber per hole, spaced two to three feet apart. Stake each immediately with a five-foot, 1x1-inch stake (you don't want to mistakenly skewer tubers later). Each hole should be almost a foot deep for sandy soils, six inches for heavy soils. Make sure the sprout, or eye, is pointing up.

Don't bury tubers completely right away, though. Begin by covering them, in the bottom of their holes, with just an inch of soil, then keep adding more as sprouts grow, until the hole is filled in.

By the end of summer, after flowering, there will be clumps of tubers to divide yet again.

SHORTENING TOO-TALL BEGONIAS

Q: Could you tell me the correct time and procedure for pruning angel-wing begonias?

—D.K., GLENDALE

A: Cut back cane-type or angel-wing begonias, such as 'Irene Nuss', with its big, drooping clusters of coral-pink flowers and dark-red leaves, in March or April, according to Lew Whitney of Roger's Gardens in Corona del Mar. This means you'll have to look at a bedraggled plant all winter, but you want to protect them from a late cold snap, which will "really fry any new growth," says Whitney.

I cut off only the top one-third of the canes, just above growth nodes, because I like tall angel wings—mine get three, four, even five feet tall. Whitney prefers them shorter and bushier, so he cuts off the top two-thirds. Either way works—they'll bounce right back if you start fertilizing right after pruning. "They are voracious feeders," says Whitney.

Save those cut-off pieces. They will easily root in potting soil in a shady spot if not kept too wet. Soon you'll be supplying the neighborhood with baby begonias.

TAMING A TOWERING WISTERIA

Q: When we planted a wisteria in a big pot three years ago, it was in full bloom. Last year it had only a few flowers and this year none at all. It's full of leaves, though, and we fertilize it often. What do we need to do to get flowers?

—G.G., TORRANCE

A: It often takes time for wisteria to settle in and start flowering. Fertilizing encourages only leafy growth, not blooms. But getting wisteria to bloom is almost as simple as pruning a hedge, despite some rather complicated instructions found in garden books.

To get wisteria to flower, you must "control the monster," says Lucy Tolmach, director of horticulture at Filoli in Woodside, a public garden in Northern California renowned for its spectacular two-story wisteria. The vines at Filoli flower as profusely as they do because of constant summer pruning.

There are two kinds of growth on wisteria: the vigorous vegetative twining stems and the shorter fingerlike spurs that form near the bases of twining stems. The spurs, similar to those found on apples, produce the fat buds that become spring's graceful flowers.

From June through September, encourage flowering spurs and manage the size of the plant, Tolmach says, by whacking back every twining stem that emerges from the canopy of leaves so it is roughly even with the rest of the plant. These will immediately start regrowing—cut them back again. Each time you cut back a twining stem, you make more flowering spurs.

When cutting back a twining stem, try to leave three or four buds, but don't worry if there are more. The gardeners who work on Filoli's towering wisteria with pole pruners often just have to approximate.

In winter, when plants are leafless, tidy them up, removing dead and crossing branches, plus stems that are growing in the wrong place. At Filoli, gardeners work to preserve the lean, evenly spaced lines of the vines with winter pruning, which is why they are so graceful and elegant.

STUMP REMOVAL

Q: Now that we've cut down a tree to a stump just at ground level, how do we go about killing the roots without harming the lawn area?

—T.F., Los Angeles

A: Although products are sold that supposedly dissolve trunks, I have never heard of one that works. Pioneers used to slowly burn stumps out, but that is not advised either.

With the tree already cut flush to the ground, you need to have a tree company with a machine called a stump grinder chip up the roots. With enough workers and enough time, it is possible to dig out the stump, but grinders are quicker and cheaper.

A stump grinder will not damage the surrounding area because it can be tipped down onto the stump and remaining roots. As it works, it fluffs up soil with sawdust, which then needs to be treated with extra nitrogen fertilizer so it does not steal nutrients from the surrounding soil. Raw sawdust can be toxic to plants.

Next time, if you don't plan on grinding, leave about three feet of trunk for leverage when it comes to digging it out. Rent a come-along, or cable hoist, to winch out stubborn stumps. Attach the other end to something very sturdy.

CUTTING DOWN YUCCA

Q: My neighbor has a large yucca tree that is pushing against my block wall. The wall is now cracked, and I'm afraid it will fall. The neighbor is not reluctant to remove the plant. Do you have any suggestions on the easiest method?

—C.N., Inglewood

A: Although above ground a yucca is ponderous, its base goes down only about eight inches and there are no large roots underneath.

Cutting down a yucca is slow work because the wood is wet and heavy. Arborists Don Case of Fullerton and Bob Hansen of Santa Monica both suggest cutting off small pieces at a time. When you reach the base, dig to undermine one corner, then chip off manageable chunks with a Pulaski (an ax-handled digging and cutting tool).

❧ ❧ ❧

Container Gardening

QUALITY POTS RING TRUE

Q: My clay pots tend to turn white at the bases, or the clay chips off. Even if

I wash them and put gravel in the bottoms for drainage, I still have this problem. Can you help me?

—T.T., MONTEREY PARK

A: Plants prefer growing in terra-cotta pots because the clay is porous and "breathes." A wicking action causes calcium and other minerals found in our water or in fertilizers to accumulate on the outside (the white deposits you see), where they do not harm the pots or plants.

On inexpensive pots, this action causes pots to erode and flake, generally because the clay is soft or was not fired in a kiln, according to Gloria Lopez, of Pottery Manufacturing & Distributing in Gardena. Many rough, inexpensive, low-fired Mexican pots have asphalt painted inside—an attempt to prolong their lives—but once tar has been painted on, the pots can no longer breathe, so you lose the benefits of clay.

To find quality pots that last, Lopez says, give them a sharp tap. Those that have been high fired ring like a bell. Short-lived, low-fired pots make a dull ring (if they don't ring but thump, the pot is probably cracked).

Lopez says American and Italian pots are high fired and will last a very long time. Most other imports, whether from Africa, China or Mexico, should be protected with special pottery sealers (available at nurseries). Be aware that these sealers give pots a sheen. Do not use Thompson's Waterseal or concrete sealers—these are toxic to plants.

Many gardeners like the look of the mineral deposits, and green algae and other things that make a terra-cotta pot appear old. Some actually paint on lime to hasten the whitening.

But if you find the deposits unsightly, you can try to get rid of them on your sound pots (not ones that are already eroding). Remove as much as you can with a wire brush. Then apply linseed oil, which makes the powdery deposits invisible and the pots look shiny and new. Or try to dissolve them with vinegar and water, or with a 10 percent solution of hydrochloric acid (at pool-supply stores). Rinse well afterward.

Putting a layer of gravel or broken pieces of pots at the bottom of a container to improve drainage is a garden myth that refuses to die. In fact, these two practices can hinder the health of a plant. Gravel simply takes up valuable root space, and pieces of broken flower pots allow soil to wash out and bugs to crawl in.

All that is required at the bottom of a pot is some kind of screen to cover the drainage hole. This keeps soil in as water easily passes through, and prevents slugs and bugs from hiding up inside. I use nylon window screening, which lasts forever.

Some gardeners like to use cut up coffee filters, though I don't know that they last long.

See Week 24 in 52 Weeks in the California Garden.

A GOOD POTTING MIX AND OTHER MUSTS

In summer, it's just too darn easy to kill potted plants with either too much or too little attention. In the case of my sad, shriveled terra-cotta-colored million bells, sitting lifeless in its pot on the back steps, it was too much water. But it looked just like it had been watered too little.

No wonder over- and under-watering are often confused: They have the same symptoms. Keep the soil too wet, and the roots rot right off the plant. Without viable roots, the plant appears to be wilting from lack of water. Watering at this point only hastens the plant's demise.

But I blame the death of my little million bells on lousy potting soil.

Years ago, a researcher with the University of California tested commercially available potting mixes and found that many performed poorly. The brands have changed since then, but I think most of today's mixes are even worse. They wear out way too fast and often drain poorly from the start. If you keep having problems with plants in pots, consider looking for a better potting soil.

A good quality potting mix holds the right amount of water and nutrients, and lasts for several years in a pot. It contains organic matter, such as ground bark or peat moss, which stores water. Inorganic components, such as sand and perlite, serve mostly as particle separators, so air can get into the mix.

I have never found an inexpensive mix that works well, though one I tried years ago was quite amusing. With colorful shreds of telephone wire in it, the soil looked like the day after New Year's. Presumably the bits of wire were in the mix to speed drainage. Most inexpensive mixes I've tried need to be replaced almost every year, and some of them get so soggy they are useless for anything but bog gardens.

However, there are some very good potting soils (as of spring 2002). I've had good luck with Uncle Malcolm's, LGM brand, Nurseryman's and Miracle-Gro. These are what potting soils ought to be. The ones by Miracle-Gro contain fertilizer so growth is quite fast the first few months, which is perfect for annuals but not for things you want to just maintain.

Miracle-Gro also has a mix that contains coir, or coconut fiber, which tends to store a little extra moisture. Another way to get a mix to store extra moisture is to add a soil polymer such as Broadleaf P4. Follow directions carefully so you don't add too much.

These mixes are also good for starting seeds. Before sowing, run the soil though a potting screen, or riddle, with quarter-inch openings. The sifting takes out the chunkier pieces that improve drainage but interfere with germination. Nurseries sometimes sell these, or you can make your own.

Watering: When and How

The best way to tell when to water a pot is to pick it up . If it is heavy, the soil is too wet. If it weighs next to nothing, it's too dry. In summer and in fall, the surface of potting soil dries almost immediately. If you respond to this visual clue by watering, you might overdo it—the soil just below the surface could be soaking wet.

If a pot is too big to pick up easily, the finger-in-the-soil testing technique is necessary. Push your finger down into the soil to determine whether it is wet or dry. Never rely on how the soil looks.

Ideally, you shouldn't have to water container plants daily. A pot should store water for several days, and plants are often happier if the soil begins to dry. As soil dries, air, which is as necessary to roots as it is to leaves, is pulled down.

When watering, use some kind of diffusing device on the end of the hose. Not only will it prevent valuable potting soil from washing out, but it will keep the water from churning the soil, thereby destroying its porous structure. A wand makes it easier to reach plants, and an on/off valve saves water between pots.

Fertilizing: Striking the Right Balance

As an artificial medium, potting soil has no natural nutrients. Plants confined to pots need to be fertilized, or they go hungry, which is not necessarily a bad thing. Some plants bloom and fruit better when they are a little hungry, but not annual flowers and most vegetables. Fertilize annual flowers and vegetables regularly, but fertilize less often if you don't want plants to outgrow their pots.

The easiest way to feed is to use timed-release fertilizers in pellet form (such as Osmocote, Sta-Green and others), which mete out nutrients. Or use liquid fertilizers in a watering can once a month or even less. Mild liquid fish is hard to beat, but it smells awful. Chemical fertilizers (such as Spoonit, Peters and Miracle-Gro) are stronger and should be diluted by about half to prevent crazed growth.

Repotting: Giving Plants a Fresh Start

Even the best potting soil won't last forever. After a year or two, potting soils just wear out and become too compacted. Drainage slows, and the soil becomes airless, which encourages root diseases and rotting.

It's time to repot when water doesn't drain quickly. Use the same container—trim the roots and the top of the plant and add some fresh potting soil—or move it up to a larger size. In either case, shave off some of the old potting soil so the plant gets a fresh start. You have the same choices when a plant becomes root-bound or too big for its container.

Put a screen over the drainage hole, and don't fill the pot too full (leave room to water) or bury the plant below the new soil level (which can cause crown rot).

When repotting in summer, keep plants in partial shade until they become accustomed to their new quarters (a week or two). You can also move plants into partial shade on really hot days or while on vacation. Try not to move them abruptly from one to the other, but in stages.

Used potting soil can be revitalized by adding quality peat moss or soil amendment, but it will never be quite as good. Use it on less fussy plants, or in the garden as a soil amendment or mulch.

SPECIALTY MIXES FOR CACTUS AND SUCCULENTS

Q: Last year I tried making my own soil mix for succulents and cactus, with disappointing results. It dries out quickly, stays very loose and is somewhat water repellent. Can you suggest a good formula?

—J.S., ARCADIA

A: Cactus collectors Seymour Linden and Henry Varney devised the following mix for their several thousand succulents, many of which are rare and quite finicky: 4 parts fine pumice; 3 parts LGM planter mix; 1 part decomposed granite or washed builders' sand. Both swear by the pumice and say LGM makes for a mix that is "dry, even when it is soaking wet." They water fairly often with this mix; one with less pumice and more sand or granite, they suggest, will require less watering.

For the Huntington Botanical Gardens' enormous collection of cactus, curator of desert collections John Trager mixes: 60 percent pumice; 20 percent forest humus; 20 percent builders' sand. In place of forest humus (the Huntington has access to special commercial composted barks), Trager says, substitute any good indoor-plant potting mix, such as LGM or Supersoil. For especially water-sensitive plants, increase the amount of pumice.

A mix for California's native succulents, the dudleyas, was suggested to me by collector Kei Nakai: 1 part generic kitty litter (with plain diatomaceous earth, not clay or other additives); 1 part decomposed granite; 1 part ordinary potting soil; a touch of a composted sewage-sludge product (such as Kellogg's Nitrohumus).

The Desert Garden at the Huntington Botanical Gardens, 1151 Oxford Road, San Marino, CA 91108; telephone 626.405.2141; on the web at www.huntington.org.

PESTS INDICATE A WEAKENED PLANT

Q: I have a one-year-old brugmansia (angel's trumpet) in a large outdoor container that is afflicted with whiteflies to the point that the leaves are yellowing and dropping. Is there some kind of systemic soil drench that might work, and is there a risk that the infestation might spread to a big brugmansia in the ground nearby?
—C.M., Santa Monica

A: I'm not a fan of systemic poisons, but you can check at the nursery for those labeled for ornamental shrubs other than roses. You can also try hanging yellow sticky cards (available at better nurseries) on the plant—they are meant to attract and detain the pests.

However, in my experience, there's no surefire organic control or poison for whiteflies.

Poison sprays tend only to aggravate problems in the garden. With each generation, whiteflies—which reproduce in quantity so very often—become tolerant of poisons. In the meantime, poisons are killing their predators. Lots of insects in the garden eat whiteflies, from lacewings to ladybugs. So with every application, you have more whiteflies and fewer predators. You can see how the pests quickly get the upper hand!

Whiteflies usually pick on weakened plants. The fact that there is a big, healthy brugmansia nearby indicates that the plant's problems have to do with its being grown in a container. Otherwise, the whiteflies would be all over the other one as well.

Your plant might be over-potted, meaning it's in a container too large for its

Don't move a plant into too big a pot, or it may rot. The new container should be about four inches wider and two to four inches deeper than the previous pot.

roots. Without enough roots to remove the excess water from the soil, it tends to stay wet too long. The roots rot, and leaves yellow and fall off.

In general, as a plant grows, it should be moved to increasingly larger containers, a couple of inches at a time. A plant in a gallon nursery can should go into a pot about two inches wider and a little deeper. After it fills this pot, move it again to a slightly larger container, and so on.

Your plant could also need fertilizing. Even though fertilizer is seldom the solution to problems of garden-grown plants, container-bound plants (at least those grown outdoors) frequently suffer from malnutrition, since there is little built-in nutrition in the artificial potting soil. Watering washes away fertilizers, which must be replaced regularly. So, while garden plants manage to find nutrients somewhere, a potted plant—unless it roots though the drainage holes and into the soil—is dependent on the kindness of strangers.

If the plant is not growing in too large a pot, try fertilizing every two weeks with half-strength fertilizer, or at least once a month with full-strength, and see whether the whiteflies move on. Use a liquid, or the kind mixed into a liquid. Timed-release kinds, which dissolve slowly and fertilize every time you water, should be reapplied much less often.

FERTILIZER, TOO MUCH OF A GOOD THING

Q: As a bonsai enthusiast, I have several flowering cherry trees (*Prunus serrulata*) planted in a large dish. A couple of trees have rust-colored rings around the edges of their leaves. The plants are watered every day and fed regularly. Is there something I might add that will alleviate this problem?

—C.H., FULLERTON

A: It's more likely you need to subtract something. The leaves you sent were a bit shriveled by the time they arrived, but, even in this condition, their edges clearly indicate an excess of mineral salts. A number of deciduous plants that really aren't suited to growing here—including your cherries, some magnolias, Japanese maples and birches—get this salt damage. Near the end of summer, the minerals accumulate at leaf edges, turning them that rusty-brown color.

You may be fertilizing too often—excess nitrogen from fertilizers can burn leaf edges—or these minerals may simply be in your irrigation water. A good rainy winter will help flush salts out of the pot, but you can help by watering containers every now and then with pure distilled water. Make sure plenty of water comes out the drainage hole.

If the salts are flushed out, the new spring leaves will be fine. Next summer fertilize less, and flush the soil with pure water every so often.

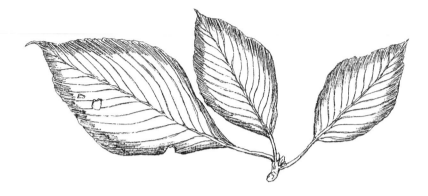

Brown, burnt-looking edges on leaves are a sign that water or
fertilizer has been too high in mineral salts.

An aside: To remove salts around trees that are growing in the ground, thoroughly irrigate once in summer, applying about six inches of water over a few days.

NORTHERN EXPOSURE

Q: I have two potted bougainvilleas that were in bloom when I bought them
but haven't bloomed since. They're on my patio outside my apartment and are
growing quite nicely. The patio faces north, and I get sun in the early morning, but
it will be in shade during the winter months. Will they ever bloom again?
—A.N., Los Angeles

A: Bougainvillea needs a lot more sun than that. Tough plants like bougainvillea will grow in poor light, but they will not flower. That's one reason shady gardens
are full of foliage but bereft of flowers. If you have no sunny place to move them to,
replace them with something that will do well. You'll find that no shade plants
bloom as heavily as a bougainvillea does when it gets enough sun and heat, but at
least they will flower.

Very few large plants flower well on the north side of a building. Here are some
to try:

• A potted camellia will do very well for a number of years. A friend of mine
has several on his north-facing balcony, and they look elegant in any season, though
they flower for only a month or so in winter or spring.

• Yesterday-today-and-tomorrow (*Brunfelsia*) has similar foliage and grows to
about the same size, with flat lavender flowers in spring.

• Abutilon, or flowering maple, will outgrow a container in a few years, but
it flowers for most of the year and is easy to restart from cuttings.

• Hydrangea will work, but it is dormant in winter, or nearly so.

• Upright fuchsias are great container plants and bloom for most of the summer, but they too are nearly dormant in late winter (when they need to be cut back by about a third).

• Several annual flowers, such as primroses and impatiens, will flower with a northern exposure. Or try shade plants valued mostly for their foliage, not their flowers, such as palms and *Fatsia japonica*.

BOUGAINVILLEA FOR BALCONIES

Q: I have two bougainvillea plants in pots on my balcony. While they bloom profusely, they drop leaves continuously. Can you suggest a solution to my problem?
—K.R., LAGUNA BEACH

A: Leaves could be falling for several reasons. In winter, many bougainvillea drop leaves; in summer, sea breezes may make it too chilly for heat-loving bougainvillea. One of the better bougainvillea near the coast is 'San Diego Red'. However, it is known for its abundance of blooming bracts (what people call flowers) and, at the same time, lack of leaves.

Over- and under-watering are always possible factors. Keep the potting soil evenly moist, not too wet or too dry. If it dries out completely for even a day, the leaves can fall while the flower bracts remain. Fertilize once a month but not more often, since bougainvillea don't need much fertilizer. In the ground, fertilizing is not necessary at all, but in containers some kind of regular feeding is. Use a simple all-purpose liquid fertilizer intended for container plants—fish fertilizer or one of the chemical kinds to be mixed with water, such as Peters, Spoonit or Miracle-Gro.

The most likely reason for your leafless condition: You are growing varieties not suited to container culture. According to Lew Whitney of Roger's Gardens in Corona del Mar, only two varieties really do well in pots, the multicolored 'Rosenka' and its red cultivar 'Oo-La-La'. Small and bushy, both will remain happy in pots for years.

The recently introduced pink 'Silhouette' and white 'Ms. Alice' are bushy kinds from Singapore that reach three to four feet across at maturity. New growth on mature plants tends to be thornless. Bracts last a long time, and plants are said to bloom even in the cooler coastal areas. Their hardiness is not known, but they can take at least 30 degrees. And, it's said, they are great in hanging baskets.

CYMBIDIUMS, THE STATE ORCHID?

If there were a state orchid, chances are it would be the cymbidium. It's one orchid that is easily grown outdoors in much of California and nowhere else in the continental United States, not even in Florida, which is too humid and too warm at night.

Native to China and other parts of Asia, cymbidiums are now standard garden fare here, commonly available at nurseries from October to June, when so many bloom. "They thrive on benign neglect, a little food, a lot of water and half a day of sunlight," says Jo Ann Farrar, who cares for about 350 at Sherman Gardens in Corona del Mar and an additional 200 at her home.

Cymbidiums are a snap to grow outdoors in most of the Los Angeles basin, and in Orange, Santa Barbara and San Diego counties—wherever temperatures don't drop below 28 degrees for very long. Some inland areas, though, can get too cold. Hobbyists advise that extra protection of some kind may be needed east of West Covina or in the San Fernando Valley. To bloom, they need the cool night air and a difference of about 25 degrees between day and night temperatures. "You can take them indoors for the day, but, like a cat, let them out for the night," Farrar says.

Cymbidiums require lightning-fast drainage. For this reason, they are almost always grown in pots. Most hobbyists favor black plastic pots, which don't dry out as fast as clay. The plants can be grown in large containers, but these are unwieldy when repotting time comes every few years.

To get the proper drainage, growers of cymbidiums use pure, chunky orchid bark, with maybe a little perlite and charcoal added. At Sherman Gardens, Farrar's mix is three parts seedling bark (one-eighth- to one-quarter-inch size), two parts perlite and one part horticultural charcoal.

In the city of Orange, cymbidium hobbyist Bill Austin, who grows his plants in gallon cans, mixes eight parts small-size bark, one part perlite and one part charcoal. A dry mix can damage the roots, he says, so he always moistens his before using or storing.

As for watering, never let cymbidium orchids go completely dry. "It's probably the most important part of caring for cymbidiums," Austin says.

Cymbidiums like lots of fertilizer, and cymbidium fanciers have a million ways to keep their plants happy. The easiest, suggested by Farrar, is to use timed-release fertilizer pellets designed to last nine months—Osmocote, Sierra and Sta-Green are some. Add pellets to the pots in spring and fall, and cover with about an inch of bark.

Standard cymbidiums need about half sun and half shade in most areas. If the leaves get little white spots or streaks, it's a sign of sunburn, Austin says. Black tips and streaks usually have to do with salts and minerals in the water. Leave them or trim them off. When plants are in flower, though, they should be kept in a fair amount of shade so the blooms will lasts longer and won't bleach.

Rules for Repotting
Mostly because the bark in the potting mix begins to get mushy and

drainage degrades, cymbidiums need repotting about every two to three years. It's a must when they approach being pot-bound. There is an old gardener's tale that pot-bound cymbidiums bloom best, but, says Palos Verdes hybridizer Bill Bailey, who's been growing them for 40 years, they actually do better when regularly repotted.

Farrar says to repot when the pseudobulbs—the bulblike swellings at the base of the plant—get within an inch of the edge of the pot, "or there will be no room for new bulbs or blooms." As the plant grows, pseudobulbs get used up and no longer produce leaves, at which point they become known as backbulbs. Cut them off at repotting time and toss.

The time to repot is immediately after a cymbidium blooms, so it will have enough time to grow and flower again the next year.

To get the cymbidium out of its pot, Austin uses his "potting stick," which he fashions from a broom handle cut to about two feet long. One end is sharpened to resemble a knife blade; the other end is blunt. With this end he taps against the sides of the pot to loosen the root mass.

Once the roots are out, he shakes all the bark away and trims them to about two to three inches long (he holds them like a barber grabs a hank of hair, then cuts). He removes the dark dead roots, saving only the white new ones. With a blast of water, he washes out any remaining bark.

To repot, he uses both ends of his potting stick to force soil between and around roots so the plant is really packed into its pot. "You should be able to pick up the plant by its leaves and not have it come out of the pot," he says.

Cymbidiums for Hanging Baskets

The hot items among cymbidium hobbyists now are those with pendulous bloom spikes that spill down over the sides of hanging baskets. In Ventura, self-professed obsessed hobbyist George Hatfield, a vice president at avocado marketer Calavo, lauds them as "the greatest thing to happen to cymbidiums in a hundred years."

The individual flowers on pendulous cymbidiums may be smaller—about 60 percent the size of standard cymbidiums—but there are more blooms per spike, and more spikes per plant. For one cymbidium show, Hatfield had to outfit his wife's van to carry an amazing 10-inch hanging plant with 38 spikes and a total of 754 mahogany-red flowers (actually counted by judges).

Having debuted in the orchid world during the 1970s, pendulous cymbidiums are available mostly at orchid specialty nurseries. They are usually grown in six-inch plastic hanging pots; otherwise, they are treated like ordinary cymbidiums. Hatfield grows his on the bright but nearly sunless north side of his house, "which is a no-no with regular cymbidiums."

CHAMELEON CYMBIDIUMS

Q: I have a wood planter with seven cymbidium orchids. When I planted them, there were several different colors—yellow, green, pink, burgundy and white. When they bloomed the following season, they were all pure white. They are very beautiful, but I would like to know why they changed color.

—C.M., SANTA MARIA

A: It's impossible—flowers can't suddenly and radically change color, according to John Ernest, of cymbidium growers Gallup & Stribling Orchids in Santa Barbara. They might be more intense or faded looking depending on the light they get, but, says Ernest, "We grow hundreds of thousands [26 acres of greenhouses], and they always look basically the same. A burgundy orchid can't change into a white." The plants were either mislabeled, or somebody swiped yours and substituted whites.

MAKING MOTH ORCHIDS BLOOM

Q: I received a phalaenopsis as a gift and don't have the vaguest idea how to care for it. Could you give me information so I can take care of this beautiful, exotic plant?

—E.M., CANOGA PARK

A: The trick to growing any flowering plant indoors is getting it to bloom. But give a phalaenopsis (moth orchid) a little care, and it may bloom several times each year, according to Julie Norman, orchid curator at the Arboretum of Los Angeles County in Arcadia.

Find a place where it will get good light but no afternoon sun. Morning sun is good; so is tree-filtered light coming through a window. Keep it in the bathroom or kitchen, usually the most humid rooms in the house, or set it on a humidity tray, a wide dish or tray filled with pebbles and water. Make sure the water does not touch the pot—it may rot the roots.

Fertilize every two weeks with an orchid fertilizer (available at nurseries), following label directions. Water about once a week in winter and twice a week in summer, whatever it takes to keep the soil evenly moist at all times. Water in the morning so foliage dries quickly and doesn't develop fungus, or keep water off the foliage.

The first flower spike will appear in spring. When it is finished, you can get the plant to bloom again by snapping off the stalk just above where the third or fourth flower appeared. The stalk will fork and flower again. After the fork flowers, cut off the stalk at the base so it can't bloom yet another time, which would "cause the plant to bloom itself to death," says Norman.

However, there's a good chance the plant will produce more stalks, at other locations on the plant, and bloom again in summer or fall.

The orchid can probably live in its pot for several years; moth orchids do fine when they're a bit root-bound. When you do repot, increase the size of its container by only a couple of inches, say, from a four-inch to a six-inch container. Use a bark and perlite orchid potting mix (at nurseries). Don't crowd orchids together; they need good air circulation.

AFRICAN VIOLETS: THE MORE, THE MERRIER

Q: I used to propagate African violets by putting the leaves in water, but this doesn't seem to work anymore. Have the growers done something to prevent this, or have I just lost my touch?

—K.S., Riverside

A: I suspect it's your technique that needs a little fine-tuning. Diane Miller, a member of the Orange County African Violet Society, propagates 300 to 400 violets at a time in an upstairs bedroom. She roots the plants under a tier of plant lights, but, she says, an east-facing window works equally well.

To take a cutting, choose a healthy leaf from one of the middle rows on the plant, not from the outer edges. You want about three-quarters of an inch of stem attached to each leaf. Make cuts at a 45-degree angle.

As containers, Miller uses paper cups with holes punched in the bottoms. Fill the cup with a starter mix of half perlite and half vermiculite. It is possible to root African violets in water, she says, but the roots tend to be weak and mushy.

Push the stem, but not the leaf, into the starter mix. Support the leaf with a toothpick so it is not lying flat on the mix, which can cause it to mold. Simply skewer the leaf and prop it up.

Water the cutting. To create its "own little hothouse," says Miller, place a plastic bag loosely over the cup in a balloon-like fashion so it is not touching the leaf. Don't water again until it starts to dry.

Little plantlets will form around the leaf. Cut them off when they are an inch wide or larger. Separate them so each plant has only one crown, then pot them individually.

African Violet Society of America is on the web at www.avsa.org.

REPOTTING ROSES

Q: I have three rosebushes in large whiskey barrels that were extraordinary last year but mediocre this rainy year. They get sun from late morning through the afternoon. I water them every five to seven days and feed them monthly with a systemic product. Because of rust and mildew, I had to cut them back several months ago. Now, although the rust and mildew are gone, the plants are droopy and the flowers' life spans are extremely brief, when they used to last well over a week. Can you give me any suggestions to turn my roses around?

—N.D., PALMS

A: Everybody has a tough time growing roses after a long, wet spring. Mildew and rust are everywhere; even black spot is common. Where the sun finally comes out and the weather warms, roses will recover. But in coastal areas such as Palms, these diseases may not depart until late in summer.

Roses should quickly recover after being cut back, even in summer. Your roses may have been weakened by disease, enough to have been hindered in their comeback. You did the right thing, though: Just about the only way to battle rust is to pick off the affected leaves or cut the plants back. There really are no other effective controls.

Horticulturist and rose hybridizer Tom Carruth of Weeks Roses in Upland, who grows lots of roses in containers in his own garden, agrees with this assessment. He adds that the roses may need repotting, which should be done every two years in winter, when plants are semidormant.

If your roses are not too far gone (if they are, start with new plants), take them out of the pots. Shake most of the soil from the roots, prune some of them, and replant in new potting soil. Once they leaf out, fertilize with a complete fertilizer high in nitrogen.

Carruth fertilizes once a month with a 16-16-16 blend, though he says an 8-8-8 or something similar will work. Many special rose foods, he says, especially systemics such as you're using, are surprisingly low in nitrogen, the basic plant food. He also suspects that going five to seven days between waterings may be too long. Try more frequent irrigation, even every other day during the heat of summer.

POINSETTIAS THAT LAST

Q: Why do the green leaves on my poinsettias fall off as soon as I get them home, with only the red ones remaining? I admit I always buy bargain plants at the market. Could this have something to do with it?

—B.S., LOS ANGELES

A: Years ago, bargain poinsettias were often older varieties, sometimes called by growers "those lovely strippers" because they shed their green leaves so quickly. However, almost all the modern varieties, even the inexpensive ones, should hold on to theirs.

Surprisingly, the most common cause of leaf loss is too long a time in shipping sleeves, whether paper or clear plastic, according to Jack Williams of the Paul Ecke

Ranch, a huge poinsettia grower in Encinitas. Williams encourages retailers to remove sleeves immediately and even discourages consumers from buying plants that still have them.

Varieties with light-green leaves tend to drop leaves more quickly than those with dark-green leaves, says Williams. The darker-green varieties photosynthesize better and so are less affected by changes in light and other factors that stress poinsettias.

Better-grown poinsettias are less likely to shed leaves because they are stronger plants. Bargain plants are more likely to have been poorly grown. Check the roots by tipping the plant out of its container. Avoid plants that have few or damaged roots, or that have completely dry or overly wet soil.

Extremes in temperature can cause poinsettias to shed leaves. Don't bring poinsettias home to a hot, stuffy house or set them in front of a lighted fireplace. Poinsettias prefer temperatures in the upper 60s, though they will get used to temperatures in the low 70s. And don't leave them outside overnight. It's too cool.

What Bug Is That?

❦ ❦

Pests, Diseases and Weeds

ARDENS SHOULD TEEM WITH LIFE, like pond water under a microscope. People and plants are only part of the picture—there should also be shiny black ground beetles hiding under fallen leaves, birds on the branches above and maybe squirrels leaping from limb to limb. Lucky gardeners may have opossum visitors at night, or fish in ponds.

All of these creatures need something to eat. That is why gardens also contain a number of creatures not usually thought of as desirable, such as slugs for the beetles or snails for the opossums. Birds feed on aphids and weed seed, and fish eat algae. Squirrels can be quite amusing (and I'm sure if I think long and hard enough, I'll come up with another reason for their presence).

Healthy gardens keep all of these vital elements in balance. Occasionally, though, something gets out of whack, and some creature, disease or plant becomes too numerous. If it comes from another part of the world, your garden might not have built-in defenses. Weird weather can bring on surprises. Or something you or someone else does may begin a chain of events that eventually rocks the garden. Spraying poison over the entire yard to control your dog's fleas, for instance, could kill valuable predatory insects that have been keeping something else in control, such as whiteflies.

When things get badly out of balance, and for more than a few weeks, the gardener must step in like the town marshal and restore order in an attempt to set thing right. Today, good gardeners first look for a logical and natural way to balance the books. They try to make things right culturally by paying more attention to gardening practices like watering. They'll look for natural predators and try to encourage them, or even round some up for the posse. Or they'll use sprays and other controls that do not poison everything in sight.

The goal is never to eliminate pests and diseases completely, but simply to bring them under control (weeds you can try to eliminate, but good luck). If you really did get rid of every single whitefly, don't you think the good bugs that eat whiteflies and keep them in check would move on, rather than face starvation? And then, when the whiteflies did sneak back into town, the troops would be gone and the marauders would sack your vegetable city.

Besides, there are no silver bullets, no cure-alls, even though advertisers might like you to think so. In fact, gardeners should be very wary of any advice when it comes to pests, disease and weed control. Do a little homework on the web, and consider possible consequences. Think it all through, even the advice on the next few pages.

🦋 🦋 🦋

What's Eating California?

SNAILS AND SLUGS

Here they come, up and over the fence, across the sidewalk and out from under old boards, pots and garden debris. As days get warmer in spring and nights dewy, snails and slugs go on the prowl, looking for tender young seedlings, even crawling up into citrus to munch on flowers, leaving their silvery telltale trails. The common garden snail can patiently travel up to 100 feet a night in search of food.

Of all the pests that have arrived in California—from the fire ant to the giant whitefly—few are as destructive to gardens as snails, also an introduced pest (as are many slugs). In the 1850s, a Frenchman brought snails to San Jose hoping that Californians might learn to eat them. Unfortunately, he brought the wrong species—according to *Tiny Game Hunting: Environmentally Healthy Ways to Trap and Kill the Pests in Your House and Garden,* by Hilary Dole Klein and Adrian M. Wenner (The University of California Press, 2001)—and soon the escaped escargots were eating California.

But take heart. In the last few years, fighting snails and slugs has become much easier and safer. Perhaps none of the following strategies alone will completely eliminate the mollusks, but a combination of techniques should bring prompt relief—and with no poisons.

Use Organic Baits

The newest line of defense is a product used just like the old poison baits, only it is not a poison. It's made of naturally occurring iron phosphate mineral ore combined with a cereal-like bait attractive to slugs and snails. Because they prefer the bait over plants, once they eat it they stop feeding and die within a few days. And since it is not a fast-acting poison (it interferes with their ability to make mucus), they have time to crawl back to their hiding places before dying, leaving no trace.

At one time, avid gardener Sharon Milder could handpick as many as 30 snails and slugs a day from her Westwood garden, a wonderful mix of perennials and old roses. After using iron phosphate, she found almost none.

Considered an organic product, iron phosphate won't poison pets, children, birds or other wildlife. After breaking down, it essentially becomes a fertilizer. Said to work best in early spring, it should be scattered about, not put in piles. The directions suggest using one level teaspoon over one square yard, or one pound per 1,000 square feet. A common brand is Sluggo; another is Worry Free.

Introduce Predators

Snails have very few natural enemies, with the exception of opossums and roof rats. Opossums can rid an entire garden of snails, given the chance. At one point my garden was completely snail-free, thanks to an opossum. Unfortunately, it moved on.

The next-best predator is the decollate snail, a pointy-shelled carnivorous snail. According to John Calman, integrated pest management specialist at the Los Angeles County Agricultural Commission, decollate snails eat common garden snails and their eggs (though they do not eat slugs). What makes them effective, though, is that they come to displace the common garden snail in the garden, occupying the same niche. But unlike ordinary snails, which target only the leaves of your favorite plants, they are scavengers, eating at all sorts of things and causing much less visible damage.

However, decollate snails will nibble on young bedding plants that have just been set out. Protect these areas selectively—with snail bait or a physical barrier of crushed eggshells, sharp sand or wood ashes. Do not use any kind of bait out in the garden. What kills ordinary snails also kills these.

Spring is a good time to release carnivorous snails.

Slugs have even less in the way of predators, but there is one—the shiny black ground beetles found under garden litter. Cherish them.

Create Barriers

Solid lines of crushed eggshells, oyster shells and wood ashes have long been used as physical barriers against snails and slugs. The Los Angeles County UC Cooperative Extension Common Ground program suggests another barrier that's easy to find in some neighborhoods: liquidambar balls. Popular as street trees and known for their colorful fall foliage, liquidambars drop their hard, spiky seedpods all year. A minefield of liquidambar balls would certainly deter me!

Mulching plants with organic matter also hampers the mobility of snails, according to research conducted by the Ventura County UC Cooperative Extension. Mulches make it difficult for snails to crawl through the garden.

But the most effective barrier is a copper strip, especially one called Snail Barr, which has edge tabs that can be bent to a 90-degree angle. Mollusks that try to crawl across copper apparently get a mild shock from natural ground current. And the edge tabs are tricky to negotiate.

Ordered in 100-foot rolls, Snail Barr can be wrapped around entire raised vegetable beds, totally excluding snails and slugs. For years it has kept the pests from the vegetable beds in my garden where we grow lettuce, a favorite food of these slimy creatures.

It can also be wrapped around the trunks of citrus to keep snails out of the trees. However, make sure the branches and leaves of the protected plants do not touch the ground, fences or walls—these pests use them as living escalators.

Set Traps

Many gardeners swear by beer, placed about the garden in shallow dishes, for trapping and drowning snails. But here in Southern California's dry climate, where liquids quickly evaporate, it doesn't work as well as it's said to, at least in my experience.

Trapping slugs and snails under old boards, however, is surprisingly effective because both need cool, dark hideouts during the day. Here is the method recommended by the University of California: Place a couple of two-inch-wide strips of wood as runners on either side of a piece of 1x12 board, so the bigger board is kept off the ground. Set the trap near places where snails and slugs are active (snails are likely to be found around or in agapanthus, iris, ice plant, ivy, jasmine and nasturtium). Check it every day—you'll find lots hiding on the underside. Smash the creatures with a stick, scrape them into a plastic bag, and put that in the garbage. The remains still stuck to the boards will likely attract even more the next night, according to UC research.

Common Ground Garden Program, part of UC Cooperative Extension, is on the web at celosangeles.ucdavis.edu/garden.
A mail-order source for decollate snails and Snail Barr is Mary's Decollate Snails, 912 Cassou Road, San Marcos, CA 92069-9233; telephone 760.744.9233.

SALTED SNAILS

Q: I have been struggling with snails since I purchased my house three years ago. I sprinkle pellets and the snails disappear for a while, but then they come back. A friend suggested that sprinkling salt on flowers will kill them just as effectively.

Is this true? Also, does my watering the garden at night attract snails?

—P.S., WOODLAND HILLS

A: Don't ever put table salt on the garden! It harms, even kills, plants. Watering at night does lure snails and especially slugs out into the garden since both like to travel on moist ground. Try switching to early in the morning, so the ground dries by evening.

SOW BUGS AND PILL BUGS

Q: Those cute roly-poly sow bugs are destroying my garden—killing daisies and poppies and even eating my strawberries. What can I do?

—L.O., SIMI VALLEY

A: Sow bugs and pill bugs (pill bugs roll up into tight balls, sow bugs don't) primarily feed on rotting and decaying matter, though they will nibble on young seedlings. If they really are doing damage to living plants in your garden, you have an epidemic-size problem that is probably cultural in origin.

Sow bugs and pill bugs "get blamed for more than they do," notes Mary Louise Flint in the excellent book *Pests of the Garden and Small Farm: A Grower's Guide to Using Less Pesticide* (The University of California Press, 1999), because they are often found on fruit or flowers initially damaged by some other creature. Snails, for instance, may eat plants at night, but by morning all you'll find are sow bugs feeding on the already damaged and decaying sections.

First, check to make sure other creatures are not responsible for the initial damage. Then look at environmental factors. Sow bugs—soil-dwelling crustaceans related to crayfish that breathe through gills—require moist conditions. Watering too often keeps the ground moist (and may actually initiate decomposition), encouraging their activity. A thick, chunky mulch, such as pebble bark, provides ample hiding and breeding space, especially if it's kept damp.

Cut back on watering, water early in the day, encourage good air circulation in the garden, and consider using another kind of mulch. Don't spray or use poison pellets. These little creatures actually have an important role to fill in the garden—helping old vegetable matter break down.

Figure out how to elevate fruits lying directly on moist ground so they do not rot. Strawberries are particularly susceptible to rot, which is why they are usually mulched. Mulch with black plastic or clean hay, and keep it on the dry side. Or put berries in raised beds so the clusters can hang over the sides, off the ground, and dry out.

CRICKETS

Q: You've written about other insects, but what about crickets? Are they beneficial? What do they eat?

—I.C., LOS ANGELES

A: There are several kinds of crickets living in Southern California. The most common, tree crickets, do feed on plant matter but are considered beneficial because they prefer to eat garden pests such as aphids, leaf hoppers and scale. These songsters that lull us to sleep in summer are almost impossible to find. "Its voice, like that of a ventriloquist, is difficult to trace to its source," noted the late Charles L. Hogue, author of the excellent *Insects of the Los Angeles Basin* (Natural History Museum of Los Angeles County, 1993). What you're looking for are thin, greenish crickets, only half an inch long.

Easier to spot, though less common, are the chunky dark-brown or black field crickets. Although they often get inside houses and continue to sing, they usually live under litter on the ground. They can become very minor pests if there are lots of them.

Another field cricket, the European house cricket, is light brown and smaller (three-quarters inch long). Introduced from Europe, they are often sold as fish bait or animal food, and they have come to live in or around houses. I don't know what they eat in the wild, but pet stores feed them cornmeal or raw potatoes and carrots.

WHITE GRUBS IN THE GRASS

Q: My lawn seems to be infested with larvae that develop into June bugs. Crows fly in, attack and rip the lawn to get to the larvae. Needless to say, we have a lot of June bugs in June. How can we treat the lawn to get rid of them?

—D.G., SANTA MONICA

A: Similar and related to the larvae of the fruit beetles mentioned above, but about half the size, the larvae of June beetles eat roots and can harm lawns and ornamentals, although they are normally not numerous enough to worry about. Crows and raccoons can be much more destructive when looking for them. There are many kinds of June beetles, with four types common here. All have very similar larvae, often called white grubs.

When there are too many, there is a biological control, a type of beneficial nematode that preys on larvae. These microscopic wormlike creatures also attack cutworms, flea larvae and other larvae that live in the soil. Results do not come overnight, but a dramatic difference is noted as time goes by. The nematodes will be around for at least two years and maybe longer. To find sources of beneficial nematodes or any other beneficial organism, obtain a free copy of "Suppliers of

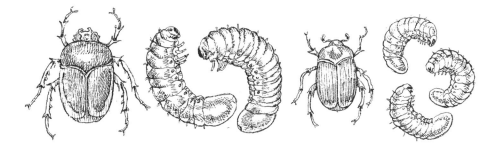

The large white grubs found in compost piles grow to become iridescent green fruit beetles (left), while the small kind found in lawns become June bugs.

Beneficial Organisms in North America."

If you want a chemical control, diazinon spray and granules are poisons that kill grubs—but also earthworms and other soil organisms. Read and follow directions very carefully, and never use them near edibles.

Manuel Gonzales of Pacific Green, a lawn-care company in Chino Hills, says to ensure that the poisons work, lure grubs to the surface by thoroughly watering the lawn the day before, apply the diazinon, and water again to force the material into the soil.

"Suppliers of Beneficial Organisms in North America" is available by writing to the California Environmental Protection Agency, Department of Pesticide Regulation, Environmental Monitoring and Pest Management Branch, 1020 N Street, Room 161, Sacramento, CA 95814-5604; telephone 916.324.4100; on the web at www.cdpr.ca.gov.

BIG GRUBS IN THE COMPOST

Q: There are quite a few healthy white grubs in my compost pile. I have read that they are the larvae of beetles. Will they eat the roots of my plants if I put the compost in the garden without removing them?

—S.H., LOS ANGELES

A: These huge grubs—about two inches long, white with dark-brown "helmets"—are the larvae of fruit, or fig, beetles (*Cotinus mutabilis*), a relative of the sacred Egyptian scarab and June bugs. The larvae are usually found in winter curled up in compost piles; the beetles in late summer. Although they look fearsome, the larvae eat decaying plant matter, so they actually help the composting process and won't harm your garden if they get added along with the organic matter.

GREEN BEETLES

Q: What I thought were just carpenter bees turn out to be some kind of beetle. They have an iridescent green shell and hang out in my sycamore tree. Could I have the dreaded Japanese beetle?

—S.Z., LOS ANGELES

A: This inch-long, metallic-green insect is the fruit beetle, so named because it may nibble on ripe fruit (it's uninterested in your sycamore). Only occasionally, though, does it cluster on and damage fruit; otherwise it is seldom a pest. It's also harmless but may fly clumsily, sometimes running into people and startling them.

Native to Arizona—where it presumably feeds on cactus fruit—it arrived here in the 1970s. While the adults are pretty enough to be jewelry, the larvae are those fat white grubs found in compost piles and mentioned above.

GERANIUM BUDWORMS

Q: Geranium budworms have chewed up the leaves on my geraniums, along with the buds, which then do not materialize into flowers. I keep getting new geraniums, and they keep eating them. What can a person do about a moth that comes in the night and lays eggs?

—C.D., LOS ANGELES

A: You need to break the egg-to-adult cycle, according to Louis Andrade, who runs Grand View Geranium Gardens, the largest wholesale grower in the West. There, they mostly regularly apply liquid *Bt* (*Bacillus thuringiensis*), a nonpoisonous biological control (Safer is one brand), which works best on the young larvae.

First spray the damaged plants with a pyrethrin-based spray or Orthene to kill the large adult worms, Andrade says. Then, a few days later, spray several times in a row with *Bt*—he suggests spraying every three days for a total of nine days, early in the morning or early in the evening. From then on, spray with *Bt* once every couple of weeks to prevent new budworms. When you think the problem is under control, you might stop spraying. But keep an eye out for new damage, and apply *Bt* at the first sign.

Andrade does not use the *Bt* straight. To a gallon of water, he adds a couple of liquid ounces of white vinegar, to "sweeten," or soften, the water. Then he adds the *Bt*, plus a couple of drops of household detergent, which makes the water "wetter" so the spray sticks better to foliage. Use this solution to spray the tops of the leaves and flower buds.

Orthene, a systemic insecticide that gets into plant tissue and thus into the flower buds where worms secrete themselves, is the best chemical approach. But don't use Orthene near anything edible, and follow label directions carefully.

INFECTIOUS FUCHSIAS

Q: Last spring I bought two small fuchsias from a nursery. When I got them home, I noticed an abnormality in their leaves, which have a drawn, kind of gathered-at-the-edges look, especially at the bud tips. By summer, most of my other fuchsias were infected. What is this condition, and what should I do to eradicate it?

—E.S., LAWNDALE

A: The condition could simply be caused by aphids, which are easily controlled with a horticultural soap spray. If the leaves are severely twisted, swollen and blistered (often accompanied by redness), it is probably caused by the fuchsia gall mite (*Aculops fuchsiae*). This tiny, worm-shaped mite, barely seen even with a hand lens, can severely disfigure fuchsias.

First, try cutting the infected foliage off and sending it to the dump (not the compost pile)—that works for moderate infestations. If plants are severely disfigured, the University of California recommends pruning in spring to remove all galled growth and then applying carbaryl (Sevin) or a miticide (such as Kelthane). Add a wetting agent (sometimes sold as a spreader/sticker) to help the solution stick to the leaves, then spray to thoroughly wet foliage. Repeat two to three weeks later. These two applications should provide control for several months. For further information, obtain "Pests of Landscape Trees and Shrubs: An Integrated Pest Management Guide," by Steve H. Dreistadt (University of California Division of Agriculture and Natural Resources, #3359, 1994).

Fuchsia expert Ida Drapkin says that most members of fuchsia societies use endosulfan (Thiodan). Follow the same procedure as above, but spray once each week for three weeks. This will finish the mites for the season. Although this poison is more effective, it is also more toxic to humans. Be sure to follow all precautions on the labels on these sprays.

Those who object to poisons can try pruning off all the infected growth, then spraying once a week with a light horticultural oil (such as SunSpray or Saf-T-Side), thoroughly wetting the foliage.

In some gardens, predatory mites have brought this pest under control. Also, 'Baby Chang', 'Chance Encounter' and 'Space Shuttle' are large-flowered fuchsias that are naturally resistant to the mites, as are many of the small-flowered kinds and such species as *Fuchsia thymifolia* or *Fuchsia arborescens*.

WHITEFLIES EVERYWHERE

Q: Help! Whiteflies, the giant variety, are everywhere in south Torrance. They are on coleus, common ivy, feverfew, begonias, hibiscus and even tall trees.

—G.B., TORRANCE

A: The "giant" whitefly is actually pretty small, about three-sixteenths of an inch long. But it makes a big mess, covering leaves with white, waxy deposits and dripping waxy filaments that look like holiday flocking. Black sooty mold fungus quickly follows, living on the whiteflies' honeylike excrement.

The whitefly dines on a long list of plants—from acacia to xylosma—but favors hibiscus. It's also found on giant bird of paradise, orchid tree, banana, mulberry, even Japanese anemone.

While there is no silver-bullet cure, help is on the way. In some areas, it has already arrived—in the form of three different parasitic microwasps (don't worry, they are harmless and don't sting). Collected in Mexico and Texas, these wasps were raised here by the millions and then released in the coastal counties. Already well established in places such as Tustin and Long Beach, they may actually be in your yard, according to John Kabashima, an advisor at the UC South Coast Research and Extension Center in Irvine.

Look on the undersides of leaves. If the oval-shaped whitefly pupae have turned quite yellowish, black or gray, they have been parasitized, which means that very tiny wasp larvae are living inside. You can also check for tiny emergence holes in the pupae, signs that the wasps have exited their hosts (just like in the "Alien" movies). You might need a hand lens to see them.

Kabashima says the wasps have taken hold in Orange County, where Master Gardeners helped disperse them. Los Angeles County should see improvement soon. People living right on the beach may still have problems, even after the wasps become established, Kabashima says, because the parasites don't seem to do as well there. They are not at their best in deep shade, either.

Don't expect all traces of the filament-spinning giant whitefly to vanish from your garden. There will always be some near the base of the plant, says Kabashima. The wasps always leave a few to eat later on so they never run out. "It would be like eating everything in the cupboard," says Kabashima.

In San Diego County, parasitic wasps have been released for several years. "Control can be spotty," cautions Vincent Lazaneo, home horticulture specialist at the San Diego County UC Cooperative Extension. "And you won't see results overnight, even if you do everything right." It may take a year or more before there is a real difference. In San Diego, some feel that a faster, more aggressive parasite is needed, similar to the one that almost immediately brought the ash whitefly under control a number of years ago.

While we wait for noticeable results, it's important to stop using any kind of control. Ignore advice to spray with light paraffin oil or summer oil—these also kill the parasites. Ditto for any kind of pesticide, including systemics. Whiteflies always recover faster than their parasites do after sprayings, and you will set into motion an ever-tightening spiral of increasingly more whiteflies and fewer and fewer parasites.

The only UC Cooperative Extension–recommended control for whitefly colonies is plain water, used to break the egg-to-adult cycle. Strong blasts of water from the hose aimed at the undersides of leaves work if you are persistent. Whitefly larvae cannot crawl back up to the plant once they are knocked off. But other adults will lay new eggs (often inside those rings of waxy, white concentric circles), so you must blast them again, and again if necessary, until the parasites begin to help out. One gardener reports that she has successfully controlled the giant whitefly by blasting it off plants twice a week.

Keep careful watch on the garden because the pest is fairly easy to control if you act fast. Colonies tend not to fly or wander (they drift into your garden on the wind) but cluster on the undersides of leaves. Simply picking off the leaves, putting them in a plastic bag and sending them to the dump is often enough to eliminate them.

This advice applies to any whitefly: Poisons seldom work because whitefly populations recover so quickly; it's better to stop using them, spray with strong blasts of water, and wait until natural predators get the upper hand.

CURLING LEAVES

Q: I have a ligustrum hedge with leaves that are green but curling. Some turn yellow and have spots as well. I have tried spraying, to no effect. Some advice?
—G.I., PACIFIC PALISADES

A: Usually, curling leaves indicate some kind of sucking insect, such as aphids or thrips. Your case is surprising because privet (*Ligustrum japonicum*) is one of the more bulletproof plants. The dwarf Texas privet (*Ligustrum japonicum* 'Texanum'), one of my favorite hedge and background plants, is incredibly tough and virtually trouble-free.

If it is a sucking insect, you're going to have to catch the critter before the leaves curl. By then the damage is done, and the pests have moved on, have been controlled naturally by predators or are hiding inside the rolled leaves. Control them in their unprotected state with horticultural soap or oil sprays. Always follow directions carefully.

However, I doubt your plant is a ligustrum. The leaves of *Ficus microcarpa* (sometimes sold as *Ficus retusa* or *Ficus microcarpa nitida*) are very similar, and ficus is commonly used as a hedge because it grows so quickly (though it also gets rather large, needs frequent pruning and has invasive roots). A quick way to tell the difference is to look at the leaf tip. Ligustrum has a sharp pointed tip; ficus also has a pointed tip, but the very end is blunt. Or break off a leaf or twig. The ficus will bleed a white, sticky sap.

This ficus is frequently covered with curled leaves (especially in summer), caused by Cuban laurel thrips, a sliver of a pest also often evidenced by tiny black calluses on the leaves. When the pests are numerous, you'll find small, narrow black bugs on your arms and clothing after you walk by.

Since the insects hide inside the leaf rolls, they are hard to control because most sprays can't reach them. If you can tolerate the disfiguring, the ficus will eventually shrug off and outgrow the attack. In winter you can try trimming or shearing the plants and disposing of the infected leaves. This will get rid of most of the thrips, which have a hard time surviving winter outside their blanket roll of leaves.

Spraying is not effective, but if you're seeking a chemical control, Orthene may be the best bet. A systemic, it is taken up by leaves and so is ingested by the thrips.

PINE TREE PESTS

Q: My mature red pine has some kind of pest problem. The tips of the branches get black, the roots of the needles get sooty, and eventually the limbs get brown and die out. Is there any insecticide I can use?

—H.H., TORRANCE

A: Most people have probably seen the sooty mold fungus on citrus, but it is also common on pines. This black fungus lives on the sugary excrement of leaf-sucking insects, which are the actual problem here. On pines, these may be aphids, pine scale or even pine mealybugs.

Most vigorous trees can stand some damage. But if too many branches are yellowing and dying, blast these creatures off with a strong spray of water. Or use a horticultural oil spray, but not the so-called dormant oils. Look for oils listed as "supreme" or "superior," those called summer or year-round, or paraffin oil. The label should say that the spray can be used on conifers during hot summer weather. Saf-T-Side and SunSpray Ultra-Fine are two brands.

Scale are the most difficult to get rid of because they are protected by hard shells. Only a few parasitic wasps and ladybugs can get under (or drill through) that shell. The defenseless new hatchlings, or crawlers, are your target, so you must discover when they are crawling about. Use a hand lens to spot them (they're about the size of the period at the end of this sentence), or double-sided tape to trap them. When there are a lot, spray with oil. Begin checking as early as February and continue into early summer.

If ants are climbing the tree trunk (they feed on the honeylike excrement of scale and protect them), stop them with a band of sticky gel, such as Tanglefoot.

CYPRESS: WHEN THE BOUGHS BREAK

Q: What can I do to minimize the effect of borers in the Italian cypresses that line our driveway? Short pieces of branches fall, presumably the results of the bugs.

—B.K., ANAHEIM

A: The damage is the work of the cypress bark beetle, according to arborist and pest control advisor Tom Wurster of Mitchell Pest Control in San Gabriel. First, adult beetles feed on tender twigs and nearly chew through them, causing twigs to break off; later, they burrow into the bark of the tree to the critical phloem layer.

Because cypress bark beetles are so difficult to control, says Wurster, the best course is prevention. Keep trees adequately watered with infrequent but deep irrigation.

A "brood" tree, where most of the bark-burrowing occurs, is usually in the vicinity, he says. A professional tree care company may be able to locate the brood tree and should remove it. The damage caused by the burrowing beetles is so severe—and control essentially impossible once they are inside—that the damaged portion of the tree will almost certainly die.

Beetles chewing on the twigs are easily killed by a spray such as carbaryl (Sevin), but new beetles quickly take their places if the brood tree remains. Spraying a tall tree, usually planted on a property line, is a job best left to a professional. If you attempt it yourself, make sure to notify neighbors.

EUCALYPTUS PSYLLIDS

Q: My eucalyptus trees have an infestation of red-gum psyllids, those nasty little suckers that live under some type of shell on the leaves. The bugs cause a lot of defoliation, and their shells drop everywhere. What can I do?

—J.G., MENIFEE

A: It used to be that eucalyptus were one of the few pest-free trees in California, but several insects have arrived here from their native Australia to change that.

There are now borers, which typically attack already weakened trees, and—at last count—four kinds of psyllids. Perhaps the most widespread is the red-gum lerp psyllid (*Glycaspis brimblecombei*), first found in 1998. Red-gum lerp psyllids are sucking insects found only on eucalyptus. The magnificent red gum (*Eucalyptus camaldulensis*) is their favorite host, but they're also found on lemon gum (*Eucalyptus citriodora*), sugar gum, red ironbark, *Eucalyptus nicholii* and others. The lemon-gum lerp psyllid (*Eucalyptolyma maideni*), found in 2000, attacks lemon gum and *Eucalyptus maculata*.

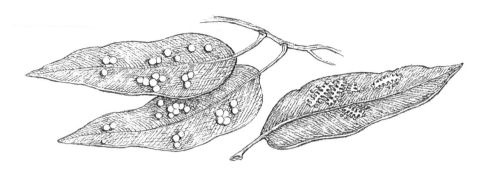

Several kinds of psyllids attack eucalyptus in California, and they build various kinds of protective shelters, called lerps, under which they live.

Both types of psyllids live under lerps, a kind of cover, or shelter. The lerp of the soft-bodied red-gum psyllid is a hard conical shell, while the lemon-gum psyllid lives under something that resembles a latticework tent. Several lemon-gum psyllids may hide under a lerp, often dashing in and out. Only one psyllid resides under the snug, cemented-down red-gum lerp.

A red-gum psyllid lerp looks a lot like the armor of a scale insect but is only a temporary shelter made by the nymph from crystallized honeydew secretions. Sometimes lerps and leaves are covered with green or black sticky mold that grows on those secretions. Often these lerps rain down from the trees as they are abandoned, or they cling to the dying leaves as they fall. Nymphs can also dribble honeydew from on high. Adult psyllids look similar to light-green leafhoppers, but only their bodies are green; the wings are clear.

Psyllids are tough pests to control. Fielding the first calls to come in to his company about the psyllid, entomologist Harold Mitchell, of Mitchell Pest Control in San Gabriel, asked people "where they wanted us to pile the firewood"—only partly in jest. In his 50 or so years in the pest control business, Mitchell says, he's never seen anything take hold so quickly.

But during the last several years, the company has found that it can save and completely clean up trees by using a systemic named Merit in specific treatment programs. Although it's possible for homeowners to get Merit in a product called Bayer Advance, treating eucalyptus is a big job probably best done by professionals.

Homeowners can take preventative measures, though. Make sure the tree doesn't get too dry in summer. Water occasionally but deeply, perhaps once a month. Don't overdo it—a wet soil can be just as harmful as one that is too dry. Keep water away from the trunk, and don't fertilize. If a tree is small enough, you can try spraying insecticidal soap and horticultural oils, but that probably won't do much good.

The red-gum psyllid can defoliate trees. A repeatedly defoliated tree may not have the energy to recover. A stressed tree then becomes the target of the other recent arrival from Australia, the eucalyptus long-horned borer, which can kill it. Dead and dying trees can be seen along many California freeways.

But things may soon begin to turn around. Native predators, such as green lacewings and certain ladybugs, seem to like to sample the psyllids, and a number of small birds will flock to trees to feast on the sugary lerps. The state is also releasing tiny parasitic encyrtid wasps from Australia—completely harmless to humans—which should begin to control the psyllids.

UC Berkeley Center for Biological Control program for the red-gum lerp psyllid is on the web at www.cnr.berkeley.edu/biocon/dahlsten/rglp.

FLIES IN THE OAKS

Q: What can I do to get rid of slow, hovering flies (bigger than gnats) that hang around in the shade of our oak tree and on the front porch?

—S.Z., LOS ANGELES

A: Those sound like false stable flies, which hover aimlessly and never seem to land. They breed in rotting organic matter, but I know of no way to get rid of them. They do not bite, if that's any consolation.

OAK ROOT ROT

Q: Oak root fungus is a big problem here, and there is little one can do about it. Some say there are no plants that are 100 percent resistant to it. Do you know of any?

—C.A., PASADENA

A: Oak root fungus is a serious problem, but there is much one can do about it, and there is a very good list of resistant plants. Entomologist Harold Mitchell has been battling oak root fungus for 50 years. He says that half of the dead trees he has "autopsied" have died of this fungus disease. It is very common in the foothill communities.

You can find descriptions of oak root fungus, also called armillaria root rot, in many books and articles. Seldom mentioned is that *any* perennial plant, not just trees and shrubs, can get the disease. It is not spread by spores, like most fungus diseases, but by rootlike mycelia that fan out from the infected roots of other plants, which can be up to 30 feet away. Overwatering favors the fungus.

Infected plants can be saved. Mitchell proudly points out trees that are still strong 50 years after he began treating them. "If there's anything I want to be remembered for, it's all those trees I've kept alive," he says.

The booklet "Resistance or Susceptibility of Certain Plants to Armillaria Root Rot" (University of California Division of Agricultural Sciences) contains a list of well over 100 ornamental plants that are considered immune or highly resistant enough to easily make a garden, even where oak root fungus is a serious problem.

"Resistance or Susceptibility of Certain Plants to Armillaria Root Rot" (Leaflet #2591) is available from the University of California Division of Agricultural Sciences, $1.75 plus shipping; telephone 800.994.8849.

TERMITES IN PATIO FURNITURE

Redwood lumber is not the tough stuff it once was. I still have my great-uncle's redwood garden bench, which he built and dated on the bottom. The year was 1914, and that bench has been out in the weather ever since.

I doubt my new outdoor redwood furniture—six chairs and a big table—is going to last even 10 years. Today most construction redwood is from second-growth trees, which are full of white sapwood. Sapwood has few of the natural defenses found in heart redwood—it doesn't resist rot or bugs very well. In fact, it's a favorite food of drywood termites.

The Western drywood termite (*Incisitermes minor*) is the most common termite in Southern California. And it's found not just in structures. Urban entomologist Hanif Gulmahamad, of the pest and termite control service Terminix, has observed damage indoors on furniture, pool tables, pianos, picture frames and (horrors!) books, and outdoors—in patio furniture, wood spas, gazebos, power poles (maybe they'll get rid of the ugly pole in my back yard), fences, firewood, boats and even a classic Ford woody.

The way to tell whether the drywood termite is eating your fence or furniture is to look for the piles of tiny wood pellets it leaves behind. Look closely at what appears to be sawdust, and you'll discover six-sided, barrel-like pellets. The white-colored termites hide inside the wood, but outside, in exposed tunnels or beside the occasional pin-size exit or entry hole, they leave their telltale pellets. In late summer and fall, the male termites swarm. They are chocolate brown and about half an inch long from the tops of their brick-red heads to the tips of their dark, veined wings.

To get rid of our termites, I used Term-Out, a material similar to WD-40 in the way it quickly spreads. It's an aerosol with a small hose attached, the tip of which is inserted in the termite holes. Every time I saw a few termite pellets, I'd find their holes and give them a blast. In a short time, the termites were eliminated; no new holes appeared. Follow the directions on the can.

When the termite tunnels become large enough (mature 15-year-old colonies can have more than 2,000 members) and are close to the surface, the wood gives way, and you have a big hole to repair. I used PC-Woody (made by PC-Products), a two-part wood epoxy paste that can be used outdoors. It cures hard and strong but can easily be sanded smooth.

Spoon out equal parts of the two pastes, and then mix together on a piece of board. Using a putty knife, stuff the paste into the holes and roughly shape or smooth it. The paste sticks to the knife, so it's difficult to do a very good job on big holes (a couple of my patches looked like choppy seas), but after it cures for 24 hours, it is easy to sand flat. A few pieces of wood split off or had fallen off my furniture, so I glued them on with Titebond II, a water-resistant wood glue that can be used outdoors.

Gulmahamad says that a stain or finish of some kind usually keeps drywood termites out. We decided to stain the furniture a dark grayed-green. I discovered (by calling several manufacturers) that deck stains work great on outdoor furniture. I was cautioned, however, not to use siding stains because they often contain additives that shouldn't come in frequent contact with skin. The solid-color acrylic latex deck stain I bought came only in gallon cans—half a gallon covered the whole lot.

Before applying the stain, the wood should be clean (I lightly sanded everything), dry and absorbent, one reason this is a good job to tackle in the fall when the air can be so dry. Work in the shade, as these stains dry much too quickly in the sun. When dry, they have a flat, dull finish. They raise the grain of the wood a bit, but lightly sanding with 220-grit paper makes them smooth again.

FUMIGANTS AND YOUR PLANTS

Q: We are planning to have our house tented for termites, and I am concerned about the herbs and raspberries planted up against the house. Will these chemicals contaminate the plants and soil?

—S.C., LOS ANGELES

A: According to Donald Reierson, staff research associate in the UC Riverside department of entomology, the most commonly used fumigant for termites is sulfuryl fluoride (Vikane), which has just about replaced methyl bromide. The former shouldn't "contaminate" plants or their roots (it is not absorbed), but direct contact may damage or kill them.

Vikane is manufactured by Dow Agro-Sciences, in Indiana. A company spokesperson says that roots can be given protection. Right before the tent goes up, thoroughly wet the soil—water works as an effective barrier to the gas. When the tent is taken off, the lighter-than-air gas "goes straight up," the company says, not down into the soil, and dissipates very quickly. There are no known short- or long-term effects on the soil.

Plants three feet from the house or closer may be burned or killed if the escaping gas actually hits foliage. Careful handling of the tent can minimize this.

Tenting and fumigating a house is still considered the best way of killing dry-wood termites, usually found in house timbers, dead tree limbs and patio furniture. If you have wood patio furniture—even redwood—put it inside the building before the tent goes up so it gets fumigated too.

THE BEES WE NEED

A Burbank gardener telephones a county agricultural official to ask where all the bees have gone. Another wants to know why he no longer gets many squash or peppers in summer and why there are so few apples on his tree. Are these incidents related?

One-third of the food on our tables comes to us thanks to the pollinating efforts of the common, everyday honeybee, according to Michael Pearson, Los Angeles County apiary inspector. And though it seems familiar enough to be, it is not native. Honeybees were brought from Asia to Europe ages ago, and then to the Americas in the mid–17th century, raised by farmers for their honey and pollinating efforts.

They are also an important pollinator of commercial crops. Bee scientist Adrian M. Wenner, professor emeritus at UC Santa Barbara, calls the honeybee the "ultimate generalist," pollinating all sorts of blossoms, from alfalfa to zucchini. The mostly mild-mannered feral honeybee has made its home in the wild, in trees or in walls of buildings, and through the years has pollinated many home fruits and vegetables—all of the stone fruits, apples and kiwifruit, for example, and such vegetables as eggplant, peppers and squash.

But honeybee populations are in trouble. "It's a disaster, actually," says Wenner. Two predatory mites—the vampire, or varroa, mite, introduced by accident in 1988, and the tracheal, introduced in 1984—are decimating wild honeybee colonies by the bucketful. And efforts to protect honeybees in commercial hives (such as those little white boxes seen dotting the country landscape) have made beekeeping ever more costly.

The result is drastically fewer bees. The nationwide population of ordinary honeybees has shrunk from about 5.9 million colonies in 1945 to roughly 1.9 million today, according to Stephen Buchmann, researcher with the Forgotten Pollinators Campaign, an Arizona group that promotes the unsung native bees.

Africanized Bees

It's more likely, though, that Africanized bees will take the place of feral honeybees because they are more resistant to the mites. Africanized bees started their northward trek way back in 1957, after imported African bees escaped from a Brazilian laboratory. Colonies have been found in all of Southern California, as far north as Kern and Ventura counties. Los Angeles in considered completely colonized, though not every bee is Africanized.

Honeybees become Africanized when their queens mate with descendants of these escapees. Honeybee colonies are not actually booted out by new bees; they are simply absorbed and converted by a new hybrid queen. Similar in appearance to honeybees but slightly smaller, Africanized bees are much more aggressive.

If avid gardeners are concerned about the disappearance of honeybees, the average homeowner (especially one who already fears bees or has allergies) is quite anxious about the arrival of Africanized bees. Calling them killer bees—an unfair moniker, given the facts—hasn't helped.

Although Africanized bees must be respected, they should not be feared. An individual out foraging for pollen or water is like any other honeybee, docile unless pinched, swatted or stepped on. And like an ordinary honeybee, each can sting only once, and the sting is no more potent. Potential danger arises when a large group becomes riled.

Africanized bees move, or swarm, more often than honeybees. When they are swarming, they are not particularly aggressive. It's when they start building a new hive that they become fiercely protective. People, animals, even the vibrations and smells from leaf blowers and power mowers (they cannot hear) set them off.

"Concentrated bee activity" (in other words, lots of busy bees) suggests a nearby hive, says Pearson, and that's your cue to "run the other way" and get inside a building or vehicle. It is possible to outrun Africanized bees—they fly about 11 to 12 miles an hour and defend an area only the size of a football field.

Established colonies can kill, although incidents are extremely rare. In this

---

IN AN EMERGENCY ...

- Report Africanized bee swarms to your local Mosquito and Vector Control District office. Look in the Government pages of the phone book or on the web at *www.mvcac.org*.
- Call 911 only if someone is attacked.
- If you are stung, run indoors. Remove stingers quickly by scraping them out with a blunt butter knife or a credit card; do not pull.

country, eight deaths have been attributed to Africanized bee stings since the bees' arrival in October 1990, one in California (in Long Beach). Since the Africanized bees arrived in Tucson, Arizona (in the late 1990s), "people's life styles really haven't changed that much," says Steven Thoenes, former U.S. Department of Agriculture bee scientist and owner of BeeMaster Systems, a bee management company, there. About 5,000 swarms are reported each year, according to Thoenes.

Africanized bees nest in the protection of a cavity, which can be surprisingly small, such as a curbside meter box, an empty cardboard box or flowerpot, or an attic. To keep them away from your home, Pearson says, "really clean up the yard," and cover openings in buildings with one-eighth-inch or finer wire mesh. If promptly removed by a pest control company, a colony is not a threat.

Native Bees

Southern California is home also to a myriad of native bees—about 500 species and subspecies. Of these, says entomologist Robbin Thorp, professor emeritus at UC Davis, at least 100 are common in and around our gardens.

Some can be very helpful in the garden, pollinating all sorts of fruiting crops. Buchmann, of the Forgotten Pollinators Campaign, asserts that native bees are better than honeybees at pollinating certain crops, including eggplant and tomato. Many native bees start earlier in the season; some are early risers or emerge on cloudy days, venturing out when no self-respecting honeybee would—more reasons they make good pollinators.

Casually observed, many native bees look like flies, and most are somewhere between the size of a housefly and a honeybee. Often they are dull brown or gray in color; a few have bright metallic, flylike colors. Most females can sting if provoked, though they rarely do.

Most, including sweat bees and alkali bees, are solitary, living in ground burrows rather than in colonies. Some live in deep, narrow cavities, such as those left by burrowing beetles. This includes leaf-cutter bees, which make those fascinating perfectly cut half-inch circular holes in rose leaves to cap either end of their nests.

Yellow-striped bumblebees and shiny solid-black carpenter bees are the biggest and best known of the native bees. If a bumblebee is nearby and you hear a high-pitched buzzing, it is shaking pollen out of flowers with its wing muscles. This "buzz pollination" is so effective with tomatoes that the bees are being raised to pollinate greenhouse tomatoes. Bumblebees live in small colonies in the ground. Not easily provoked, they do deliver a severe sting. It doesn't last long, though. I know—I pinched one once while weeding.

Carpenter bees are also good pollinators. Occasionally a lucky gardener will spy a male, which is dramatically covered with golden hairs. Slow to anger, females deliver a mild sting. The bees get their name because they burrow into soft wood, even telephone poles, to make their nests. The half-inch-wide holes appear to have been drilled by a precision power tool.

Squash, zucchini and pumpkins are pollinated by squash and gourd bees, which advanced north along with these crops from Mexico and Central America thousands of years ago. These ground-dwelling bees rise very early, often before daybreak, well before the flowers close at midmorning.

Sweat bees are good general pollinators, especially of melons. These housefly-size bees, just under half an inch long, are bright metallic colors. Males have striped abdomens. If provoked, females can sting, but the sting is less painful than that of a honeybee.

Mason bees are acknowledged orchard pollinators, even doing their work when ordinary honeybees are fast asleep on cloudy days, one reason farmers in the Northwest work to attract them to their apple orchards. Here, mason bees also pollinate apples and stone fruits (apricots, peaches and the like), even during wintry

GIVING NATIVE BEES SAFE HARBOR

Can native bees replace the dwindling honeybees as pollinators? Native bees often reproduce only once a year, and adults die before the young hatch. To rebuild their populations, they need places to live. In Southern California's dense neighborhoods this is difficult, but you can help things along.

- Leave a little uncultivated soil, some moist, some dry, where native bees can make homes, suggests Thorp. Bee scientist Adrian Wenner leaves bare dirt between flagstones in his garden where they can burrow. "Most native bees like the kind of place people are always trying to get rid of," he says: bare ground, dead accumulated brush and the like.
- Keep plenty of flowers in bloom, so bees have a constant pollen source.
- Limit the use of pesticide sprays. "People need to realize that every time they get rid of some pest with sprays, they also get rid of bees," Thorp says.
- Build bee homes or shells. Take a chunk of 2x4 or 4x4, and drill holes with the grain, four to six inches deep, spaced rather closely. Several diameters attract different bees. Put the block of wood on the north side of the house or under eaves where it is at least partly shaded. Various native bees will line the holes with leaves or mud and move right in. For mason, or orchard, bees, buy a bee house. Search on the web for mason bees.

weather, which is when blossoms often open. They are gentle, do not swarm and sting only when swatted.

To identify insects in your garden (and learn more about them), get the excellent, amply illustrated "Insects of the Los Angeles Basin," by Charles L. Hogue (Natural History Museum of Los Angeles County, 1993).

WASPS' NESTS IN THE LAWN

Q: Every early spring, my yard is invaded by some form of wasp, which makes its nest in the dirt and grass. I see many little holes with mounds of dirt. I am afraid to go barefoot in my own yard. Is there any way to discourage them?

—M.G., DOWNEY

A: Many native bees and wasps make nests in the ground, but I wouldn't be afraid to go barefoot (though I might worry about stepping on other things, like nails or glass). Most are so-called solitary wasps and bees, which rarely sting. Even when they do, it is often mild. There are exceptions, of course. Before you decide to get rid of them (which is very difficult, in any case), identify them—they may be beneficial creatures.

There are two you want to be careful of. Yellow jackets (aptly named) are bothersome and easily provoked. Big, black tarantula hawk wasps (up to two inches long with orange wings) feed on those furry spiders. The female's sting is painful, though she is not easily provoked.

If they are the inch-long, turquoise-striped sand wasps, rejoice—they eat houseflies. These have lived in my garden for years, and my wife, who frequently works barefoot in the garden, has never stepped on one. I've actually watched them catch flies and carry them back to their burrows.

❋ ❋ ❋

Back-Yard Fauna

KEEPING GARDEN BRIGANDS AT BAY

Wouldn't it be nice to go to sleep at night, or off to work in the morning, and know that your fruits and vegetables are safe? Safe from robber raccoons and burglar birds, sneaky squirrels, tunneling gophers, rabbits, deer, digging dogs and cats? If you had a big enough garden, you could afford to share your edibles with the wildlife. But in the typical Southern California garden, there is precious little produce to spare.

With a few minor carpentry skills and a modest budget, it's possible to build a critter-proof vegetable bed. You may be able to put away that plastic owl and the ultrasonic devices (which don't work anyway) and still pick strawberries and tomatoes at the end of the day.

Several years ago I observed such a structure in Arizona, home of the ultimate garden pest, the javelina, a wild pig that makes all other creatures look like they walk on tiptoes through your garden. With its snout and claws, it tears up gardens like some peccary corps of engineers, moving mounds of soil in the process. The owners of the garden I visited had built a garage-size enclosure with welded wire on the top, sides and underneath.

I've seen similar versions here in Southern California, one in Pomona and the other in consumer reporter David Horowitz' back yard. At his previous house, Horowitz had a huge 75x200-foot vegetable garden. "I could afford to share," he says, "even though the animals used to scarf about 25 percent of the crops." Now he has a much smaller space for vegetables, and keeping critters out has become more important. Since he frequently travels for work, he can't keep watch on the chicken coop, so to speak.

On his property, tree rats pillaged freely at night, sometimes even in broad daylight, and there were gophers as well. Horowitz' solution: Build a "fortress," simple, affordable and appropriately scaled for the smaller back yard. He built a 4x10-foot raised bed, nailed uprights to the bed's redwood boards, put in pipe rafters and covered the thing with one-inch chicken wire. It looks like a playhouse with a pitched roof, sheathed in chicken wire.

Additional galvanized chicken wire is buried about 10 inches deep around the sides to keep gophers and other digging animals from undermining the bed. (The bottom could even have been lined with wire.) The openings in the chicken wire are wide enough "for bees to freely fly through and do their work," he says, and the sides roll up so he can harvest or work inside. Slugs and snails are not a problem in Horowitz's garden; they're the favorite food of the roof rats he's keeping out. But a citadel like this could be made slug-and-snail proof by wrapping copper strips, which they will not cross, around the outside of the raised bed.

The critter-proof bed in Pomona is closer in scale to the one in Arizona. Gardener Natasha von Rathjen, who lives in the hills above Cal Poly Pomona, had problems with squirrels, rabbits, skunks, opossums and blue jays. Her solution was to have a builder of aviaries put together a 25x30-foot "aviary" that would keep birds out instead of in.

The structure is made from galvanized poles and wire aviary netting. Because it is so large, von Rathjen enters through a regular screen door, and she can comfortably walk around the individual beds on paved paths (no muddy feet when picking dinner!). She had bubblers installed in the beds and put on a timer. In 11 years, no animals have ever gotten in.

She had additional problems of hillside wind and inland heat, so the sides of the structure can be covered with shade cloth to protect vegetables. Shade cloth can also be laid over sections of the top when extra shade is needed, for lettuce in summer, for instance, although she shades many of the vegetables year-round.

This is the closest thing I've seen to a back-yard vegetable factory, though I might go one step further and keep a few small seed-eating birds inside. The company would be fun, and their droppings would enrich the garden. Sounds like a place for a hammock, too, under one of those shade-cloth panels. You could just lie back and watch the tomatoes ripen.

PEPPER SPRAYS

Q: Neighborhood cats stop by my garden to urinate in some of my favorite places. Last fall I tried spreading around an expensive powder, which was not effective for more than a few days, if at all. What can I do to keep those cats out of my garden?

—B.C., Los Angeles

A: Cats spraying onto the foliage, which is what this sounds like, are males marking their territory and are tough to deter. We have one neighborhood rogue who regularly hits a clivia near the back door, leaving a disagreeable odor. Try this: Fill a quart spray bottle with water, add one tablespoon Tabasco sauce, and spray the foliage. Or dust the ground with cayenne pepper.

Peppery products deter all sorts of pests, but they have to be reapplied each time you water. Better for the whole neighborhood: See if the cats' owners will get them fixed, which usually, but not always, stops this behavior.

On the subject of pepper: I know one gardener who battles deer with 15-pound commercial tins of cayenne. At Soka University of America, in Calabasas, landscape contractor Tom Hollow came up with a variation on the old pepper spray theme to protect roses from deer. He mixes a commercial-grade pepper-spray repellent called Hot Sauce with an antitranspirant named Vapor Guard (both sold by AG Rx in Oxnard). Antitranspirants are routinely used to keep foliage from losing moisture too quickly. In this application, they coat foliage so the pepper solution isn't washed off quickly by rain or watering.

Hollow suspects other pepper sprays, even Tabasco, mixed with other antitranspirants might also work. He cautions that, even though the substances aren't poisonous, gardeners should stand upwind during applications and avoid direct contact with the pepper solution. It can really burn, even though, he reports, it won't harm even the most delicate rose petals.

PHYSICAL DETERRENTS

Q: I need an easy, inexpensive way to keep cats out of my flower bed. What do you recommend?

—N.J., WESTCHESTER

A: Carefully cultivated, easy-to-dig soil quickly becomes a litter box for cats. Nurseries and mail-order companies sell dog and cat repellents, but I've never heard of any getting rave reviews from gardeners. Most say they don't work.

I have found only one surefire way to keep neighboring cats (or even your own) from digging in garden beds, and that is to lay branches across the empty dirt until plants fill in and cover most of the soil. Having saved woody, pruned branches from hedges, trees and shrubs, I simply lay them flat on any bare soil, just close enough to discourage digging and squatting. I suspect you'll find the slightly untidy look (although branches can be arranged quite artfully) preferable to the smell of cat poop.

I know of several gardeners who use this simple method in their raised vegetable beds, but it also works in flower beds. Also, consider planting more densely so less soil is exposed.

Another clever idea: "Empty nursery flats discourage pet damage until the plants can hold their own," says gardener Nora Kuttner of Fullerton. A plastic grid forms the bottom of the flats, so, inverted over the area, they make perfect little

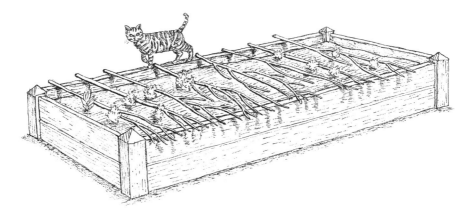

Laying bare branches across vegetable beds will keep cats
from using your carefully prepared soil as a litter box.

cages that still admit lots of sun and water.

Gardener Anita Work of Sylmar employs a method that keeps her two cats, dog and rabbit out of the garden beds. She pushes bamboo stakes, cut into 12- to 14-inch lengths, into the soil about six inches apart to form a grid resembling a bed of nails. At first the stakes are pushed so deep they are barely visible, but as plants grow they can be pulled higher until the plants become large enough to fend for themselves. The stake grid may sound like a fearsome medieval defense, but it makes it impossible for animals to dig up the area without harm, she says.

SCARE TACTICS FOR BIRDS

Q: Birds perching on a utility pole are making a mess of our pool deck. The utility company refuses to put up a fan-rotor device, like those on top of billboards. What can we do to scare the birds away? On a trip, we saw Mylar streamers in farmers' fields. Would that work? How about a fake owl?

—P.O., Valley Village

A: In my experience, fake owls, cats and other scarecrows do not work. However, flashy streamers do—if they catch birds by surprise. Modern Agri-Products, one manufacturer of bright red and silver Mylar streamers, recommends they be used only temporarily. At first the birds are startled by the flashy tape, but they soon get used to the color and motion. In agriculture, the streamers are taken down immediately after fruit ripens, in order that birds will be scared away again in following years.

Pasadena gardener Sharon Clark came up with something similar to keep birds out of her apricot trees. "I saved all those free AOL-installation CDs," she says.

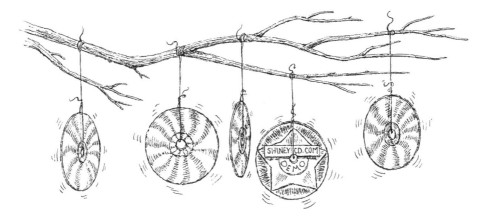

Birds are scared off by shiny CDs hung on branches,
but after a while the creatures become accustomed.

"When the apricots started to ripen, I tied 50 discs to the branches. In every sun-lit breeze they sparkled and shined. I lost not one apricot—canned 60-plus pints, shared with neighbors and friends, dried some, froze some, ate some."

Because reflective materials tend to work only for short periods, you may be more interested in permanent things, such as the rotor device you mention (which is why the billboard companies use them) and bird spikes. Bird spikes are those wicked-looking metal or plastic spikes attached to long strips. Like razor wire for birds, they are used wherever roosting birds are a major problem, including on urban buildings and marinas, on ledges and roof ridges and atop fences and pilings.

A number of different kinds of spikes are available (do a search on the web), including less-noticeable spikes made of clear material. But you must ask your utility company first if these can be put on that pole.

RACCOONS ROLL UP THE SOD

Q: I live in Topanga Canyon, and in October I put down sod. About a month later, raccoons began to roll it up at night, presumably looking for grubs. I've tried cayenne pepper sprays and even live trapping. I'm about to give up. Any suggestions?

—A.B., TOPANGA

A: The raccoons are, indeed, looking for grubs and are clever enough to roll up the sod in their search. There's really no way of stopping them. Even using beneficial nematodes to control the grubs will have limited effect—the raccoons will still come to look. One Topanga resident managed to bar them from a new sod lawn with a short electric fence.

In your lovely canyon setting, plantings more natural than a lawn and less water dependent (water is harmful to native live oaks) might be more appropriate and less likely to suffer at the paws of raccoons.

Consider planting a yarrow lawn, as has grown for years at the historic Lummis Home, just off the Pasadena Freeway. Or try perennial ornamental grasses left unmown, at least until fire season. These look beautiful in a wild kind of way, shimmering in the slightest breeze. Use a variety of types and heights. One example I have seen: buffalo grass as the basis planted with other grasses and interspersed with other wild-looking plants—tiny bulbs, perennials, even herbs.

Another option: Many new gardens just have paths surrounded by low perennials, shrubs and herbs, with wide areas here and there for outdoor dining or sunning. Gritty decomposed granite would look quite at home in the Santa Monica Mountains. Things could grow in the paths as they do in trails, and rainwater can soak into the granite. Make the paths wide enough so rattlesnakes—one of the hazards of gardening in Topanga—can't rest unseen at the edges.

The raccoons should approve of these schemes, and then you can enjoy their antics, not be at war with them.

Lummis Home, 200 East Avenue 43, Los Angeles; telephone 323.222.0546.

SKUNKS GO FOR THE BORDER

Q: My garden near the edge of Eaton Canyon labors under many disadvantages, including oak root fungus and Irish wolfhounds. The final straw—skunks are digging up the perennials and annuals in my front border in search of grubs and other comestibles. My neighbors have suggested several solutions, including mothballs. Do you have any advice?

—T.J., ALTADENA

A: The only proven deterrent I've heard of is a fence. Apparently skunks are poor climbers, and a simple two-foot-tall wire fence will keep them out.

Do not put poisonous mothballs in the garden. They are highly toxic to pets and small children—especially the older kinds, which are 100 percent naphthalene; some contain less-toxic paradichlorvos. Who knows what they do to the soil? I have heard that they are not terribly effective as animal repellents, anyway.

MOLES MUCK UP THE LAWN

Q: My lawn is suddenly full of slightly elevated burrowing trails, which might be the work of moles. Can I use one of those sound devices I see advertised on the web to chase them away?

—J.S., LOS ANGELES

A: Despite advertising claims, all of the various sound devices "do absolutely nothing," says Raymond Smith, supervising agricultural inspector for the Los Angeles County Agricultural Commission.

It has been proven many times over that the devices do not get rid of moles or any other creature. "There are virtually no controls that reliably work," says Smith. "If moles were in my garden, I'd leave them alone."

Unlike gophers and rats, moles are not rodents. They do not eat plants, but are insectivores with a voracious appetite for bugs, grubs and earthworms (this is what drew them to your lawn). Their damage is merely cosmetic—raised soil and an occasional exit hole.

One way to tell a mole from a gopher is by the shape of the exit holes. Moles come straight out of the ground, so their holes resemble miniature volcanoes, with the dirt evenly distributed. Gophers, on the other hand, exit at a

45-degree angle, which makes a lopsided mound. "It's easy to tell the two apart," says Smith.

The traps for moles are rather expensive and aren't often successful. No poisons are approved for use on moles. There is one organic solution that Matt Buckmaster, of Island Seed & Feed in Santa Barbara, finds temporarily effective—a yucky castor oil solution called Mole Med that is soaked into the lawn.

That there are so few controls is the bad news. "The good news," says Smith, "is that moles are not very common" in Southern California—unless, of course, "they happen to be in your yard—then it seems like there must be hundreds."

Island Seed & Feed is on the web at islandseed.com.

GOPHERS AND GUM

Q: Can you help those of us who garden in gopher-infested areas? Other than narcissus, are there any plants gophers avoid? I back up to the hills and have tried various means. I'm even thinking of ringing the garden with narcissus bulbs.
—J.M., GLENDALE

A: I have never seen a list of plants that gophers avoid, although it is known that they do not touch garlic or the toxic narcissus and daffodil bulbs. Gophers don't like the spindly five-foot-tall gopher plant (*Euphorbia lathyris*), the sap of which can also severely burn humans, but there is no proof that it repels them, despite frequent claims.

Macabee and other pincher-type traps are the most reliable controls, but follow instructions closely—two traps are necessary. Living so close to wilderness, though, you will make only a temporary dent in the population with traps. The same is true of gas bombs, special fumigating pellets (available only to professional pest control companies) and homemade windmills and whirligigs that transmit vibrating sounds into the soil, none of which is as effective as trapping. Ordinary poison baits, such as Go-Die Gopher Bait, work reasonably well.

Landscape contractor Tom Hollow has come up with what he claims is "the most effective gopher product ever." Hollow should know. Gophers are a constant problem at Soka University of America, in Calabasas, where he takes care of the 40-acre campus, surrounded by the wild Santa Monica Mountains.

Hollow's nifty and nasty solution: Punch a hole in their tunnel, and drop in a stick of Juicy Fruit chewing gum (unwrap the gum with gloves on to keep your scent off). When the gopher comes to investigate the light, it will try to eat the gum and choke to death. "It works better than any poison," Hollow says.

You can try protecting the roots of valued plants by planting them in buried homemade baskets of chicken wire. You can also line the bottom of raised beds with it.

RODENTS CHEW THROUGH DRIP TUBING

Q: Many plants on a deck in my back yard are watered by a drip system with standard quarter-inch tubing. I found that one supply line was leaking from many (more than a hundred) small bite holes that I assume to have been caused by mice or some other small rodent. Is this a common problem?

—R.W., RANCHO PALOS VERDES

A: It's not a common problem, but rodents will gnaw on tubing; it's one of the few drawbacks of drip irrigation. In this case, it may be the work of the common roof rat, which can hear the water running inside the tubing and will bite through for a drink.

In the garden, the tubing can be buried (though gophers will puncture it if they are around), but on a deck, the lines are vulnerable to rodents. Provide them with a bowl of water, and hope that satisfies their craving, or cover the exposed tubing with wood tunnels or loose rock.

Better yet, suggests drip irrigation expert Robert Kourik, use PVC irrigation pipe for all the supply lines, and use the small, soft tubing only to supply individual pots.

SQUIRRELS: IF YOU CAN'T BEAT 'EM, ENJOY 'EM

Our first introduction to the squirrel was at the kitchen door. I had just built a simple wood handrail on the back landing, and apparently she thought I had put it there expressly for her. It was very handy since it began right next to a big tree. She could hop on the railing and follow it to the kitchen door. There, she could lean out, look around the door frame and peer at us in the kitchen. All we could see was this little pointed head and two tiny ears. Well, hello.

That was the same day we spotted a squirrel pillaging our delicious fraise du bois strawberries and some nearly ripe 'Anna' apples. It took a while before we realized that these remarkably different creatures—one nice and the other naughty—were actually one and the same. You've heard of Dr. Jekyll and Mr. Hyde. Meet Dr. Squirrel and Mrs. Rodent, the Eastern red fox tree squirrel with the split personality that lives in our yard.

Don't confuse the bushy-tailed tree squirrels, which run up trees when frightened, with the scrawny ground squirrels, which dive underground. Ground squirrels live in close subterranean quarters that may foster serious diseases and are a public health concern; tree squirrels may be pesky, but they are not a health risk.

But tree squirrels do annoy—and even scare—some people.

On her good days, Dr. Squirrel is a well-behaved creature that scampers merrily across the lawn and takes peanuts from my hand gently and carefully, making sure the peanut is not a finger.

(Please note: It is not a good idea to teach squirrels, or any wild animal, to eat from your hands. They can bite hard, as my oldest son once found out. But someone else had trained the amazing Dr. Squirrel, and trained her well, though I suppose she could be an escaped stunt squirrel from nearby 20th-Century Fox.)

She can do some amazing feats. I discovered quite by accident that this squirrel will sit on my arm with her head in my shirt pocket as if it were a feed bag. After she grabs a peanut, she looks me right in the eye, as if to make sure I won't object, then fearlessly climbs onto my shoulder and finishes off the nut.

If my arm is not positioned correctly, she simply hangs from my shoulder by her back feet and drops headfirst into my pocket, her fluffy tail going up my nose. "What a clever squirrel!" I say.

But this very squirrel can be quite annoying—the very definition of *varmint*. I've seen her other persona, Mrs. Rodent, grab onto a too-curious cat and give it a nasty bite. My cats are actually scared of the squirrel.

She seems to find it amusing to chew loudly on the rooftop furnace vent, so

SQUIRREL FACTS, IN A NUTSHELL

In Southern California there are two kinds of tree squirrels. Eastern red fox squirrels (*Sciurus niger*), gray brown with a rusty glow, were introduced to the area many years ago. "Gourmets," according to one reference, they eat a variety of seeds, nuts and fruit. Native gray squirrels—big, bushy and very gray—primarily hoard and eat acorns, and spend time frolicking. Both species nest in trees, in cavities or piles of twigs about 30 feet above the ground. Both bear two litters of three to five young annually, in late winter and late summer, and live as long as 15 years.

In designated areas, tree squirrels are hunted. Like deer, they are classified as game mammals by the California Fish and Game Code and can be taken only by following hunting regulations. The native gray tree squirrel is protected in most urban areas. Eastern fox tree squirrels found to be damaging crops or property may be trapped by property owners or tenants with modified lethal box traps used for gophers.

In the city of Los Angeles, the Department of Animal Services claims jurisdiction over squirrels. You can rent a humane trap from a city animal shelter, which will relocate the captured animal. State and local law prohibits the poisoning of squirrels.

that the sound echoes throughout the house. She thinks it's funny to drop like a fur bomb into a hanging pot of impatiens, snapping off the crisp stems. She's the one who digs up the potting soil, looking for nuts hidden by the scrub jay.

For a number of years, we had a bright blue scrub jay that wouldn't put up with this nonsense and chased squirrels from our garden, squawking at them the whole way down the street. But that jay moved on, and the new jay is not so protective, despite regular bribes of peanuts from me.

It's a peanut economy in our back yard—whole, unsalted and unroasted peanuts passing as currency. They are begged, borrowed, stashed away and stolen. We give nuts to the jay, which consumes a few and buries the rest. The squirrel comes along, digs them up, eats some and reburies the others. I complete this economic loop when I find the nuts as I garden and give them back to the waiting jay.

I must say, both animals are expert nut hiders. The jay pounds nuts into the ground with her beak, then picks up dried leaves and neatly covers the hole. The squirrel digs holes at warp speed, tossing dirt everywhere, but then she pushes it back in and pats it down with her paws, completely covering the nut. She looks like a gardener firming the soil around some new bedding plant, but this lightweight has to put her whole body behind each pat.

It can be said of the nefarious Mrs. Rodent that her nose is remarkable, and not simply for the way it wiggles. She finds peanuts by sniffing and can smell one in the next yard. We know because once, while trying to get rid of her, we threw

GARDEN VANDALISM: WHO DONE IT?

Squirrels often get blamed for the bad deeds of other creatures, probably because their antics are so visible during the day. But squirrels do not tunnel or dig extensively (they do bury and uncover nuts in planted containers and in the garden). They do not eat leaves, but they do nibble on avocados, some deciduous fruits such as apples and apricots, tomatoes, strawberries and, of course, nuts and birdseed. They do peel and eat several kinds of citrus.

Other perpetrators to suspect: Raccoons and skunks dig at night, usually for grubs in lawns, flower beds and pots. Opossums do some digging but seldom cause serious damage, and they eat snails, so they could be considered helpful. The most destructive diggers, especially in freshly cultivated soil, are cats and dogs, both day and night. Birds of various kinds eat holes in fruit and consume seed or even small seedlings. So do nocturnal snails, cutworms and other larvae that hide in the soil by day.

some peanuts over the back fence. She stood there on her hind legs, weaving back and forth—nose working a mile a minute—until she smelled those peanuts on the other side of the block wall. Over she went and was back in just seconds sitting on top of the wall with one of the peanuts, somehow finding it in the neighbor's ivy. I was impressed.

Still, Mrs. Rodent can be a real pest, and there's not much that can be done about it. Whole books have been written on the subject. "Squirrel Wars: Backyard Wildlife Battles and How to Win Them," by George H. Harrison and Kit Harrison (Willow Creek Press, Inc., 2000), is one such chronicle. But although the cover copy says the book tells "how to win," I only found ways to keep squirrels out of bird feeders.

The only gardener I know who has won this war did so by building a giant metal cage around his prized apricot tree to protect the fruit, and only that tree was safe—squirrels still had the run of the rest of the garden.

Repellents seldom work, and because squirrels and people have similar tastes, it's self-defeating to cover fruit with distasteful products such as pepper sprays. These may work when you're trying to keep flowers safe from various creatures, but squirrels aren't all that fond of flowers, though they do relish the tightly closed buds of Iceland poppies.

Despite her dual personality, we're quite fond of our Dr. Squirrel, though at the moment we are squirrel-less. We assume she is nesting and rearing her young, and we hope she'll be back soon. We'll keep the peanut jar full.

☙ ☙ ☙

Weed Worries

A NEVER-ENDING CHORE

Most people look at my garden and see no weeds. I, on the other hand, often look at the very same garden and see *only* weeds. I'll be looking at some lovely plant and suddenly spot a weedy leaf poking out. Can I ignore it and continue sipping my iced tea? Of course not! I must get up from my comfortable chair, open the garage to get a trowel and dig it out, roots and all. I am perhaps a bit obsessive, but that's the only way to keep a garden so it at least appears to be weed-free. Get after weeds as soon as you spot them.

It's important to act before weeds scatter their millions of tiny seeds. Otherwise, the weeds will be worse next year and the year after until they have won and their flag flies over your garden. If you never let them set seed, the opposite happens: There will be fewer weeds every year, until you have pushed them back into the sea, so to speak.

Of course, there's no such thing as a weed-free garden—weeds can grow in the middle of an asphalt freeway. Some are nearly impossible to get rid of once they get a foothold. Let one of the bad boys—nutgrass, false garlic (*Nothoscordum inodorum*) or the yellow Bermuda buttercup—get started, and you may have no choice but to move away to be rid of them. I have known good gardeners who have actually relocated after certain persistent weeds got the upper hand, making it impossible to grow anything more interesting than a weedy lawn and big shrubs. Hopefully the new owners weren't gardeners and were content to have a green back yard.

Weeds with underground bulblets or spreading rhizomes must be dug out, not hoed or pulled, because they will come right back. To get rid of Bermuda grass, for instance, dig up every single root and rhizome. Even the smallest piece left behind will resprout. This is why some gardeners resort to the herbicide Roundup (glyphosate), which kills roots and rhizomes along with the leaves. It works well on Bermuda but isn't as effective on other weeds.

A few weeds, including some grassy kinds and the reddish, spreading oxalis, come apart when tugged on and leave a piece behind to regrow. Clever.

My garden's current scourge is an oxalis I have yet to completely identify. I can't find it in my weed bible, Tom Yutani's hand-drawn "Garden Weeds of Southern California" (now hard to find). I may even have planted it on purpose, having been told by someone that it was a highly ornamental, desirable little plant. It does have pretty white flowers on stems about eight inches tall, but seedlings have been popping up all over. They aren't easy to get rid of because their bulblets easily break away and sprout anew. Since they are near the soil surface, though, I have a chance of getting rid of this oxalis. I won't have to move.

Those gardeners cursed with another oxalis—the pretty spring-blooming Bermuda buttercup—have a very hard time getting rid of it because its bulblets often grow a foot or more underground and are difficult to find.

To dig weeds out, you need some kind of small, strong trowel or pry bar. My current favorite is an inch-wide trowel made from a solid, unbendable slab of stainless steel. Because it is narrow, it hardly disturbs the roots of neighboring plants. Weeds are easier to pry or dig out of damp soils because underground pieces are less likely to break off and stay behind. Searching for tiny detached bulblets in a dust-dry soil is no fun.

Quite a few weeds, such as annual bluegrass, chickweed, crabgrass and spurge, are annuals, which means they have no persistent, ever-living underground parts. With a hoe, simply skim across the soil's surface, cleanly severing weeds from their roots. Hoeing in a dry soil on a hot, sunny day guarantees that weeds immediately wither.

My current choice of weapons (they are legion) when it comes to hoes is the Weed Shredder, made by the Organic Company in Turlock, California. It looks like a lightning bolt on a pole and works about as fast—on the push and on the pull—its edges catching and severing weeds. With a nice long handle, it's extra light, easy to use and comfortable to carry around, so I have no excuse like, "Gee, it's a long way to the garage ... I'll get that weed later."

It may be tempting to put all those succulent green weeds in the compost pile, but don't—ever. The seeds will not decompose in most piles, and as you spread the finished compost you will also be spreading weed seed. For similar reasons, do not leave weeds on the ground to dry. The trash and recycling bins are the only places to put them.

THE ROUNDUP CONTROVERSY

Q: Can I use Roundup to eradicate mint plants that are strangling my roses?
—A.D., Whittier

A: Never use Roundup (glyphosate) around roses. Roses are particularly sensitive to this herbicide, and strange, stunted growth often follows its use. Digging plants such as mint out by hand is not difficult, and it is a whole lot safer for the roses.

Roundup works best in situations where the target is a deep-rooted persistent weed without any other plants close by, a Bermuda grass lawn, for example. Carefully follow label directions.

Although Roundup is the number one–selling herbicide in the country, some people will not use it, period. There is evidence that it has residual effects and that it is not as safe as previously thought, though the jury is still out.

BYE-BYE, IVY

Q: Could you tell me how to get rid of the roots of ivy? It threatened to swallow up the place before I paid to have two truckloads hauled away. Now it's back.
—H.F., Ventura

A: Obviously the roots weren't removed along with the tops. Algerian ivy is shallow-rooted, so you should be able to remove most roots by digging down a few inches. They are tough, though, and there are lots of them, so this can be quite a job. It may be the only way, however.

Herbicides don't work terribly well on ivy. For one thing, its leaves are protected by a waxy coating. Adding a surfactant, or spreading agent, to an herbicide, though, will improve its effectiveness.

TRIUMPH OVER FALSE GARLIC

Q: My yard is becoming overrun with a bulb plant that my neighbor has identified as wild onion (her yard is filled with it, too). What can I do to rid our garden of these plants?

—M.S., SOUTH PASADENA

A: This onion relative has already overrun the shores of the island of Bermuda and has become naturalized in parts of the Southeast, threatening to do the same here. It is called false garlic (*Nothoscordum inodorum*) because its gray-green leaves look like garlic's or onion's but have no scent. Herbicides roll off the foliage like water off a duck's back, so it must be carefully dug up by hand. Carefully, because the main bulb is covered with tiny baby bulbs that easily break off. Any left behind quickly become new plants. The little cluster of white flowers also sets seed, which readily sprouts.

In my own garden, I finally got it out by digging out each and every one of the bulbs and sending them to the dump, along with some of the surrounding soil to ensure I got it all. For the next couple of years I diligently dug out every overlooked baby bulb and watched for the tiny seedlings, which begin as twin thread-thin grayish leaves. It takes time and a lot of digging, but false garlic can be vanquished.

NUTSEDGE, NUTGRASS

Q: We had topsoil brought in before having sod installed, and now we have discovered a nasty, strong grass coming up in spots. We've been told it is nutgrass and that we can do nothing about it. I can't believe that. What can you tell me?

—D.K., NORTHRIDGE

A: Your sources are partially right, and this should make one think twice before ordering topsoil of unknown or suspect origin. Nutsedge (it is a sedge, not a grass) is extremely difficult to get rid of because it grows from spreading chains of nutlets, or tubers, deep underground.

First, it's important to know whether the lawn is infested with yellow or purple nutsedge, because each requires a different herbicide. Yellow nutsedge is more common in Southern California. Its seed heads are yellow, and new tubers are produced singly on the ends of rootlike rhizomes. Purple nutsedge has purple seed heads and produces strings of tubers on wiry rhizomes.

Basagran (BASF Corporation) and Nutgrass 'Nihilator (Monterey Lawn and Garden) control yellow nutsedge in lawns and are registered for that use. Hire a company to apply the herbicide, or do it yourself.

The herbicide Manage controls purple nutsedge, but only professionals are licensed to apply it. To find a company for the job, look in the telephone book under Lawns.

Elsewhere in the garden, the only way to get rid of nutsedge is to dig deeply and pick out every nutlet. Many are buried a foot below, connected in chains by thread-thin rhizomes. You won't find them all, so you'll have to keep after them. Or try starving them to death by diligently removing every leaf as it appears, so the plant cannot manufacture food. This may take two or more years, but many University of California experts recommend this crude tactic for the eradication of many persistent weeds.

OXALIS, FRIEND OR FOE?

Q: Why is oxalis referred to as a weed? Each spring it brings its bright, effortless color to my garden, which is planted mostly with natives.
—F.B., SHERMAN OAKS

A: Not all oxalis plants are weeds. A weed, after all, is simply something growing where it's not wanted by that particular gardener.

I suspect your oxalis is the Bermuda buttercup (*Oxalis pes-caprae*), with its bright yellow flowers clustered on top of stems up to a foot tall, and bright green, cloverlike leaves, often spotted dark brown. Kids sometimes chew on the leaves; in my neighborhood they call it sourgrass. The Sunset *Western Garden Book* (Sunset Publishing) lists *Oxalis pes-caprae* as an ornamental. But because it spreads so rapid-

Of all oxalis, yellow Bermuda buttercup may be one of the prettiest,
but it's also one of the most persistent of weeds.

ly, the book also suggests growing it in pots, not out in the garden.

I would add that it is impossible to get rid of, since it grows from a deep, easily detached bulb. The only way is to keep trying—never leave any above-ground growth. After several years, the energy stored in the bulb will be exhausted—it will starve to death.

The Grand Duchess strain of *Oxalis purpurea* is also sold as an ornamental plant. With glistening pink, white or lavender flowers more than an inch across, it's the first thing to bloom in the new year in my garden, dying completely back by summer. It too grows from bulbs and can become weedy, but it is less likely to spread and is not difficult to dig up should you decide to.

Occasionally several others, such as *Oxalis crassipes* and the native redwood sorrel, are grown as ornamentals. However, very few gardeners would consider the flat, spreading *Oxalis corniculata* and the taller one that roots as it spreads as anything but persistent, irksome weeds. Spend a weekend trying to dig them out of an otherwise handsome clump of native iris or a ground-cover planting of the tidy little dymondia, and you'll agree.

One clever gardener did use the weedy red-leaved oxalis between paving stones, mixed with clumps of bright-green Scotch moss, a handsome combination. As I said, one gardener's weed is another's treasure.

WHAT'S A WEED, ANYWAY?

A weed is unwanted, its appearance unkempt, its proliferation rampant. For certain gardeners, though, there are plants that cross that ill-defined boundary from designated weed to garden volunteer, useful and desired plants bestowed with the weedlike trait of coming back from seed on their own. In garden jargon, they self-sow.

The six-foot-tall *Verbena bonariensis* is the perfect example of a volunteer. It reseeds with abandon. In spring, seedlings come up like grass, and, while I would never be without a few of these oddly proportioned plants, I confess I spend a good deal of time weeding out the unwanted.

Seeding about like this may be too much for the tidier gardener. One tells me she wishes she had never planted *Verbena bonariensis*, which I had suggested as a very pretty and useful plant for the garden. Some of us, however, are thankful for any help we get from nature and, indeed, don't consider a garden mature and in order until this kind of disorder breaks out.

Several steady volunteers verge on being total weeds in my garden. If *Aristea ecklonii*—a bulblike perennial from South Africa—weren't so pretty and useful, I'd take every one out, just to stop it from seeding about. But aristea grows in the shade with grassy iris foliage and true blue flowers, so I put up with the hundreds of seedlings.

Ditto with the Santa Barbara daisy (*Erigeron karvinskianus*), a perfect filler but prolific reseeder. *Lychnis coronaria* 'Alba' is another self-seeder I couldn't live without. Its pure white flowers and gray leaves that resemble feltless lamb's ears look good wherever they come up.

Some plants that pop up suddenly are not from seed; they are actually sprouting from underground roots or stolons that have crept in from someplace else. One of my favorites, the roving, royal purple *Verbena rigida*, behaves like this (although it also self-sows).

Many plants in my garden that are wont to volunteer came from friend Chris Rosmini's huge and varied garden. This respected Los Angeles garden designer grows more kinds of plants than anyone I know, more than some botanic gardens, I suspect, so her volunteers are often surprisingly exotic.

Her tradescantias and sisyrinchiums volunteer, as does the ferny, gray-leaved *Corydalis heterocarpa*. "It is as pretty as any ground cover you can plant," she says. "I like to think of it as my version of the English *Alchemilla mollis*," which gardeners there use as a dramatic edging or filler to great effect.

Rosmini has observed that "when something seeds itself, it grows faster and more vigorously than if you had bought and planted one." This is certainly true of the many true geraniums that come up from seed, *Geranium incanum* in my garden and *Geranium sanguineum* 'Album' and *Geranium robustum* in hers.

The viney blueberry climber (*Ampelopsis brevipedunculata*) is one that verges on being a weed, if it weren't for those red-and-white-splashed leaves and bright blue berries.

Many consider the incredibly delicate Mexican feather grass (*Stipa tenuissima*) a weed. "But it's an awfully nice one," Rosmini says.

Most of these garden volunteers "are easy to get rid of if you don't want them," she adds. "They're not deep rooted or tenacious, like those weedy palm seedlings that come up everywhere."

As to the more obnoxious but pretty reseeders, she says: "There are parts of the garden where I simply let these thugs fight it out."

All of the volunteers mentioned so far are perennials, but many annuals come back from seed in the garden. We often call these wildflowers, such as our own California poppy and clarkia or the red corn poppy from Europe, which comes back from seed with regularity in my garden. In spring, Rosmini's garden is full of nigella, also known as love-in-a-mist, and the striking *Cerinthe major*. Annual sweet alyssum is so persistent that it is considered by some a weed.

I know I've left some reseeders out; there are many. I'm starting a list—my next garden may be all volunteers.

Why Is My Tomato Sick?

The Kitchen Garden and the Back 40

FARMERS MUST WORK LONG AND HARD to bring in the produce. I know. Some members of my family farm California's Central Valley, growing everything from almonds to berries to corn. But back-yard farmers shouldn't have to work that hard.

As with many gardeners, my very first plot was mostly vegetables. I was renting an old house with a large back yard that once held a barn, though the only plant left in the yard was an apricot—huge, gnarled but still bearing bumper crops. There was also an old tool shed, and before I even finished clearing my first 100 square feet for vegetables, I strung a hammock between the cot and the shed. In it I rested between my labors and admired my handiwork. I planned to enjoy my farming experience and those proverbial fruits of my labors. So what if caterpillars chewed my cabbage and got into my corn?

I've tried to maintain this relaxed attitude about fruits and vegetables ever since. Some of my relatives may be farmers, but I am not. If my crop is a failure, I am not going to lose the farm. Growing fruits and vegetables should be fun and relaxing for us amateurs, not something to fret about. Face it, you're never going to make a living or even save much money growing your own, not with the price of land and water being what it is in this state. Figure those into your farming budget, and back-yard agriculture is a money-losing proposition.

There's a very good chance, though, that what you grow is going to taste a *whole* lot better than what you can buy, even if you frequent farmers' markets. With very few exceptions, home-grown is tastier than store-bought. Home gardeners can grow varieties bred to be tender, not tough enough to withstand transit, and they can harvest at the peak of perfection, not a week earlier to allow for shipment. If they want salad greens that night, they can simply walk outside and snip some off.

Understandably, gardeners do worry that a pest might wipe out their efforts. Many might wish to spray and be done with it. But that is seldom a good idea in the vegetable garden or fruit orchard. There are many ways of battling pests and diseases that fall short of all-out chemical war. You may lose some skirmishes, and there is no lasting victory, but you can accomplish what you set out to do—grow tasty, healthful fruits and vegetables.

The University of California has pioneered intelligent pest control with helpful ideas such as IPM, or integrated pest management. Farmers have led the way, using parasites, traps, careful cultural practices and sometimes sprays. All these can work together to control pests and diseases with little harm to the gardener or his environment.

❦ ❦ ❦

The Vegetable Patch

RAISED BEDS

Imagine a vegetable garden in which seeds sprout readily, carrots grow long and straight and the soil is a pleasure to work in. A garden free of snails and gophers.

Picture raised beds.

Using just about any kind of building material, you can easily make small raised beds yourself, fill them with the best soil and amendments, and virtually pest-proof them. "It's the way to go," says organic gardening expert Janie Malloy, of Home Grown, Edible Landscaping, in Pasadena, who has installed dozens of raised beds for clients.

The folks at the Los Angeles County UC Cooperative Extension Common Ground Program would agree. Every week they build a few more raised beds for community gardens in the Los Angeles area. In these gardens, raised beds are home to everything from flowers to herbs. But what they really do wonders for are finicky vegetables, especially where the existing soil is poor. For school gardens, raised beds have even made blacktop gardening possible, says Rachel Mabie, Common Ground urban horticulture advisor. Landscape logs are stacked four high, log-cabin style, to make topsoil-filled vegetable beds 16 to 18 inches tall.

In home gardens, Malloy makes much shorter beds with 2x6 boards. Instead of bringing soil in, she improves what's already there by adding lots of compost. This makes the soil loose—almost fluffy—and easy to work in. It also ends up a few inches higher, partially filling the raised bed frames.

In home and community gardens, raised beds make vegetable gardening neat and attractive, nice enough even for the front yard. Arranged in tidy formal pat-

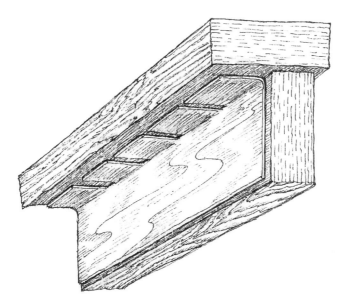

Special copper strips keep snails out of raised beds. Cap the beds with 2x4s,
and fold and tuck the strips under the overhanging ledges that face out.

terns—much like old Dutch and French potagers or early American kitchen gardens—they can become the centerpiece of the garden.

Best for smaller crops, raised beds can also contain tomatoes, even corn. Trellises for beans, peas and cucumbers can be nailed to the sides. Pumpkins and winter squash generally grow too big for raised beds and are better grown elsewhere, though even they can be planted in the beds if gophers are a problem.

With raised beds, vegetable gardening becomes a year-round, daily activity, rain or shine. "I use them constantly; every day, in fact," says gardener Liz Doonan of La Cañada Flintridge. She's got decomposed granite paths between her raised beds. With paths of shredded bark, gravel or decomposed granite, you can harvest on rainy days, or after irrigation, without getting your feet muddy. And because the beds are elevated, the soil doesn't get soggy.

Build raised beds out of just about anything—from concrete blocks to timbers. "We've tried all sorts of materials and designs," says Mabie, but Common Ground has settled on stacks of 4x4s or landscape logs. Concrete blocks or large river rocks also work and last forever, but two-inch-thick wood is the easiest to work with. After a few years, ordinary wood begins to rot, but beds made of construction redwood easily last seven years.

Simply nail boards together, and bury a little of the bottom in the ground so the beds don't leak soil at the base. Burying a bit also helps keep the sides straight.

If you use two-inch-thick boards, try capping them with horizontal 2x4s so you have a wider ledge to kneel or sit on while working.

Vegetable beds are usually four feet across so the centers can be reached from either side. Any wider, and it's hard not to step inside the beds, which compacts the soil and so defeats part of their reason for being. Mabie points out that lumber is often sold in eight-foot lengths, so cutting a board in half gives you two four-foot end pieces to work with; beds are usually eight feet long for the same reason. Most gardeners find several beds this size make a large enough garden.

If you have lousy soil, make taller beds and fill them with topsoil, ignoring the soil underneath. Use 2x12s or 2x10s or stacks of sturdy 4x4s. For a Long Beach community garden with impossibly heavy, sticky clay soil, Peter Beaudoin, of Common Ground, made 18-inch-tall raised beds of 4x6s stacked three high. He placed each of the boards log-cabin style, fastening one layer to the next with eight-inch spikes (he had predrilled starter holes). He then filled the big beds with imported topsoil.

Be a careful shopper when ordering or bringing in topsoil, Mabie cautions. A sandy loam is best, but one that is too sandy will dry out quickly after irrigations. If amendments have been added to the topsoil, make sure they are thoroughly composted or that nitrogen has been added. (Otherwise this important nutrient, rather than being available to your plants, is caught up in the decomposition process.) No matter how good the topsoil is, augment it with bagged soil amendments or compost, plus fertilizer.

In fair to good existing soil, simply add lots of amendments or compost, and fertilizer, to make it soft and fluffy. Start with a six-inch layer thoroughly tilled to a depth of about 18 inches. Add even more if the soil isn't easy to work. Always work the soil when it is damp, not wet or dry.

To exclude snails, nail copper barrier strips along the top of the outside of the beds, then fold the flaps over flush with the wood, facing in. The strips are designed to face outward, but in this position they are hazardous to a gardener's legs. Even better: Cap the beds with a 2x4, then tack the copper strips under the ledge so the fold is facing out, like it is supposed to. Copper strips can be found at nurseries. The best kind, with the fold-over tabs, are made by Snail Barr. Make sure no vegetables grow to hang over the sides (becoming siege ladders for snails).

If gophers or moles are a problem in your garden, make the sides of the beds 12 inches tall (gophers can climb into a bed any shorter), and line the bottoms with half-inch aviary wire or galvanized hardware cloth with quarter- or half-inch openings.

Many gardeners water by hand, but installing drip lines or using pop-up sprinklers with small-radius nozzles makes watering a snap. Irrigation expert Robert Kourik's book "Drip Irrigation" has a section devoted to raised beds that details a nifty removable system.

With the soil improved, sprinklers in place and snails and gophers excluded, you will quickly discover why Malloy insists this is the only way to go. "I love them," she says. "They're efficient and attractive; maintenance is low, and they're easy to water."

"Drip Irrigation," by Robert Kourik, is available through Metamorphic Press, PO Box 1841, Santa Rosa, CA 95402; telephone 707.874.2606.
A mail-order source for decollate snails and Snail Barr is Mary's Decollate Snails, 912 Cassou Road, San Marcos, CA 92069-9233; telephone 760.744.9233.
Common Ground Garden Program, part of UC Cooperative Extension, is on the web at celosangeles.ucdavis.edu/garden.

NO RAILROAD TIES NEAR EDIBLES

Q: We are using railroad ties as a border around vegetable beds on a moderately sloping hill. It is evident that they are heavily treated. A friend from Germany was concerned about the treatment leaching into the soil and affecting the plants. Is my friend's concern valid?

—J.R., PALOS VERDES

A: Although people have been using them for years to hold back hills and make raised beds, railroad ties should not be used near vegetables. Any material that prevents wood from rotting cannot be good for the vegetables or you. Railroad ties are treated with creosote, which is toxic, says soil scientist Garn Wallace, of Wallace Laboratories in El Segundo, a soil consulting and testing firm. Creosote, a wood tar, is an organic compound that decomposes and dissipates in time, at which point the wood begins to rot.

Pressure-treated wood, treated with chromated copper arsenic, also leaches toxic materials, including arsenic, only these minerals last a long time in the soil. In its research on pressure-treated wood, *Organic Gardening* magazine (January 1994) concluded that no type of chemically treated wood should be used near edibles.

It looks as though the Environmental Protection Agency is going to halt the manufacture and sale of chromated copper arsenic-treated timbers. Other kinds of wood treated with nontoxic materials such as ACQ (alkaline, recycled copper and quat, a fungicide) are expected to take its place. These may pose no problems for people or gardens, though it remains to be seen.

In the meantime, the best bets for raised vegetable beds are natural redwood or cedar boards. Redwood is the most commonly used, though it will begin to rot after several years. Concrete blocks work as well, though new concrete leaches calcium hydroxide into the soil for about six months, inhibiting plant growth. Best on a hillside is old, broken concrete slabs, laid in layers to make short retaining walls. These hold back the soil but let excess water pass through and are nearly inert chemically.

COVER CROPS BOOST FERTILITY

Q: The soil in my garden is varying consistencies of sand and clay, all comparatively hard and sterile. I am considering planting some sort of winter ground cover in my vegetable garden, which I could then dig in. Do you have any suggestions?

—M.L., BAKERSFIELD

A: Plants grown and tilled into the soil for their nutrient and organic value are called cover crops, and there are many. Various grasses, including cereal grasses, are used, as are wild clovers, vetches, beans and peas. The common yellow mustard that now blankets our hillsides in spring was previously a cover crop in orchards and vineyards, though it is now considered too weedy. As they grow, these plants accumulate nitrogen from the soil. When they are dug back in, that nitrogen becomes available to the vegetables that follow, or to trees or vines already growing in an orchard. Since the plants are tilled in, they also add valuable organic matter.

Some plants are much better at this than others, and seeds for true cover crops that do well in California are hard to find. One excellent source is Peaceful Valley Farm Supply. For homeowners, the company recommends its Green Manure Soil Builder Mix, which includes seeds for wild beans, peas, vetches and oats. The company suggests sowing three to five pounds per 1,000 square feet, and says this returns up to 290 pounds of nitrogen and up to 49 tons of organic matter to each acre. It does sell the mix in small amounts.

The reason cover crops are not used by more home gardeners is obvious: Nothing else can grow in that spot until the plants are tilled under. However, if you plan to let the vegetable garden rest for a season, fall is the time to sow many cover crops, including the mix mentioned above. It will grow with the rains, and in spring you can dig it all under, adding fertility and tilth to the garden.

Peaceful Valley Farm Supply, PO Box 2209, Grass Valley, CA 95945; telephone 916.272.4769; on the web at www.groworganic.com.

HORSE MANURE DOESN'T MAKE SENSE

Q: I am interested in starting a vegetable garden, and I have been offered several tons of composted horse manure. I was told that it is okay to plant vegetables in composted manure without any other amendments. Is this true?

—J.G., AGOURA HILLS

A: Even when it's been composted, and even when it's from a horse, straight manure can be toxic to plants. Horse manure is better than steer manure but is still relatively low in its ability to hold moisture and nutrients and is high in salts. Horse manure is especially high in boron, although it may not have as much sodium as steer manure, according to soil scientist Garn Wallace, of Wallace Laboratories in

El Segundo, a soil consulting and testing firm.

Use well-aged composted horse manure only sparingly. Wallace has found that one cubic yard tilled in to every 1,000 square feet is about the maximum that can be safely used. If you want to pursue this further (since the manure is free), have a sample tested by a soil laboratory. It can tell you how much you can use safely.

TOMATOES: THE GARDENER'S OBSESSION

Okay, maybe it was the weather that allowed me to have ripe tomatoes on Memorial Day. But you never know. Maybe it was the location I picked for them.

I planted 'Early Girl' in late February in what I thought was a special spot that would give me extra-early fruit. I picked a sheltered, warm piece of ground against a south-facing wall of the house, looking for maximum heat and light in my cool, somewhat coastal West Los Angeles garden. By the end of April, plants were four feet tall; they had big green fruit by May 1, with fully ripe tomatoes on Memorial Day. I thought it quite an achievement.

Then I thought it would be fun to find out from other tomato gardeners around Southern California the hows and whys of getting early tomatoes. So I asked.

"It was just an early year for tomatoes," Jim Holley of Torrance said via e-mail. "I plant 'Early Girl' each year, and it usually does not produce until late June to July 4. This year I had the first on June 1. Dang, they are good."

Linda Chisari wrote from Del Mar: "I began picking tomatoes on May 25." It was June when she wrote, and she was getting fewer tomatoes than in May, which, she said, "suggests that the warm temperatures were at least as important as the varieties." It had been a warm, fogless spring.

Ingrid Elsel from Ventura wrote in June: "I planted my tomatoes against a south-facing garage wall this time and have had ripe tomatoes for weeks. I imagine this is due to our wonderful warm spring weather."

Maybe it was the weather; maybe it was that special south-facing spot. I'm convinced that location has a lot to do with getting early tomatoes, especially for those who garden near the coast.

"I garden near the coast and have been able to bring in ripe tomatoes around Memorial Day most years," Daryl Cella from San Pedro wrote. "My usual successes are from plants I put in the ground in February or March, planted next to a south-facing concrete-block wall painted white."

In Northridge, where orange groves once grew, Ernie Schroer grows tomatoes year-round against the south wall of his house. "The microclimate is very different there," he said. "In late February, I picked 10 pounds of tomatoes one afternoon from four plants." I'm jealous.

He grows 'Carmello', a tasty French variety from Shepherd's Garden Seeds. As proof, he sent along a photo of a plate full of tomatoes with a February photo-date stamp in the corner. These he had planted in early fall, but that's another story.

Late February is the time to put in plants of an early variety. 'Early Girl' is the most common, available at virtually all nurseries. Chisari had luck with several others that actually ripened before 'Early Girl' (though by just days). She planted 'Stupice', a Czech variety gaining popularity in California; 'Enchantment', a prolific egg-shaped tomato, and 'Sun Gold'.

Morris Cutler tried two newer early varieties, the tall 'Oregon Spring' and the short, bushy 'Burpee's Early Pick'. Both produced nice crops but later than 'Early Girl'. Seed catalogs are full of newer early varieties for the adventuresome, including 'Northern Exposure', 'Early Cascade' and 'Fourth of July'.

In Pasadena, Jill Polsby even starts 'Better Boy' (which is not an early variety but happens to be her favorite) "no later than February 10," she said. Fruit forms by May in a special spot along a south-facing wall.

The consensus: Find a spot in the garden where it stays sunny all day. Against a south-facing, light-colored wall, tomato plants will be protected from cold north winds and Santa Ana winds and will get additional reflected heat and light. If you don't have a handy wall, just make sure the plants get full days of sun. Dottie and Bill Philles managed to get tomatoes by June 4 from plants that sit in the middle of a community garden in Torrance, only two miles from the beach and unprotected from chilly ocean winds, though they did lose about half the plants to the elements.

Other reader tips: Cella suggested an interesting planting method. "I use a posthole digger to make a hole deep enough to plant the seedling up to the top few leaves, removing all others. At the bottom of the hole I put a generous handful of composted steer manure covered with a thin layer of soil. After the plants are established, I fertilize them with a 'tea' made by soaking manure and compost in a bucket of water for several days. This elixir seems to give the plants a boost, but I'm careful not to add too much nitrogen, as this results in great plants with little fruit."

Some gardeners ignore the conventional tomato wisdom and don't plant their tomatoes deep in cool weather. Instead they plant them like anything else—at the same level they were in the nursery containers—so the roots are growing in the warm soil near the surface.

Schroer doesn't start with nursery plants; he sows seed directly in the spot where the tomatoes are to grow. His trick? Prepare the soil, adding fertilizer or amendments. Scoop out a little depression, and fill it with an inch-thick layer of seed-starting or potting mix. Sow the seed on this, and cover with a hot cap (he gets these clear plastic caps from Gardener's Supply Company), which provides enough heat for germination. Leave the hot caps on until plants outgrow them.

Priscella Blakely from West Los Angeles doesn't even bother to plant seed. She simply nurtures the seedlings that pop up on their own in February and still manages to get "at least a dozen tomatoes" by early June in her five-foot-wide south-facing garden.

There is no one trick that nets early tomatoes, which should encourage gardeners to experiment and come up with their own patented, surefire methods.

Shepherd's Garden Seeds, 30 Irene Street, Torrington, CT 06790-6658; telephone 860.482.3638; on the web at www.shepherdseeds.com.

Gardener's Supply Company, 128 Intervale Road, Burlington, VT 05401; telephone 888.833.1412; on the web at www.gardeners.com.

TOMATOES AND CROP ROTATION

Q: Regarding growing tomatoes in the same spot year after year—I know this is a bad practice, but space is a real problem for city gardeners with only one area of sufficient sun. I was told by a nurseryperson that I might dig in sulfur granules, which would act as a fungicide against soil-borne pathogens. Have you heard of this?

—K.F., PACIFIC PALISADES

A: It's true that diseases can build up in soils if tomatoes grow in the same spot year after year. That's why certain tomatoes have been hybridized to resist such things as fusarium wilt and verticillium wilt (listed as F and V, respectively, on the labels). Organic gardening guru Andy Lopez says that digging in soil sulfur would cause more problems than it would cure. The sulfur, which acidifies soil, would kill good, as well as bad, soil organisms. Instead, Lopez says, add fresh homemade compost every year. University research has shown that homemade compost does, indeed, cut down on tomato pathogens.

Lopez says he can point to many gardens in which the locations of crops cannot be changed, or rotated, but that have no soil problems because they are regularly invigorated with fresh homemade compost. He makes a strong distinction between homemade compost and compost available at many nurseries, adding that, although some specialty nurseries do offer quality organic compost, the kind made in home compost heaps is as good as it gets.

Some gardeners go so far as to dig a hole about 18 inches deep, fill it with only compost and then plant the tomato directly in the compost, changing it out each year.

Another trick, which has been shown successful in university research, is to plant garlic in winter where tomatoes grow in summer. Apparently the garlic helps

Leathery scarring on tomato bottoms is called blossom-end rot,
a disease caused by inconsistent irrigation.

cleanse the soil of tomato diseases. And then there is growing disease-resistant varieties. Combining all three techniques should allow you to grow tomatoes in the same sunny spot each year.

Andy Lopez is on the web at invisiblegardener.com.

PATCHY TOMATOES

Q: For 12 years I've grown the best beefsteak tomatoes, but in the last few, they've gotten black-crusted, flat-sided bottoms. I cut off the crust and the rest is fine, but they sure are ugly. What can I do to avoid this problem?

—J.S., VENICE

A: The leathery scarring on the fruit is blossom-end rot, usually caused by either sudden changes in soil moisture or a lack of calcium.

Switching between too much and too little moisture can bring on this disease. For example, if you are watering regularly—say, every week—and then stop for a few weeks, that sudden change will bring on blossom-end rot. Jim Waltrip, of vegetable seed grower Seminis Garden, recommends daily drip irrigation to maintain consistent soil moisture.

Whether or not you use drip irrigation, try to keep the soil evenly moist, with the emphasis on *evenly*. In some climates and some soils, tomatoes can grow with almost no irrigation, but if you soak them one week and let them bake the next, you are inviting blossom-end rot. Mulch plants so they do not dry out too fast, but make sure the soil drains quickly and does not stay too soggy.

Certain tomato varieties, especially pear-shaped kinds, Waltrip says, are more prone to blossom-end rot.

Though bad watering habits are the more likely reason, lack of calcium is the textbook cause, he says. Adding small amounts of calcium to the soil may help. Calcium is found in agricultural limestone and in ground oyster shells. One suggested cure is to add five pounds of pulverized limestone per 100 square feet before planting. Carefully mix it into the top 10 inches of soil.

RED SPIDER MITES ON TOMATO LEAVES

Q: For the last few years my tomato plants have been decimated by red spider mites. Do you have a solution?

—D.L., Ontario

A: Common inland, red spider mites cause stippling and then yellowing of leaves, and eventually defoliation. Nearly invisible, they look like tiny moving dots, but the telltale evidence is the minute webbing they make on the undersides of the leaves.

Several experts I spoke to agreed that the best control on vegetables for this warm-weather pest is a light horticultural oil spray, such as Pest Fighter Year-Round Spray Oil, Saf-T-Side or SunSpray. On the label, tomatoes are listed as approved for spraying; follow the recommended dilution.

A few precautions: Water beforehand so the tomatoes are not dry, spray early in the morning, and do not spray when temperatures exceed 95 degrees, or leaves may burn. Light oil sprays are not poisons but work by smothering pests, so your tomatoes are perfectly safe to eat.

Next best would be the miticide Kelthane, which has been around for years. It is a poison but one with relatively low toxicity. The label will explain how close to harvest you can use it. The same precautions mentioned above apply.

ASPARAGUS AND ARTICHOKES

Q: I live about nine blocks from the ocean and need to know how to plant asparagus and artichokes.

—T.O., Redondo Beach

A: You live in the perfect spot for growing artichokes in Southern California—close to the beach. But don't expect the same tasty, meaty buds found at the market that come from the foggy fields of Castroville. Down here, harvest them small and they'll taste better and be less stringy. Normal harvest size is plump but still tightly closed.

Artichokes such as 'Green Globe' are usually sold bare root in winter. Plant the dormant roots vertically in the soil with the top sticking out at the same level it was before it was dug from the fields—in other words, so the crown and cut-back leaf stalks are just above the soil line. Away from the coast, gardeners may have more luck with seed-grown artichokes, such as 'Imperial Star'. Planted in early spring like any other annual, they will produce the first year.

Artichokes need average watering and little fertilizer. In spring the plants produce buds—a few big ones on top and smaller side buds. Harvest all at the same time. After harvesting, cut stalks to within an inch of the ground. A new stalk will spring up and produce a second crop (of poorer quality) in late summer or fall. Unpicked buds open into spectacular purple thistles.

In late fall, as leaves begin to yellow on the kinds grown from roots, cut plants completely to the ground. They will be back next year, bigger than ever. Because seed-grown kinds often don't come back, they are best taken out each fall and new ones planted in spring. Watch out for snails and ants on artichokes.

Asparagus are reliable in all climates, but ask 100 expert gardeners how to plant them and you'll get 100 answers. Also sold in winter as dormant roots, these are buried deep underground. One of the most common methods is to plant them in trenches two to four feet apart. Trenches should be one foot deep and one foot wide with a layer of completely done compost on the bottom.

Space roots about a foot apart, and cover with two inches of soil. Gradually add more as the tips begin to grow, until the trench is filled in. Don't get ahead of the growing tips; make sure they are always exposed. Asparagus need only normal watering. The compost should feed them for most of the year, although you can fertilize through spring and summer. Add compost on top the following spring.

Don't harvest any asparagus during their first spring. The following spring, begin harvesting by cutting spears below ground with a forked asparagus knife (which also makes a great weeding tool). Harvest only for a short time, and let the rest turn into ferny, leafy stalks. Cut this foliage to the ground in late fall. Plants will produce edible spears for years and years.

BRUSSELS SPROUTS AND CAULIFLOWER

Q: This is my first time growing Brussels sprouts and cauliflower. I know to tie the leaves over the forming cauliflowers, but what do I do when the Brussels sprouts begin to form? Are the leaves edible like collards, kale and other greens?
—B.B., Los Angeles

The leaves of all cole crops, such as Brussels sprouts and cauliflower, are edible, although the bigger, older leaves are often bitter and not usually harvested.

Because Brussels sprouts need months of cool weather, it is difficult to grow this crop away from the beach. Inland gardeners should plant as early in the season as possible, even in late August, to extend the cool season. Hot weather shuts down Brussels sprouts and causes heads to open much too quickly.

The little leaves that make up individual Brussels sprouts are tastiest while the heads are still tightly closed. As soon as they begin to loosen, it's best to harvest. Heads won't ripen all at once—they begin at the bottom of the stalk and work their way upward. Where days are cool, very close to the beach, it's not uncommon to see bare, stripped stalks several feet high with buds still ripening at the top.

Modern cauliflower varieties are self-blanching, meaning leaves need not be tied overhead. Harvest them before the white flower buds begin to loosen—you want cauliflower heads to be tight. At the first sign of loosening (a prelude to blossoming), cut them off. Don't try to judge the time of harvest by the size. Some modern varieties can get huge—as much as a foot across!

THE INS AND OUTS OF BEETS

Q: Can you tell me how to grow beets successfully?

—M.C., SAN PEDRO

A: In Southern California, beets are a year-round crop, but they are easiest to grow during the cool months. Sow seed spaced about one inch apart. Don't be surprised when several seedlings sprout from each seed. A beet seed is actually a "seed ball," according to Nancy Bubel's *The New Seed-Starter's Handbook* (Rodale, 1988), "an aggregate of two to six individual seeds." Bubel suggests soaking seed before sowing and making sure the seed is in good contact with the soil by tamping it with the flat back of a hoe.

Los Angeles County Master Gardeners program manager Yvonne Savio scatters seed, pushing each into the soil up to her first knuckle, about half an inch deep.

As beets grow, thin to two inches apart, but not by pulling. Snip off the leaves of unwanted seedlings with small scissors so as not to disturb the roots of others.

It takes at least two months for the first beets to be ready to eat. Some beets grow faster than others. Harvest these first. Others will continue to grow and ripen for a month or more. This prolongs the harvest for at least several weeks.

Both the tops and the roots are edible. Should your harvest be too bountiful, it is said that the round beet bottoms (roots) can be stored for as many as four years!

KEEP THAT CILANTRO COMING

Q: I have a small herb garden in pots on my patio. Although most have done nicely—my basil and chives are thriving—I'm wondering why my cilantro plants die. The whole area gets lots of sun, and I water regularly. Any suggestions would be appreciated—I love that herb.

—G.K., SAN MARINO

A: Cilantro is my favorite, too. An annual herb from southern Europe, *Coriandrum sativum* lives to make seed, which is what cooks call coriander. A lot of gardeners have trouble keeping cilantro from becoming coriander. In the warmth of summer, it sets seed rapidly, but if you start the plants in the fall, it takes much longer and there will be plenty of leaves for fresh salsa, soft tacos and special Asian dishes.

A second sowing in early spring, say March, should keep you in cilantro until the onset of summer. In summer, plant the cilantro in a cooler place and pinch off flower buds as they begin to form. A little shade might help, and keep the soil constantly moist once the plants are several inches tall.

Start cilantro from seed (you can use the coriander sold at the market), since the little pots sold at nurseries contain way too many seedlings. Crowded, they go to seed quickly. Or pry all those little seedlings apart and give each its own spot, or pot.

Of course, being an annual, once cilantro makes seed, it dies, so start fresh every now and then to keep yourself swimming in cilantro.

RHUBARB, A MIDWESTERN TRANSPLANT

Q: Can I grow rhubarb here?

—L.B., LONG BEACH

A: Yes, although heaven knows why you would. There are better uses for the space. Although Midwesterners love rhubarb and it is pretty, the plants are big, the leaves poisonous and the red stems used only in pies. Varieties named 'Cherry' and 'Strawberry' are the two common red-stemmed types, available bare root in winter. Plant these perennial vegetables three to four feet apart.

IS OVERFEEDING POSSIBLE?

Q: In my back yard I have six bathtubs in which I grow onions, tomatoes, fennel, cucumbers and other vegetables. I seem to be getting a lot of growth with my plants, but very few blooms. Am I overfeeding?

—B.K., HOLLYWOOD

A: Most likely. Anything grown in a container (even one as large as a bathtub) needs regular fertilizing, but too much nitrogen causes excess growth at the expense of flowers and fruit.

Some gardeners fertilize at first with a high-nitrogen formulation (fertilizers with numbers such as 10-5-5 on their labels, the *10* being the percent of nitrogen), then switch to flower-and-fruit formulations, such as 0-8-8. These have little or no nitrogen and are supposed to promote flowering and fruiting, but there is little scientific evidence that they do.

Tests conducted at Cal Poly San Luis Obispo concluded that there is no difference between fertilizing with nitrogen the whole time and fertilizing with nitrogen at first, followed by a no-nitrogen formula. To get more flowers and fruit, continue using a high-nitrogen fertilizer, but use it less.

USING NEEM ON VEGETABLES

Q: I purchased a neem oil product, Safer BioNeem, to use on my vegetables and citrus, but the label says not to use it on food crops. I've heard it's organic—can I use it anyway?

—L.G., TORRANCE

A: It's against the law to disregard label instructions, even on so-called organic products. However, Safer BioNeem is registered for a great variety of edible crops, from citrus to tomatoes. You apparently have an old bottle from the days before neem was registered for use in this state.

It would be very surprising if neem weren't labeled for fruits and vegetables, since it has a very low toxicity for pets and humans. For the record, neem is less toxic than aspirin and even the nonpoisonous biological control *Bacillus thuringiensis* (*Bt* for short), and rates only a caution on its label.

Neem is derived from the neem tree in India and comes two ways—as an oil and as an extract. Both have extremely low toxicity because neither is a poison.

Neem oil smothers, kills and repels pests such as mites and, to a lesser extent, whiteflies and aphids. In addition, it controls some fungus diseases, including mildew and rust (these are common rose problems—Rose Defense is a neem oil product made by Green Light). For diseases, neem oil is touted mostly as a preventive and is apparently quite effective.

Fruit, Nut and Vegetable Spray (also from Green Light) is a neem oil product for food crops. Do not spray when bees are about, however, since it can kill them.

The more powerful neem extract products, which act as pest growth regulators and repellents, are most effective on insects that pass though all stages of metamorphosis (they do nothing to diseases). Safer BioNeem is an extract aimed at pests ranging from hornworms to sawflies. It usually takes three to 12 days before results are noticeable. Extracts can harm beneficial insects, so use with restraint.

CATERPILLAR COMBAT

Q: I have cabbage, collards, tomatoes and beets in my little garden spot. Little green worms are eating my cabbage and collard leaves, and I don't know what to do about them. I dread thinking about those big tomato worms.

—W.C., SANTA MONICA

A: The biological control *Bacillus thuringiensis* (*Bt*) is a bacterium that kills caterpillars about three days after they eat and digest it. It can be applied to vegetables up to the day of harvest. Because it is not a poison, it does not affect humans, pets, earthworms or beneficial predators in your garden or the soil.

Bt works best when caterpillars are young, so apply it thoroughly and before damage occurs (though it helps even after there are lots of holes). It kills cabbage worms and tomato hornworms, though it doesn't work on tomato worms once they get big, fat and sassy. You'll have to handpick these (or hire someone less squeamish to do it).

I like to use the dust version of *Bt* (one kind is made by Safer) because it is visible on the plant and I know whether it has been washed off by rain or watering. It requires no mixing, so it's always ready to use. I keep cole crops such as cabbage and cauliflower dusted from day one, so the worms never have a chance to get started.

To use Safer dust, hold the plastic bottle upside down, remove the small plug that's set off to one side, and gently squeeze, aiming the little nozzle up so it covers the undersides of leaves (where the worms hide). Dust is hard to find at nurseries, though the liquid form of *Bt* is commonplace.

That white butterfly (the European cabbage butterfly) fluttering around gardens in summer is the adult of the worm and is busy laying next winter's eggs. An interesting tidbit: Cabbage worms prefer green cabbages over the red varieties, perhaps because the green worms are not invisible against the red leaves. Red cabbage also is prettier shredded into salads. It might be the wiser choice if cabbage worms are a real problem in your garden.

CORN-EAR DAMAGE

Q: I grow a plot of sweet corn each year and have a lot of damage from the large green worms that invade the ears. How can I control them?

—D.G., ENCINO

A: Those green caterpillars are corn ear worms, although they are not always green—they exist in a variety of dusky colors. Some have side stripes, and all have short hairs growing from wartlike bumps (look very closely). They not only tunnel through ears of corn but also leave holes in tomatoes (they're sometimes called tomato fruit worms), lettuce, even beans.

The easiest way to deal with corn ear worms on corn is to cut off the damaged ends after harvest. Ear worms usually eat less than a third of the ear, so slice that off and you'll never know they were there (cutting off the ends also makes it easier to skewer cobs on corn holders, so it's a win-win situation). Send all damaged fruit to the dump, not the compost heap, to prevent the pest from spreading. That goes for infested tomatoes, too.

The nonpoisonous biological control *Bt* (such as Safer Bt Caterpillar Killer) works well on tomatoes and beans and can be dusted or sprayed on corn silks every few days from formation to when the silks dry.

The University of California also recommends a technique that entails dribbling 20 drops of mineral oil from an eyedropper into each ear, three to seven days after the silks appear. Both approaches kill baby worms as they enter.

RX FOR EGGPLANT

Q: The leaves of my otherwise healthy eggplants, Japanese and Italian, are shriveling and dying. I have grown them nicely for years and never had this blight. I've tried a variety of sprays, but none works. What can I do?

—J.L., WEST LOS ANGELES

A: Never spray without identifying the problem. It's like shooting in the dark. In this case, it's probably not a bug that's the cause, but a disease—verticillium wilt. This is a soil-borne fungus, and the solution is to plant somewhere else every few years so it can't build up in the soil. Sprays do not help; instead they kill innocent, beneficial bugs such as bees, wasps and ladybugs.

To check for verticillium wilt: After a plant dies, split the lower stems and the roots lengthwise. Brown streaks inside are caused by the fungus.

If you've already pulled the plants out and can't check, grow eggplant in another location next time. It sounds like you've been growing eggplants in the same spot for too long. The same thing goes for tomatoes, which also get verticillium wilt in time, though there are somewhat resistant tomato varieties. Or try adding lots of homemade compost to the soil each season, which seems to cut down on disease.

SQUASH LEAVES TURN WHITE

Q: My squash and pumpkins start out just fine. Then white patches appear on the leaves, and soon they are coated with a white powder. Can you help?

—M.F., WEST LOS ANGELES

A: Powdery mildew is common on all cucurbits, including squash, pumpkins, cantaloupe and cucumbers. A built-in resistance is the first and best line of defense. Some varieties, such as 'Early Pride Hybrid' cucumbers (Burpee Seeds) and 'Amber Hybrid' cantaloupes (Park Seed), have bred-in resistance. I've run across only one squash that claims resistance: 'Park's Crookneck PMR Hybrid' (Park Seed), a small, space-saving bush, three to four feet across.

Aziz Baameur, vegetable crops advisor for the Riverside County UC Cooperative Extension, also suggests growing plants in full sun, watering well but avoiding overhead watering (to keep the spores from germinating) and excess fertilizer.

Also prevent powdery mildew by dusting or spraying with sulfur. Safer makes an improved sulfur formulation that is reportedly more effective. Never apply sulfur when temperatures threaten to rise above 90 degrees—it will burn the foliage.

Burpee Seeds Company, Warminster, PA 18974; telephone 800.333.5808; on the web at www.burpee.com.

Park Seed Company, 1 Parkton Avenue, Greenwood, SC 29649; telephone 800.213.0076; on the web at www.parkseed.com.

❦ ❦ ❦

Fruit Trees

THE NOT-SO-SMALL ORCHARD

In his Northridge back yard, Tor MacInnis grows 63 varieties of apples—all on one tree. Not only that, he grows 22 kinds of pears (which aren't even supposed to grow in his climate), 18 different apricots, 19 types of Asian pear, 31 plums and 28 plumcots. All of this fruit grows on only six smallish trees—making his back yard a textbook example of the age-old propagation technique called grafting.

The tanned MacInnis says lack of space is what started him grafting. Although his back yard is almost two-fifths of an acre, he wanted to grow dozens of fruit trees. The solution? Put dozens on one tree. His garden is in Sunset Zone 18— defined in the *Western Garden Book* (Sunset Publishing) as the coldest parts of the inland valleys and considered a good area for deciduous fruit trees.

In grafting, a branch or a bud from one plant is attached to a living, compatible plant, the splice healing like a cut heals on your skin. While it may sound vaguely Frankensteinian, grafting "is really pretty easy," says MacInnis.

So what started out as a 'Dorsett Golden' apple is now part 'Gordon', 'Beverly Hills', 'Anna', 'Ein Shemer', 'Granny Smith', 'Fuji', 'Gala', 'McIntosh', 'White Winter Pearmain', 'Winter Banana' and so on. From each branch hangs a metal tag so MacInnis can keep track, which makes the pyramidal apple look like a decorated Christmas tree.

The different varieties ripen consecutively, so the tree is never covered with apples, but there is fruit on it for an amazing six months of the year.

Saving space and spreading out the harvest aren't the only reasons to graft back-yard trees, says MacInnis. Another is that many fruit trees need another like variety, a pollenizer, growing nearby in order to produce sufficient fruit. For example, the apple named 'Anna' does better if the variety 'Ein Shemer' or 'Dorsett Golden' grows in the vicinity. In addition, a well-established, existing tree that produces poorly can be completely grafted over to become essentially a different variety, or several different varieties.

Apples and pears are the easiest of the deciduous trees to graft, MacInnis says, and apricots the hardest. Pears supposedly need much more cold than Southern California can provide, but he has found that some do fine, at least in his area.

The method MacInnis used is called whip grafting, simple to make with a sharp knife, grafting wrap and a little hot wax. Scions (pronounced "sigh-ons"), the branches that are appended to the living tree, can come from neighbors' or friends' trees. Nurseries must prune their bare-root fruit trees each winter, and this is where MacInnis gets many of his. Each winter the California Rare Fruit Growers holds scion-wood exchanges, where its 3,100-some members swap branches. Mail-order companies, such as Sonoma Antique Apple Nursery, also sell scions. (They must be kept cool and moist before use.)

In addition to the apples, pears, Asian pears, apricots, plums and plumcots, MacInnis has grafted genetic dwarf peaches and nectarines, figs, jujubes and grapes. He even has a grafted wisteria that blooms in three colors and a multicolored crape myrtle in the front yard. "I couldn't help myself," he says.

Grafting Made Simple
Grafting, at least with deciduous trees such as apples, is best accomplished in

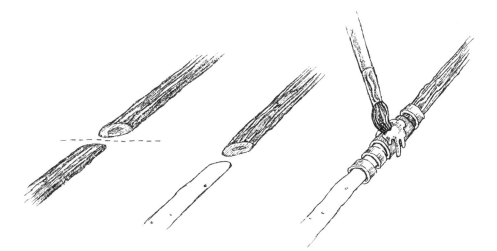

To graft, cut off some scion wood, make a matching diagonal cut
on the tree branch, then attach the two with grafting rubbers
or electrical tape. Protect with hot wax.

late winter. To make a graft, the branch of the living tree and the scion must be of similar thickness, between a quarter inch and a half inch thick. The idea is to join their cambium layers—that thin layer just beneath the bark that conducts water and nutrients. "Nothing happens anywhere else," says MacInnis—the center of a branch is essentially dead wood and the bark simply protection.

•   Using sharp shears, cut off the end of the tree branch to be grafted. Choose a scion of about the same thickness, and shorten it with shears, leaving about three or four buds.

•   With a sharp knife (preferably one with a straight blade edge), make a long diagonal slice on each. Be careful to keep the cuts flat, and avoid what's called shoveling, or curved cuts, so the two will fit tightly together. Make cuts away from buds since branches are distorted near them.

•   To join, move the branch and scion around until they fit snugly, then wrap the splice with special grafting rubbers or with stretchy plastic electrical tape. Don't use green garden tape or rubber bands—neither is strong enough.

•   Once the two pieces are tightly wrapped, coat the last inch of the branch and the whole scion with hot melted wax. This keeps the graft from drying out until it takes. MacInnis says grafting wax is best, lasting months, but ordinary paraffin will work. He melts the wax in a small pot with a butane torch outdoors. You can melt it in a microwave but not on the stove, since flames might ignite the wax.

•   Label the new graft with a long-lasting metal tag. In the following weeks, resist testing the graft by touching or pulling—it may break. MacInnis says that even birds landing on a newly grafted branch can snap it off.

California Rare Fruit Growers is on the web at www.crfg.org.
Sonoma Antique Apple Nursery is on the web at www.applenursery.com.

MAKE THE MOST OF A GOOD PEACH

Q: I have a peach tree that I grew about 20 years ago from the pit of a supermarket peach. How can I find out what variety it is? It produces delicious fruit.
—N.W., ALTADENA

A: For something to be a named variety, it must have been grown vegetatively— from cuttings, buds or grafts; it cannot have been grown from a seed. Since your peach is seed-grown, it has no name or identity. Every plant grown from a seed has two parents and so is distinct and unique, even if it varies in only small ways from its parents.

You're actually lucky your peach produces tasty fruit, since it could just as easily have been a poor producer of insipid or tiny fruit. One frequently hears of avocados grown from pits that bear small fruit or very few.

Plants propagated vegetatively, however, are exactly alike every time. In the world of horticulture, these cultivated varieties are designated cultivars, with their names appearing in print inside single quotes—such as the apple named 'Anna', or the bougainvillea named 'California Gold'. Every 'Anna' is identical to every other 'Anna'.

If your peach is a winner, why not propagate it vegetatively? Graft it onto a young peach tree in the winter. You can even give it a name, like 'Altadena Beauty'. Grafting is not difficult to learn, but many professional gardeners can do it for you.

HIGH DENSITY, HIGH YIELD

Q: I've read about planting dwarf deciduous fruit trees (such as apricot or peach) very close to each other and about planting them in the same hole. Any advice?

—A.W., SYLMAR

A: High-density planting is the name of the fruit game now. That means stuffing two to four trees in the same hole, or planting them only 30 inches apart in a line as a hedge. The idea is to get several varieties in the space usually occupied by one.

In my grandfather's time, it was quite commonplace for gardeners to graft different varieties onto one tree. In my parents' yard, in Northern California, he turned one apricot into a tree of many fruits, with grafts of several varieties of apri-

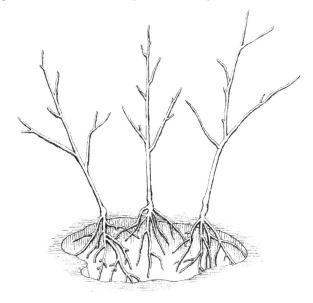

To get a lot of fruit for the buck, plant three different kinds
or varieties of bare-root fruit tree in a single hole.

cots and even peaches. With today's dwarf trees, however, planting several different kinds in one hole is a quick, easy way to get more variety in a small space and might be more reliable (tissue compatibility is not a concern, as it is with grafting).

Different varieties of fruit are chosen because they ripen at different times (so as to spread out the harvest) or because they are needed as pollenizers, planted to ensure sufficient crops. For instance, in my garden I planted an extra-dwarf 'Anna' apple and an extra-dwarf 'Ein Shemer' variety in the same hole. While 'Anna' technically needs no pollenizer, I had been told that its yield almost doubles if there is an 'Ein Shemer' nearby. Planted with their trunks almost touching, they may grow together in time.

As many as four trees can be planted in a single big hole with the trunks spaced about 18 inches apart, according to Dave Wilson Nursery in Hickman, California—one of the largest wholesale growers of fruit trees. With careful pruning and the right varieties, the resulting "tree" will occupy only a 10x10-foot area. The density of planting will further dwarf the trees.

With the same-hole technique, or when grafting, it is important to make sure that one variety does not grow faster or stronger, eventually coming to shade out the others. This takes a little research. In the case of grafted trees, look for those that have already been budded, such as the three-in-one, low-chill apples or peaches offered at some nurseries. Bay Laurel Nursery offers helpful tips on high-density planting and pruning on its web site; look for Backyard Orchard Culture.

Flat, espaliered trees, planted about 10 feet apart along a fence or wall, are yet another way to fit more fruit in a small space. In one hypothetical plan, Dave Wilson Nursery proposes planting 10 trees in only a 12x20-foot area—two sets of four trees (four to a hole) plus two espaliered trees against the wall. Choose the right varieties, and fruit should ripen from spring to fall.

Bay Laurel Nursery, 2500 El Camino Real, Atascadero, CA 93422; telephone 805.466.3406; on the web at www.baylaurelnursery.com.
See Week 2 in 52 Weeks in the California Garden.

UNPREDICTABLE APRICOTS

Q: We have an apricot tree that is more than 20 years old. Every year for the past seven years, we have gotten only one or two apricots. How can we get more?
—W.M., TORRANCE

A: Many gardeners are reporting the same sorry predicament. The answer is you probably can't get more apricots. The trees need winters that are cold enough to set fruit, and in the urban areas of Southern California the climate has changed. You'll notice that while very few low-temperature records are broken nowadays, record highs seem to be set every few weeks. The more developed an area becomes, the more pavement and houses, the warmer it gets. Call it urban warming. Even the traditional apricot-growing areas (apricots were commercially grown in the San Fernando Valley, Ojai and Hemet) are now as much as 10 degrees warmer in winter.

According to University of California pomologist James A. Beutel, apricot trees generally are difficult to grow in mild-climate Southern California anyway, and often the fruit of the trees that do grow lacks flavor. During a warm winter, apricots actually drop their fruit buds (they are all over the ground in February), and even a normal winter might not result in much fruit being set. There are exceptions: Certain trees will bear fruit, and some places do seem to get cold enough.

Deciduous fruit trees, in order to set fruit, require a certain amount of winter nighttime chill, measured as hours of chilling. Hot days tend to negate the chilling from cold nights, so inland areas aren't necessarily better off than the milder coast. Areas below some coastal canyons actually get more chilling than some inland areas.

Recently, Matthew Shugart, a member of the California Rare Fruit Growers, did some figuring that suggested that areas below hills and canyons near the coast got 425 to 550 hours of chilling, while inland valleys got 450 to 525, surprisingly similar numbers. He also figured that low-lying coastal areas with little topography get only 275 to 400 hours and that the traditional avocado areas, which are slightly inland but on sloping ground (Sunset Zone 23), get only 150 to 300. Areas at the base of the foothills get 375 to 525.

Apricots generally require at least 500 hours. You can see that very few parts of Southern California get enough hours of chilling to grow traditional apricots, though there are new varieties that supposedly need only 300 (such as 'Gold Kist'

FENDING OFF APRICOT ROBBERS

As anyone who has tried to harvest apricots (or any other fruit) in a squirrel-besieged neighborhood knows, one must go to great lengths to safeguard the precious bounty. By way of example, gardener Ron Thomson of West Los Angeles sent in snapshots to illustrate his solution. Several close-ups depict a squirrel trying to bite through chicken wire. Another shows the exhausted animal lying flat on his belly, legs splayed, atop some sort of cage. The final shot reveals what that squirrel was up against: an elaborate cage that completely envelops the apricot tree. Built by Thomson, a retired president of Anawalt Lumber, from 2x2s and one-inch poultry netting, it also keeps the birds out, so he gets every last apricot.

and 'Garden Annie'). Only truly interior regions such as Canoga Park, San Bernardino and Ramona get cold enough, with 525 to 725 hours of chilling.

In many areas apricots are things of the past. However, every few years, conditions are just right and gardeners get good crops, making liars out of garden writers. Even without fruit, the apricot is a handsome shade tree, so you might want to keep it as long as you can. Don't expect it to last forever, though. Apricots are not long-lived, and a 20-year-old tree is considered to be getting up in years.

In addition, apricots tend to be alternate bearers, which means they fruit heavily one year, then not at all the next. So there's not much you can do to increase bearing, but an old agricultural bulletin suggests trying to keep the leaves on the trees into the fall with good care and adequate water.

UNDERSTANDING 'ANNA'

Q: My five-year-old 'Anna' apple tree is already flowering while half the leaves are still on the tree. Should I pluck the leaves by hand?

—J.S., WEST HILLS

A: 'Anna' is one of the better apples for Southern California because it requires little winter chilling. Most apple varieties need a series of cold nights during winter to make fruit, which is why they do better in places like Washington. A few will fruit in our mild climate, but 'Anna' even fruits right on the coast, where nights are seldom cold.

Many of these low-chill varieties frequently flower at odd times of the year. One neighbor of mine in West Los Angeles gets two crops a year, one in spring and one in fall. The trees are frequently full of leaves when they flower. My dwarf tree seems to flower whenever it feels like it. It has no concept of spring.

Although plucking the leaves would seem to make sense (since it's done on roses at pruning time), it isn't necessary. The tree will flower and fruit with leaves or without.

ANTI-ANT TACTICS

Q: As soon as the figs on my tree begin to ripen, ants discover the fruit and crawl up the tree to feast on the bounty. Is there a way to prevent the ants from getting at the fruit without using poison?

—D.S., LA CRESCENTA

A: Absolutely. Use the time-tested product Tree Tanglefoot (usually available at nurseries) or one called Stickem—sticky substances applied to the bark near the base of the tree, in bands wide enough to halt the pillaging ants.

If the tree is young, apply the product to tree wrap or a tree collar, not directly on the bark. On older trees, spread it directly on the bark. Make sure there is no other avenue into the tree—don't let branches touch the ground, fences, walls or other plants.

The ants will try to bridge over the sticky stuff—sacrificing their own bodies if need be—so they can continue their foraging. Keep disturbing the surface to keep it tacky. Dust can also coat the surface over time.

Mail order Tanglefoot, Stickem and tree wraps from Peaceful Valley Farm Supply, PO Box 2209, Grass Valley, CA 95945; telephone 916.272.4769; on the web at www.groworganic.com.

TREATING TERMITES

Q: I have a 35-year-old 'Green Gage' plum tree that still produces delicious fruit. However, it is riddled with termites. Is there anything I can do, and will it affect the fruit?

—M.S., LOS ANGELES

A: There is no surefire way to control termites in live trees, but there are things you can try. Treatment is determined by what kind of termites are in the tree.

Subterranean termites live underground and feed on any available dead wood, including the old heartwood of living trees. If a tree is healthy, though, these termites tend to leave it alone, generally entering through wounds or dead areas in roots or branches. They don't eat the living wood, or cambium, so the tree keeps growing.

For subterranean termites, try using stakes, either the growth-regulator type or the those that contain poison (such as Terminate, made by Spectracide), around the tree—although these are intended for treating home perimeters. The materials will not end up in the fruit.

Drywood termites also enter through wounds, but live above ground. Look for the piles of tiny wood pellets the insects leave behind. If you can't prune off the infested wood, the colonies are difficult to access. After harvesting fruit, try using Term-Out, which you spray into termite tunnels through a tiny hose.

Drywood termites are the ones that get into patio furniture and wood fences, and Term-Out works great in those instances as well. Another outdoor termite product is Termite Prufe, a safe borate powder that can be painted or sprayed on fences and sheds but not on live trees.

Your plum will probably last another 10 years, even with the termites. Spur-bearing fruit trees such as plums and especially apples live a long time, unlike peaches and nectarines, which are often removed after only 10 years, especially near the coast. Plant a backup plum so you'll have a bearing-age tree when the old plum finally does fall over. And I wouldn't take a nap under, or attach a hammock to, a termite-infested tree.

MOLDY PEACHES

Q: A gray mold has completely wiped out the crops on my nectarine and peach trees and those of my neighbor. It started out as a small soft spot on the fruit as it began to ripen and eventually covered the entire fruit and some of the short branches. What should I do?

—L.L., CAMARILLO

A: It sounds like brown rot (various species of *Monilinia*), the most common disease of stone fruits, especially peaches and nectarines, and very difficult to eliminate. It thrives in wet weather, so a wet winter brings on lots of brown rot. Small, velvety gray or tan spores start on spring's flowers, which then infect the fruit. The first sign of brown rot is the shriveling of the flowers, which persist on the tree and don't fall off.

To get it under control, begin by removing and disposing of all shriveled fruit "mummies," which often hang on the tree for a year or more. Also remove all dead, dried flowers—this is where the mold spores come from, although branches also harbor them. Peek over the fence to see if any mummies hang on neighbors' trees. Offer to clean up those trees as well so they are not a continuing source of infection. Send every infected leaf and flower directly to the dump; do not put them in the compost pile.

As buds swell in spring, but before they open, spray them with a copper-containing Bordeaux mixture or Liqui-Cop, or use the fungicide chlorothalonil (Daconil). While chlorothalonil is practically nontoxic to birds and bees and only slightly toxic to mammals, it is highly toxic to fish.

These work only as preventives. If it rains after you apply these sprays, spray again at full bloom and after the flowers fall.

As flowers open, prune out any that are diseased. As fruit forms, carefully watch for the disease, which begins as brown or tan spots that quickly enlarge. Pick these, too, and send them promptly to the dump.

Once fruit forms, it may be too late to do anything, although spraying with Bordeaux one to three weeks before harvest might help (the copper in it might damage the tree's foliage).

One other tip: Keep foliage and fruit dry. Water trees from below.

Citrus

LEMONS, ORANGES, LIMES …

At one time Southern California was covered with citrus. Groves blanketed the valley floors and crept up into the hills. Yet today, in these same soils, gardeners are having trouble growing good oranges, tangerines and even lemons.

Or so it would seem.

In a four-year period, the Los Angeles County Master Gardeners hotline received 332 questions pertaining to lemons alone, making it by far the most popular topic. The contenders were tomatoes (186 questions) and roses (100). Master Gardeners program manager Yvonne Savio says the most common questions about citrus problems are usually easy to answer. But others, on the general poor health of a tree, for example, are more difficult.

In its time, *The Times* Garden Q&A also received myriad questions from readers wondering why their citrus trees were doing poorly.

A Whittier reader wrote: "I have two 'Valencia' orange trees that were here when we moved in 1958. About two years ago we noticed that the trees looked kind of sick. The leaves were scarce and the fruit very small. I feed them regularly with citrus and avocado fertilizer and they get regular water. The trees to either side of us look healthy. How come?"

Here's a comment from a Lomita resident: "We have four citrus planted in a row in a sunny bed. One of them has begun to lose its leaves at an alarming rate. We took a sample to the nursery, and they said it wasn't getting enough water, though we water every week. Please help."

Without seeing the tree, the soil or the spot where it's planted, it's difficult for anyone to ascertain the cause of the problem. However, when people ask Joan Citron, who grows a garden-sized grove of 15 different healthy, heavy-bearing citrus, what to do with their sick or nonproductive trees, she has a surprisingly pat answer: Stop watering. She even suggests gardeners quit fertilizing. In a majority of cases, she says, citrus are having problems because they are too pampered: They get too much water and too much fertilizer. "Just turn your back on them and go read a book," she says. This applies to trees growing in average garden soil, not to those that are under two years old or are container grown.

To see Citron's trees, you'd know she must be doing something right. They're loaded with juicy, sweet fruit. It may be amusing that someone named Citron should be growing fruit-laden citrus in her garden, but that is not her only claim to fame. Citron is also an avid member of the Southern California Horticultural Society, for which she edited the authoritative *Selected Plants for Southern California Gardens* (2000).

She and her husband, Jack, have been growing citrus since 1957, when they bought their house in Reseda. "We live in California, so let's plant citrus," they decided. They started with a 'Robertson' navel orange and a 'Kara' tangerine, and through the years they've added a 'Bearss' lime; 'Eureka', 'Meyer' and 'Ponderosa' lemons; 'Trovita', 'Valencia' and 'Shamouti' oranges; 'Clementine', 'Dancy' and Satsuma mandarins (tangerines); a 'Sampson' tangelo; a 'Tarocco' blood orange; a 'Nagami' kumquat, and even a lemon named 'Pink Lemonade' (it does have pink juice).

There are citrus in the front yard, in the back yard and on the property they own next door. They make juice from not just the oranges but the tangerines as well, and even have a few extra juicers to back up their trusty old Proctor-Silex. They also give much fruit away.

Watch It With the Watering

When the Citrons began, they watered often because the summers seemed so hot and dry. But soon they learned to water established trees only once a month during spring, summer and fall, and not at all in winter—and this is in one of Southern California's hotter climates. They put a fan sprinkler (or bubbler) on the end of a hose and water each tree for two hours, moving the hose to a slightly different spot every 20 minutes, so they cover all the ground underneath. This long irrigation allows water to sink several feet into the soil. And they do this only once a month. This is a far cry from automatic irrigation systems that water often and for just a few minutes.

The Citrons had found that watered frequently, some trees almost died from gummosis—a fungus disease that causes sap to ooze from the trunk. They also lost trees to root rot. So they backed off on the watering.

Vincent Lazaneo, home horticulture specialist at the San Diego County UC Cooperative Extension, agrees that overwatering is a frequent cause of back-yard citrus problems. "A whole lot more trees are killed by overwatering than underwatering," he says. "Lawns are a particularly bad spot for citrus."

When people call the Master Gardeners hotline with citrus problems, Yvonne Savio says, volunteers often learn that the callers' trees are planted in the middle of a lawn, right next to it or in flower beds—parts of the garden that get way too much water for citrus (and most other trees).

Ben Faber, subtropical fruit specialist with the Ventura County UC Cooperative Extension, agrees: Mature back-yard citrus growing in deep or clay soils need only monthly irrigations between the end of the rainy season and the beginning of the next, usually from April through November. That's when commercial groves get irrigated.

If you suspect that you have been overwatering citrus trees, don't cut them off suddenly; wean them slowly. Winter is a good time to start, since rains help cushion the transition from frequent to infrequent irrigations, allowing roots time to adjust. Begin watering less often, and you will encourage deeper rooting and better fruit production. Switch to weekly watering and then monthly, if you have a clay soil.

Keeping the soil surface dry between irrigations discourages disease, often the cause of citrus problems.

Not everyone agrees with this infrequent watering schedule, however. Several nursery growers suggest watering every 10 to 12 days during our dry season. How often you water is determined by your soil type, your particular climate and how old the trees are. Lazaneo says you'll know when you haven't been watering enough. Leaves begin to roll up at the edges, threatening to become little citrus-leaf cigars. The warning that you are overwatering won't be as conclusive; it may begin with the yellowing of leaves.

... and With the Fertilizer

Many years ago, after noticing that old, uncared-for trees in the neighborhood were producing more fruit than theirs, the Citrons decided not to fertilize. Joan does use compost throughout the garden, so her trees aren't going entirely unfed, and hers is a naturally rich, valley-bottom clay soil.

Other factors to consider in the Citron garden: The citrus trees have little competition. The couple doesn't attempt to grow other things around the trees, things that might compete with their roots or that need more water or fertilizer. For instance, growing thirsty, hungry roses nearby would definitely affect the health of citrus.

The Citrons' citrus grow much as they would in a commercial grove—with nothing underneath the trees' canopy except a thick mulch of leaves and compost. "In a back yard," Faber says, "trees don't need much nitrogen, especially if they have a good mulch underneath. Older trees may not even need fertilizing if they're thickly mulched with fallen citrus leaves." So there's science behind the Citrons' actions.

Still, Faber suggests, fertilize mature trees during and after the rainy season, in February and June, with about half a pound to a pound of actual nitrogen per year. To find out how much of a fertilizer is "actual nitrogen," multiply the percentage of nitrogen listed on the label (the *14* in a 14-8-2) by the fertilizer's total weight.

For instance, a three-and-a-half-pound bag of blood meal has 13 percent nitrogen (it's labeled as a 13-0-0), so multiply 0.13 by 3.5 pounds to get 0.46 pounds, or about half a pound, of actual nitrogen. Give the trees half in early February and half in June.

However, it's important to qualify this advice. Citrus trees are a bit like children, Faber says: "When they're young they need lots of nutrients, but as they get older, they need less and less." So fertilize young trees frequently but lightly, even every month.

With the average clay and loam soils in the majority of back yards, established citrus trees need infrequent watering and little or no fertilizing. But many newer gardens are not situated on "soil" at all, but are built in tracts or on slopes that have been bulldozed, cut and filled or otherwise rearranged so that the native topsoil is gone. Gardeners here are essentially gardening on mineral subsoils, and care for citrus is quite different and more difficult. Ditto for especially sandy soils.

On graded lots, good drainage can be a major problem. It may even be impossible to grow healthy citrus without installing some kind of drainage at planting time. On sandy soils, drainage is so quick that watering must be more frequent.

When a citrus trees looks ill, fertilizing should never be the first action taken. Fertilizing any plant that is already sick is a bad idea, since it is probably unable to "swallow" its medicine. Suspect the soil: Perhaps drainage is particularly poor, or there may be a lack of nutrients or too many growth-impeding minerals.

For a definitive answer, a homeowner must have the leaves or roots analyzed by a soil and plant laboratory, have the soil tested or call in an arborist.

Los Angeles County Master Gardeners hotline; telephone 323.838.4541. Other Master Gardener hotlines: San Diego County, 858.694.2860; Orange County, 714.708.1646; Riverside County, 909.683.6491; San Bernardino County, 909.387.2182; Ventura County, 805.645.1455.
Selected Plants for Southern California Gardens, *edited by Joan Citron, is available through the Southern California Horticultural Society, PO Box 41080, Los Angeles, CA 90041-0080; on the web at www.socahort.org.*
See Week 20 in 52 Weeks in the California Garden.

GOOD BEGINNINGS

How, when and where a young citrus tree is planted and then cared for is extremely important, with the first 12 to 18 months being most critical. Through the years, Durling Nursery in Fallbrook, wholesale grower of many citrus trees found at nurseries, has refined the planting and care of new citrus to, if not a science, a set of good rules. Here, Don Durling, of the third generation to run the nursery, shares his expertise.

• March and April are the two best months to plant citrus. Choose a spot in full sun that is out of the wind but not in a lawn or in a frequently watered garden bed.

• Make sure the soil drains quickly. Several days before planting, dig a planting hole about 10 percent shorter than the height of the root ball, so its top will end up slightly above ground level. Fill the hole halfway with water, let it drain, then fill it halfway again. This water should drain away in fewer than six hours. If it doesn't, the citrus tree will have trouble growing. Either have French drains installed (not a job for a homeowner), dig gravel-filled drainage holes on either side of the planting hole (less successful) or try another spot.

• To plant, cut away the plastic or fiber nursery can with tin snips or a knife, and gently place the root ball in the hole. Lay a board across the surface of the surrounding soil to make sure the top of the root ball ends up about an inch higher.

• Fill the hole with native, unamended soil to about six inches from the top. Add timed-release fertilizer pellets to this native soil, if you wish. Fill the upper six inches with amended soil, to which you have added about one-third organic matter, the kind sold at nurseries in bags as planting mix (don't use manure). Premix the soil and the amendments in a pile or wheelbarrow.

• With the remaining soil mix, build a several-inch-high, circular irrigation berm around the root ball. Make this basin no larger than the root ball, or irrigations may wet the soil around the plant and not the root ball.

• Remove most of the fruit; this will reduce transplant shock.

• Keep your new citrus watered for the first 12 to 18 months; this is very important. Don't drown it, but water as often as necessary to keep the root ball moist. This may mean watering every three or four days at first. To make sure the root ball is moist, probe the soil with a screwdriver or soil probe. Be especially careful to keep the tree watered during dry Santa Ana winds. After nine months, lengthen the time between irrigations to every seven to 14 days. After 18 months, deeply water every 10 to 12 days, or as seldom as once or twice a month. Of course, the frequency is determined by the weather, how hot or dry the climate and the soil type.

• Begin fertilizing right away (nursery plants have been on a constant-feed program). If timed-release fertilizer was not added to the planting hole, scratch fertilizer into the top half-inch of soil, or fertilize lightly every month for the first year or two. After the tree is two years old, switch to every other month. When it is about six feet tall, fertilize twice a year, in February and June.

• In hot areas, if the trunk's bark is exposed to the sun, paint it with flat-white, non-enamel, water-based interior wall paint, thinned by half with water. The sun can kill the cambium layer beneath the bark on an unprotected young tree.

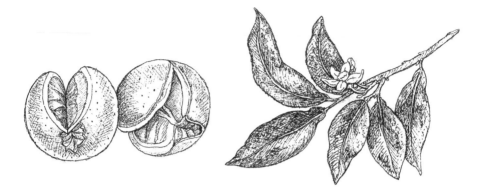

Erratic watering may cause citrus fruit to split (left). Sugary excretions left by scale and other sucking insects make for sooty-looking leaves.

WHY FRUIT SPLITS

Q: The fruit of the large navel orange tree in my back yard is splitting and falling off. What is wrong?

—M.T., ARTESIA

A: Splitting, or checking, of citrus happens to some fruit during some years. It is most common on navel oranges in September as the fruit begins to ripen. The fruit turns orange and falls off well before the rest of the fruit on the tree. The internal pressure can become greater than the rind can handle, so the fruit splits like an overinflated tire.

According to Neil O'Connell, citrus farm advisor for orange-growing Tulare County UC Cooperative Extension, no one is sure what causes this natural phenomenon. Most likely it has to do with environmental conditions, so there is little you can do to stop it. However, O'Connell says, letting trees get too dry before watering aggravates splitting. Make sure to give the tree consistent irrigation in summer and fall so the soil never gets too dry.

Other problems often associated with splitting include a fungus called black heart (*Alternaria citri*), which enters young fruit, eventually turning the interior black. Splitting fruit may also attract little dried-fruit beetles. There is no control for these problems, so hope for a better season next year, and watch that watering.

BITTER FRUITS

Q: Our lemon tree has borne lemons for many years. Last year we noticed a change in the fruit, which now is orange with the rind like that of a tangerine. The taste is very sour and bitter.

—R.M., LOS ANGELES

A: Fruit can't change that radically, say, from a lemon to a tangerine. But it can sport, meaning it can produce new growth that is slightly different from the old. (This is one way new varieties of plants come to exist.) This growth, especially if it's stronger, could have outpaced the old growth, making it seem as though the tree suddenly changed.

Much more likely, though, the rootstock of the lemon has taken over. Citrus are usually grafted to the roots of another kind of citrus, one that is tough but not necessarily tasty, so that the resulting plant is stronger, more disease resistant, more cold tolerant or has some other attribute.

At one point, lemons were grafted to a mandarin called 'Cleopatra', but the practice was discontinued because the 'Cleopatra' rootstock tended to outgrow the lemon. Other common rootstocks for lemons include Troyer citrange, rough lemon and *Citrus macrophylla*.

Suckers (which shoot up from the rootstock) that are not broken off can rapidly outgrow the grafted top. So instead of a lemon, you may now have one of the near-wild rootstocks. The fruit you describe is most likely the fruit of the rootstock, perhaps the 'Cleopatra' mandarin.

YES, WE HAVE NO ORANGES

Q: My orange tree looks healthy, but it hasn't had any fruit in a long time. Why?

—T.C., Somis

A: Citrus flowers are a favorite snack of snails, which can live up in trees, hiding on leaves by day. Copper barriers wrapped around the trunk keep snails off, provided no branches touch the walls or the ground. Snails use them as ladders.

You can also moisten the soil around the tree and bait. Or gently toss bait up into the tree, getting it to land on the leaves. This is a practice used by citrus fanciers, but one that won't be listed on the snail bait label. Try one of the nonpoisonous bait products that contain iron phosphate, which won't harm pets, children, birds or other wildlife (a common brand is Sluggo; another is Worry Free).

SOOTY LEAVES

Q: What causes black soot on the leaves and fruit of orange and lemon trees?

—I.K., Los Angeles

A: Scale and other sucking insects, such as aphids and whiteflies, cause sooty mold. The insects feed on plants and leave a honeylike excrement, upon which the black mold grows. Aphids and whiteflies can simply be blasted off regularly with a strong spray of water. They can also be dispatched with a horticultural oil spray or with insecticidal soaps. The wetting action of the pest-smothering soaps will also help wash off the sooty mold.

The insects most likely to cause sooty mold, though, are scale. They are usually controlled on citrus by several predators, including certain wasps (*Metaphycus*) and a lady beetle (*Chilcorus cacti*). However, scale gain the upper hand when conditions go against these predators, which are often killed by pesticide sprays or hindered by accumulated dust on the leaves or by ants.

First, wash down the tree to remove dust (a common problem in urban areas), then control any ants in the tree by wrapping the trunk with a wide band of a sticky barrier, such as Tanglefoot, sold at nurseries. Make sure no leaves or branches touch the ground, fences or walls, which provide ladders for marauding ants.

To kill existing scale, spray with horticultural oil, such as SunSpray Ultra-Fine or Saf-T-Side, which doesn't poison pests but smothers them. It works best on young scale, which are most active in late summer and early fall; spray at those times. Be sure to follow label directions; heed the precautions regarding temperature such as to avoid use when temperatures exceed 90 degrees or fall below 32 degrees. Even highly refined paraffin oils such as these shouldn't be used when it is very hot and humid. On citrus, besides smothering pests, oil sprays make the foliage a beautiful glossy green for a few days. A bonus!

After treatment, do not spray the tree with any other pesticides, and the natural predators should again get the upper hand. Hosing off foliage—on any plant— every once in a while is a good cultural practice.

ODDLY SHAPED LEMONS

Q: Why are my lemons so ugly?

—K.T., LEMON GROVE

A: Lemon deformation is caused by bud mites, which can be controlled with horticultural oil sprays (they also safely control many other citrus pests). Spray once in May and June, and perhaps again in fall if needed.

However, the damage is strictly cosmetic, and no control is necessary. Natural enemies of the mites usually get the upper hand in no time, and spraying might actually bring on other insect problems.

DYING BRANCHES

Q: My mature grapefruit developed splits in the bark, and sap drips out. It affects one limb at a time, and sometimes a branch will die almost overnight. Is it a fungus?

—K.S., PALM DESERT

A: The grapefruit tree probably has brown-rot gummosis, a fungus that attacks the trunk and may spread to branches and roots. The University of California suggests keeping the trunk and branches dry and preventing sprinklers from hitting the bark.

Scrape away the infected bark with a sharp knife, along with a little additional healthy bark around the edges. Allow the area to dry and repeat if it reoccurs.

CURBING RAMPANT GROWTH

Q: My lemon tree is more than 40 years old and still produces wonderful lemons. Our problem is with the continual growth of suckers, which grow very long.

—E.S., VAN NUYS

A: What you are calling suckers are actually water sprouts. Suckers arise from the roots of the tree, water sprouts from branches higher up. Lemon trees are notorious for making water sprouts. These long shoots are the norm, especially on older lemon trees. This is how lemons make new branches, which begin long, tall and straight, but bend down in time as they become laden with fruit. The 'Eureka' variety is especially prone to this.

To curb water sprout production, water and fertilize less often so the tree is not so vigorous. Mature lemons need little water and fertilizer.

You can remove water sprouts to keep the tree from getting too tall, but it's also okay to leave them. To remove a water sprout, make a cut close to the trunk or branch and it won't immediately resprout. Or just shorten it.

On other trees, water sprouts often arise from large pruning cuts, severe pruning, sudden exposure to sunlight or as a result of some injury to the tree. These are not normal and should probably be shortened or removed.

HOW LOW CAN YOU GO?

Q: I have purchased a home with a large grapefruit tree that badly needs trimming. Can I cut it back severely?

—B.H., LOS ANGELES

A: Ben Faber, subtropical fruit specialist with the Ventura County UC Cooperative Extension, notes that commercial citrus are pruned regularly to keep the fruit within reach and to allow light into the interior so fruit forms in the inner as well as the outer parts of the tree. In addition, commercial citrus that get too big are either scaffolded, to bring them down to size (say, 12 or 15 feet, down from 24 feet), or "stumped," to bring them way down.

This is all to say that citrus can withstand severe pruning. The result may not be aesthetically pleasing, but pruning does eventually result in increased fruit size and bring it back within your reach.

Cut branches just above a side branch. Protect formerly shaded bark from sunburn by painting it with a flat-white, non-enamel, water-based interior wall paint.

Be aware, however, that a tree "remembers how big it used to be," as Faber puts it. The more you remove, the more the tree will send out masses of new growth, and the longer it will take to make new fruit.

All this new growth has to be pruned and tidied up so that branches are properly spaced throughout the tree and the interior does not get too dense and dark. Also, the tree will require yearly pruning to keep it small, because it will keep trying to get back to its larger size.

A pruning this severe is a very bad idea on ornamental landscape trees. Big new branches are extremely weak and can drop without warning, creating a genuine danger.

❦ ❦ ❦

Other Subtropicals

AVOCADOS: MAKING RADICAL CUTS

Q: At what time of year can a 'Fuerte' avocado tree can be pruned? Mine is 18 to 20 years old and quite large.

—P.P., Los Alamitos

A: Prune avocados after the harvest, which in the case of 'Fuerte' is between November and April. Daniel Hagillih, superintendent at the UC South Coast Research and Extension Center in Irvine, which has a remarkable collection of avocados, suggests taking about one-third of the growth off to let more light into the interior of the tree, which greatly increases production.

The tree can also be pruned quite drastically. Avocados can "really take a whacking," more than can most fruit trees, says Julie Frink, a volunteer who records data on avocados at the UC South Coast center and who is a member of the California Rare Fruit Growers (based at the Fullerton Arboretum).

Often this is a good idea, because future fruit ripens closer to the ground and is easier to harvest. In the groves at the center, volunteers often cut tall, old trees (of about the same age as yours) with a trunk diameter of a foot or more, down to stumps about four feet tall, then let them resprout. That's radical pruning! Sometimes they graft better varieties to the new growth, but the main reason is to get the fruit back down to picking height. Protect the limbs and trunk, suddenly exposed to strong sunlight, with flat-white, non-enamel, water-based interior wall paint to fend off sunburn.

California Rare Fruit Growers is on the web at www.crfg.org.

DWARF AVOCADOS

Q: I'm thinking of taking out an old avocado tree that seldom fruits and that shades my whole garden. I can't even grow impatiens underneath. Are there dwarf avocados, like there are dwarf citrus, that won't take up so much room?

—C.L., Los Angeles

A: Some nurseries sell an avocado called 'Littlecado', which is claimed to be a dwarf. It is also sold as 'Minicado', 'Dwarf' and (rarely) 'Wurtz', its real name. Have your nursery order it for you.

Julie Frink, the volunteer at the UC South Coast Research and Extension Center in Irvine, says that the 'Littlecado' growing at the center is only eight to 10 feet tall and is a "nice-looking little tree" with pendulous branches that droop to the ground. The tree needs staking when young, says Vincent Lazaneo, home horticulture specialist at the San Diego County UC Cooperative Extension, because it grows "almost like a vine."

Gerald Carne, a Fallbrook commercial avocado grower, says that the University of California–developed variety 'Gwen' is another smaller tree. He never needs more than a stepladder to pick the highest fruit.

CATCHING AVOCADO SNATCHERS

Q: Squirrels are harvesting my avocados before I can get to them. Is there a way to thwart them?

—S.L., Pasadena

A: As all gardeners should know, avocados won't ripen on the tree. Squirrels, says Ben Faber, subtropical fruit specialist with the Ventura County UC Cooperative Extension, actually have the smarts to cut avocados and let them fall to the ground to ripen, after first taking a bite to see if they are ready for harvesting.

In my own garden, I let squirrels take a sample and cut the avocados loose. I then pick the fruit up off the ground and let it finish ripening under guard, simply cutting around the holes the squirrels have nibbled.

To control squirrels, Faber says, make a collar of two-foot-wide metal flashing and wrap it around the tree trunk, six feet off the ground. Squirrels are then unable to climb up since they can't get their claws into the metal. However, if there are other trees or buildings nearby, this won't work because squirrels can leap 15 feet through the air.

You might also try live trapping—but squirrels are protected in many communities, so first check with animal control officers to see if this is allowed. Sticky peanut butter is good bait. Faber suggests baiting the trap for a few days with the doors locked open so the squirrels get used to it before actually setting the trap.

For commercial growers, Faber says, rats, particularly roof rats, are a bigger problem, but some have had to deal with squirrels, too. Some use Jack Russell terriers to chase squirrels off. Cats are best with roof rats.

MANGOES, IN SOUTHERN CALIFORNIA?

Q: Since last year, my three-year-old mango plant's leaves have been shriveling and turning brown. Is there a cure for this?

—F.V., MONTEBELLO

A: It sounds as though the tree has been given too little water, though if the leaves first turn yellow, it could be too much water.

This is always a tough call. Check by probing near the roots to see if the soil is wet or dry. Or give the tree a gentle tug to see how well rooted into the soil it is. The roots may be drying out too fast because they are still growing within the root ball and not out into the garden soil. I once killed a new citrus this way, not realizing that the root ball was going dry even though the soil around it was moist.

If the tree pulls right out of the ground with virtually no roots, then overwatering has rotted them off.

If the leaves get crinkly and the tips and edges turn brown first, there could be either a nutrient deficiency or salts in the soil or water. As are citrus and avocados, mangoes are sensitive to too much boron or too little manganese, zinc and iron.

Surprised to hear that someone is growing mangoes in the back yard? In the warmer, nearly frost-free areas, they have been grown for years. According to David Silber, proprietor of Papaya Tree Nursery in Granada Hills, mangoes will grow where 'Haas' avocados do (where temperatures seldom go below 28 degrees) and, in time, will attain the size of a 'Valencia' orange. In Southern California, fruit ripens in fall, when there are very few in markets, an added bonus.

Don't plant a pit from a store-bought fruit—grown from seed, plants take up to 10 years to produce. Grafted kinds produce right away, though baby fruit should be stripped off trees until their trunks are about an inch across, measured a foot above the ground. Grow them in the ground or in a 15-gallon container, in which they'll produce for years, says Silber.

Papaya Tree Nursery sells several kinds, but Silber's favorite is a California variety named 'Thompson'. 'Reliable' is another, and he's had good luck with 'Edward', a Florida variety. All of these fruit heavily in Southern California. There

Strawberry and pineapple guavas, planted with Natal plums,
might make a fruitful hedge.

are also Philippine and Indian types (mangoes are native to India). Trees are self-
fruitful, so only one need be planted.

Papaya Tree Nursery; telephone 818.363.3680.

AN EDIBLE HEDGE

Q: I would like to make a hedge with strawberry guava, pineapple guava and
Natal plum. I'd like to keep it five feet tall and two feet wide. Is this possible, and
how far apart should I plant them?

—M.B., BALDWIN HILLS

A: Sounds like a great idea, an edible hedge. All three plants are tough and
grow easily in your climate zone. The only catch is that you might end up pruning
most of the fruit off in order to keep the plants hedge-like.

The variety of Natal plum (*Carissa*) named 'Fancy' is an upright shrub that
grows easily to five feet and is often pruned as a hedge, as are all the other Natal
plums. It also has the largest fruit of those commonly available.

The pineapple guava (*Feijoa sellowiana*), of similar size, also can be pruned as a
hedge. The variety 'Nazemetz' is claimed to be self-fertile, but it produces better
crops with others planted nearby, so include at least two. The fleshy flower petals
are also edible and deliciously sweet.

I've seen strawberry guava (*Psidium cattleianum*) pruned so hard it might as well
have been a hedge. This is a shame, since this 10- to 15-foot tree can be majestic,
with its beautiful bark and multiple trunks. The yellow strawberry guava (*Psidium
cattleianum lucidum*) has the densest growth and would make the best hedge.

Although all three of these can grow quite large (to 15 or more feet), it should
be no trouble keeping them at five feet. However, you may have to let them get a
little wider than two feet. Plant them about three feet, or a little farther, apart.

Help! Something's Wrong With My ...

❧ ❧

Favorite Plants and Their Plights

ARE CERTAIN PLANTS PROBLEM-PRONE? Judging from letters received by Garden Q&A, you'd certainly think so. Many gardeners would acknowledge that roses, for instance, demand more time than all other plants combined. Not only do they need regular feeding and pruning, but everything on six legs seems to savor them, and every spore that drifts by lands on their leaves. With roses, a gardener is constantly battling pests and diseases.

It's not too surprising, then, that questions about rose problems were, in fact, the third most commonly asked, right after citrus and, of course—everyone's favorite—tomatoes. But these letters actually indicate the plant's popularity, not its propensity for problems. Most asked essentially the same questions: What is the powdery stuff on the leaves, or what made all those holes? Here we have the answers and go a step further, suggesting some really good varieties that thrive in specific localities. The best way to have healthy roses, after all, is to grow kinds that like where you live and will resist invaders of various sorts.

Though some gardeners may try, roses alone do not make a garden. Gardens can be a complicated tapestry of many plants, from lawn grasses to trees. Some of us feel that the more variety of plants that exist in a garden, the merrier and the more interesting it becomes. Something new is always blooming or otherwise showing off, and there is a diversity of garden chores that require only a little attention now and then—jobs one can do in those spare moments—rather than one or two really big chores that demand help, like mowing an acre of grass. Working in a varied garden is mere puttering compared to the drudgery of caring for a big, plain landscape.

When we tore out our front lawn and replaced it with a playful mix of trees, shrubs, roses, annuals, perennials and bulbs, plus some vegetables and berries, we found ourselves spending all of our gardening time out there because it was so varied and interesting, so full of fascinating life.

What follows are some of the individual plants that make up a garden. There is plenty of information on growing specific plants and on plagues visited on particular plants—such as camellia blight and rose slugs. Also included are specific groups of plants, such as the passion vines with flowers that look like they're from another planet.

But let's begin with the beginning—how do you plant a lawn and, for that matter, do you even need one?

❧ ❧ ❧

First, Your Turf

THE PROS AND CONS OF A LAWN

Q: I live in the San Fernando Valley, and I hate my lawn. It takes too much water, and when it does grow well, it needs too much mowing and edging. Just now the grass appears to be dying, so it seems like a good time to replace it with something else. What?

—J.H., ARLETA

A: There really is no vegetative substitute for a lawn. Ground-cover substitutes were very popular in the 1970s, but none so far can compete with a lawn. They cannot survive foot traffic, require more care, are short-lived and eventually succumb to weeds. Even in areas that are not trod, ground covers can't compete. In no time, dead spots appear as plants die out, and they spread to new locations. On big commercial plantings this might not be noticeable, but in a yard it definitely is.

In my garden, I've eliminated my front lawn and reduced the back to the size of a throw rug. To walk through the current mixture of small shrubs, perennials and ground covers, you follow bark-mulched paths. The garden is much more fun, but it takes more work, if less water (although turf researchers would question this). I do the work myself—most commercial gardeners do not know how to care for this odd collection of plants.

You probably have a Bermuda grass lawn, since it went dormant in winter. (It didn't die—the roots and rhizomes are alive, but the top just died back.) Bermuda is the easiest walk-on ground cover for hot inland areas, and it shouldn't need all that much water. Bermuda grass also grows near the coast, but there tall fescues are usually preferred. Some are nearly as tough, and they don't go dormant.

Although long-lived by comparison, lawns do wear out with time. My suggestion is to redo yours. Have it renovated or replanted in spring. Stick to common

Bermuda, and overseed it with annual ryegrass in fall for winter color. Make sure there is an adequate mowing strip or barrier to keep it from spreading. A commercial gardener can do this for you.

There is no miracle substitute for lawns, unless you want to turn it into a garden. As far as kids are concerned, there is no substitute, period.

SEED OR SOD

Q: We've recently remodeled, and we'd like to replace our old Bermuda grass lawn. We don't know whether to sod or seed. What do you think?

—C.Y., VILLA PARK

A: Sod is nearly instant and seed much less expensive, but both make a long-lasting lawn if installed properly.

Both sod and seed require the same extensive soil preparation (many people think that sod can simply be laid over existing dirt). Amendments often must be added and the soil thoroughly tilled and raked as flat as a pool table.

With either sod or seed, unless you plan to plant another Bermuda grass lawn, the old Bermuda grass must be completely eradicated. Otherwise it will come back from the roots and rhizomes through the sod or sprout with the seed. The herbicide Roundup (glyphosate) is most frequently used for this purpose because it effectively kills grass roots and rhizomes. However, several applications may be necessary, and it does not kill seed lying in the soil. Read label directions carefully.

The easiest and cheapest way to redo your lawn is to prepare the soil and sow seed of common Bermuda grass. The old Bermuda stolons will sprout along with the new seed, and you'll have a lawn you can walk on in about two months. Fescues are easy to grow from seed too, but it's almost guaranteed that Bermuda seed lying in the soil will sprout at the same time. Seed can be sown only during certain seasons. Bermuda seed is usually sown in late spring or early fall.

Sod, though more expensive, does have several advantages. It can be laid practically any time and walked on almost immediately. It will keep most weed seeds lying on the soil from germinating, though sod installers often spread a pre-emergent herbicide to prevent this.

See Week 13 in 52 Weeks in the California Garden.

WHEN TO INSTALL A LAWN

Q: When is the best time of year to have new sod installed?

—A.B., LONG BEACH

A: Sod can be installed at any time—as long as there is a good sprinkler system to water it daily at first (or more often in hot weather). Here in West Los Angeles I watched a neighbor put in a new sod lawn at the height of summer, and it did fine. Inland, midsummer is probably too hot even for sod, so from mid-September on is better. Bermuda and zoysia grasses are exceptions. Since they are dormant in winter, they are usually available March through November. Most hybrid kinds of Bermuda and zoysia come as sod.

Lawn seed of the common rampant kinds of warm-season grasses, such as St. Augustine and common Bermuda, should be sown in late spring, early summer and even very early fall.

Fescues and other cool-season grasses can be sown in spring and fall. Winter is fine too, but may be too cool for seed to germinate. In the middle of spring is ideal because rains aren't likely to float seed away.

SOIL PREPARATION FOR SOD

Q: We are preparing an old lawn area for new St. Augustine sod. We thought we would "weed and feed," then bring in topsoil and lay the sod. Will that work?
—L.S., NORTH HOLLYWOOD

A: Lawn products that have herbicides and fertilizers mixed together in one package, so-called weed-and-feed formulations, are for existing lawns, not yet-to-be-planted lawns.

Most weed-and-feed formulations contain herbicides that selectively kill broadleaf weeds in lawns, distinguishing between plants with bladelike leaves, grasses, and those with broad leaves, such as dandelions. For example, they can take oxalis out of a grass lawn, but they cannot eradicate Bermuda grass (sometimes called devil grass) in a fescue lawn, because both are grasses. In addition, weed-and-feed formulations contain pre-emergents, herbicides that prevent all seeds, including lawn seed, from germinating.

To prepare an area for sod or seeding, most lawn companies use Roundup (glyphosate), a systemic herbicide that kills everything it touches; the spray must not drift onto desirable plants. Roundup is translocated from the leaves to the roots, killing them and spreading rhizomes. This makes it a very effective herbicide, especially on Bermuda and St. Augustine grasses.

A lawn can be planted just days after Roundup is applied. There's no need for topsoil. Simply rototill (add amendments if needed) or loosen the existing soil and plant.

WHEN TO WATER

Q: There seem to be conflicting opinions on when to water the lawn. I have always heard the best time is when the sun is off the lawn, as the water drops act like little magnifying glasses and can burn the grass. I typically water in the evening, but when should I?

—A.S., WESTCHESTER

A: It's an old gardeners' tale that water droplets can burn grass. In the dead of summer, overheated gardeners go so far as to spritz plants in the middle of the day without harm, although this practice probably does them more good than it does the plants.

Watering in the evening, however, is not a good idea. A lawn that stays damp at night is susceptible to rots, molds and fungus diseases, including mushrooms. According to Scot Smalley, of Pacific Sod in Camarillo, none of these do serious damage to an established lawn, but they can kill portions of new or young lawns.

Experts agree that the time to water is early in the morning. If your sprinklers are on timers, set them for just before the sun comes up. Early irrigation lets the surface of the lawn dry during the day, which cuts down dramatically on disease.

Don't water too often, Smalley warns. Watering every day for short periods encourages disease and mushrooms. Water about twice a week, letting the sprinklers run for 20 to 30 minutes each time for deep-rooted fescues, less for shallow Bermuda. Water must soak deep into the soil, where it is safe from evaporation and where the roots are.

This timing and duration can vary greatly—by season, location, kind of soil and winds. Start with these times and adjust up or down to meet your situation.

GOOD (AND BAD) GRASSES FOR CALIFORNIA

Q: Have you heard of Amazoy lawn by Zoysia Farm Nurseries? They claim it stays green year-round and needs very little watering and mowing. Is this too good to be true?

—V.R.D., LOS ANGELES

A: Stay away from those eastern zoysia creeping grasses, touted in full-page magazine ads. They're advertised the same way "tree tomatoes" are. Actually named tamarillos (*Cyphomandra betacea*), tree tomatoes can be grown easily from seed, but they are overly tart, barely taste like tomatoes and cannot be used in the same way.

Similarly, zoysia varieties from the East Coast—to which you refer—do poorly in California. No matter what ads call them, they are actually 'Meyer' varieties of zoysia. Here, these have a long dormant period, remaining completely brown for several months. They are also very slow to knit together into a lawn.

The zoysias that do well in Southern California also have these drawbacks to a lesser degree. If you want a zoysia lawn, look for sod of one named 'El Toro', developed by the University of California. It is faster to fill in and has better texture and color and a much shorter dormant period. Along the coast, it may not go dormant.

'El Toro' is recommended as a good lawn for dogs to play on, especially if it is overseeded with tall fescue grass to add some color in winter. But Bermuda grass is also a good choice for a lawn, particularly a hybrid such as 'Tifgreen'.

Korean grass is another good zoysia for California, but it's meant to be a ground cover, not walked on.

RIDDING FESCUE OF WEEDS

Q: I have recently noticed that Bermuda grass is showing up in my tall fescue lawn. Is there a product I can obtain to selectively kill the Bermuda grass and not harm the fescue?

—R.H., SAN GABRIEL

A: Surprisingly, yes. Usually herbicides kill broadleaf weeds in grass lawns, or they kill grasses in broadleaf plantings, or they just kill everything. For instance, herbicides such as 2,4-D, MCPP and dicamba, found in commonly available products such as Weed-B-Gon, kill oxalis and other broadleaf weeds in any grass lawn.

The herbicide Turflon Ester kills warm-season grasses, such as Bermuda, St. Augustine and Kikuyu, in cool-season lawns, such as tall fescues ('Medallion' and 'Marathon' are two well-known trade names). It also kills broadleaf weeds such as oxalis.

WHAT DESTROYS A LAWN

Q: My St. Augustine grass is getting destroyed. It seems to die in great patches from below. I dug for cutworms and could not find any, but the roots seem dead. What's killing it?

—H.F., SILVER LAKE

A: St. Augustine is one of the least trouble-prone lawn grasses, even in the shade, which it tolerates better than any other grass. Problems are rare unless the lawn is getting old (10 or more years). Its problem could be cultural, or it might be due to disease or pests. Before you act, make sure you pin it down.

If the lawn is watered often but not very deeply, the poorly rooted St. Augustine will die out in patches that become too dry and water repellent. Heavy thatch can also cause this; the remedy here is to have the lawn renovated with a vertical mower. Lawn services do this.

John Rector, an agronomist formerly with Pacific Sod, says the lawn may be subject to one of two fungus diseases or, perhaps, the chinch bug.

If the damage is noticeable in fall and winter, and the diseased area first turns an almost fluorescent yellow, then tan and then dies, it is probably a disease called take-all patch. Moving fast through the lawn, it attacks the roots, turns them almost black and severs them from the soil. Unfortunately, there is no control other than to try and keep the lawn healthy.

Brown patch, seen May through September, kills grass in circles larger than dinner plates. It is easily controlled with any of the lawn fungicides. Look for it listed on the label.

To check for chinch bugs, simply put a white piece of paper on the grass and brush the grass with your hand. The bugs will jump and land on the paper. They feed on the foliage of grasses and can kill large areas. Chinch bugs are easily controlled with a lawn pesticide (again, look for it listed on the label).

Before applying any of these controls, read the labels carefully and water the lawn thoroughly.

A DICHONDRA DILEMMA

Q: For the last 18 years I've had a lovely dichondra lawn, but it died out this summer. I think it was a fungus, the same one that blighted my tomatoes. Now I want to plant a 'Marathon' lawn in its place. Can I get rid of the fungus first, so the new lawn doesn't die as well?

—M.Y., LONG BEACH

A: Dichondra has many pests and problems in California, but I doubt whether any of them are related to whatever blighted your tomatoes. Dichondra is susceptible to flea beetles, cutworms and a number of diseases, including leaf spot. It may indeed have been a fungus that did it in. However, "there is no magic pill that gets rid of fungus," says Martin Gramckow, of Southland Sod Farms in Port Hueneme. Fungus spores are like bacteria, always there, just waiting for the right conditions, and nothing really gets rid of them.

Whatever killed the dichondra will most likely not bother a tall fescue lawn such as 'Marathon'. The main concern is that dichondra seeds prolifically. "While you can't keep it alive when you want it," Gramckow says, "you can't get rid of it when you don't."

Before putting in a new lawn, he says, take steps to sprout the dichondra seeds and then eliminate them by spraying with Roundup (glyphosate). You may need to water and spray several times before planting anew. Even after the new lawn is established, Gramckow says, use a weed-and-feed product to prevent dichondra seeds from germinating.

A poor soil may have hastened the dichondra's demise. Thoroughly prepare the soil before planting lawn seed or sod. Sod companies, including Southland, can provide step-by-step information and even videos.

❧ ❧ ❧

Annuals, Perennials and Bulbs

BLOOMS AND MORE BLOOMS

"What can I plant that flowers all the time?" is a question that nurserypeople hear all the time. It's like a joke, they hear it so often. Although constant blooming may seem a bit much to ask of a plant, there are a handful that will oblige.

They bloom in spring along with everything else, and they're still going strong in summer, after so many spring flowers have fainted from the heat. They may be the only thing still flowering in the fall garden, and in winter, when so much is quiescent, they're still grinding out the blooms.

I am thinking of such tough perennials as society garlic and sea statice and soft, shrubby subtropical plants such as pentas and heliotrope. There are even a few substantial shrubs, such as anisodontea, and at least one vine, the white-flowered potato vine.

These bloom all the time, with hardly a hiccup. And while regarded by some as practically extruded from plastic, they do have their uses. Planted here and there in even the most sophisticated gardens, they ensure an ever-present spot of color.

There are just enough of these ever-blooming plants to comprise an entire garden, though such a landscape might strike some as a little boring and would probably have to be replaced every few years.

You see, many tend to drop out after a few years; I suspect they simply grow themselves to death. It may take three to five years, but eventually most of these plants become woody, worn out or overgrown, and no longer flower as before. They may even die.

"So what if you have to replace them?" asks Judy Wigand, who used to sell plants from her well-known garden, Judy's Perennials in San Marcos, and is now a garden writer. "It's a small price to pay for flowers every month of the year."

The Signature Perennial

Her former nursery is where one of my favorites, *Heliotropium arborescens*, originally came from. I'm not talking about the easy-to-find cultivars of this heliotrope with names like 'Black Beauty'. Although they also flower all the time and are pretty in their own right, they are "half the plant," as one gardener puts it.

The plain *Heliotropium arborescens* is constantly smothered in light-lilac flower clusters that appear two-toned, opening as a darker shade, then fading to the palest hue. And while cultivars grow slowly to about two feet, *Heliotropium arborescens*

Scabiosa, Mexican sage, potato vine and abutilon (left to right)
are a few flowers that seem to bloom all year.

grows fast to three or four feet tall and six to eight feet across. It has been a spectacle in my garden for many years.

I got my plant as a cutting from avid gardener Beautrice Grow's flowery garden in San Clemente (she got hers from Judy's Perennials). Although cuttings are best taken from flowerless shoots, Beau and I couldn't find any—so even my cutting was in flower. At five years old, it barely pauses to catch its breath, though most of these plants do have peak seasons when they are most floriferous.

Even when I pruned it back by half to slow it down, it managed to flower within days and was back to normal in a few weeks. Pruning it back once a year keeps it relatively dense and tidy, Wigand says. Many of these types of plants need some kind of tidying up or restraining, although, she says, "It's perplexing to know when to cut back any of these, because they are always covered with flowers." Some need major cutting back every now and then, which can be a drawback to plants that are flower factories, but many of these plants grow so fast that they simply cover up faded flowers with fresh growth. Many do just fine with only a little deadheading and tidying up.

Heliotropium arborescens probably does best near the coast, where its light-lavender flower clusters glow in the misty seaside light. There it likes full sun, but inland it prefers partial shade. It can be difficult to find at nurseries, but San Marcos Growers is one wholesale source.

Did I mention that its flowers attract butterflies and are fragrant?

The ever-blooming heliotrope often named 'Alba' has white flowers that smell strongly of vanilla. In my garden, its sultry scent greets visitors near the front gate. More vine-like and scrambling, with far fewer flowers, it grows well on both sides of town. Unfortunately, it, too, can be hard to find.

Popular Nonstop Bloomers
Many nonstop flowering plants are easy to find, even commonplace, at nurs-

eries—naturally, they're quite popular.

On the shrubby side (though none of these is your typically stiff shrub), we have:

• Common shrimp plant (*Justicia brandegeana*), which has fascinating droopy, rust-colored flowers. Less common is the variety 'Chartreuse', with its greenish flowers that go with any color scheme.

• Big, bushy purple-flowered *Solanum rantonnetii*, recently renamed a *Lycianthes*, and its vining cousin, *Solanum jasminoides*, commonly called the potato vine, with white flowers.

• Abutilons tend always to have a smattering of blooms, pinks to red, plus yellows and oranges and even snappy white, and the shrubs last a long time in the garden.

• *Salvia chiapensis* has magenta spikes and will grow in the shade.

• Daisylike euryops (yellow).

• Cape mallow (*Anisodontea*), with dark-veined pinkish-salmon blooms.

• *Lavandula multifida* and the French lavender (*Lavandula dentata*).

• Star clusters (*Pentas lanceolata*).

• The familiar Mexican sage (*Salvia leucantha*).

And moving down in size:

• 'Butterfly Blue' and 'Pink Ice' scabiosas. (Beau Grow says she gets a little tired of cutting off the dead blooms.)

• The wallflower *Erysimum* 'Bowles Mauve'.

• Santa Barbara daisies (*Erigeron karvinskianus*). I like 'Moerheimii', which is less common at nurseries. It has slightly larger, light pink flowers.

• *Nemesia capensis* and *Nemesia fruticans*, with pink, lilac or white flowers.

• *Scaevola* 'Blue Wonder', though it lasts only about two years in the garden, which is shorter than most.

• *Geranium incanum* lives long enough to be used as a ground cover by some, and it never stops blooming light magenta, at least near the coast. Most other true geraniums are quite dormant in winter, but not this one.

• Sturdy *Begonia* 'Richmondensis' and impatiens, of course (impatiens really should be replaced every season, though they can go on and on). Both are best in shade.

• Purple, papery-flowered sea statice (*Limonium perezii*), a little unusual in this crowd because it tends to be a long-lived plant, as does society garlic (*Tulbaghia*), which is probably why both are so popular.

TOUGH LOVE IN AN INLAND GARDEN

When it's nearly 90 degrees outside at barely 8:00 a.m., "you know you live in a hot climate," says avid gardener Sharon Lowe one splendid but rapidly warming spring day. She is standing in her flowery garden in La Verne, which is just the other side of the low, oak-dotted hills that separate the San Gabriel Valley from the very beginnings of the toasty Inland Empire.

"We don't know 70 degrees," she says. "It's either a lot hotter or a lot colder. There are no in-betweens."

Many of the more common plants that do so well on the mild coastal plain perish here in the 95-degree heat that can last for weeks. That's why Southern California gardens pictured in magazines and books are mainly taken in coastal areas, in places such as Santa Barbara, Malibu, Palos Verdes and Corona del Mar. Yet Lowe's 25-year-old garden is full of colorful flowers even in the middle of August, living proof that many plants love the heat.

Once dubbed the Inland Garden Queen by a local newspaper, Lowe has been gardening in the heat for years. Having grown up in Covina and Glendora, she worked as a California Certified Nurseryperson at the Glendora Armstrong Nurseries for 20 years. She has consulted, taught and gardened for other people as well, developing some strong opinions on what works and what doesn't in hot, interior areas.

Growing mostly flowers ("I want color," she says), Lowe is partial to flowering plants that bloom all the time and do not require much work. Her garden has no shrubs in the conventional sense, and the few shade trees, such as the bright-gold-flowering *Cassia leptophylla* and crape myrtles, all bloom heavily.

MVPs in the Heat

The plants Lowe values most are those such as the white heliotrope 'Alba'. "It's the backbone of my garden in summer," she says. "The hotter it gets, the more it blooms." White flowers really sparkle in the heat, she points out.

She treasures the pink Flower Carpet roses, whose long, low canes she fastens to the ground with pegs, training them to flow among other plants, their flower clusters popping up unexpectedly.

She's crazy about plain old pentas and the Blizzard strain of geraniums, which bloom all the time, and red-flowered angel wing begonias.

Lantana is another favorite. "It likes me," she says. This is her way of saying that gardeners should choose plants for their ability to grow well in their particular climates or areas—not just because they like them. A case in point: Though Lowe loves ranunculus, she no longer plants them because they don't come back the following year.

She grows some daffodils but prefers tough, half-wild bulbs—such as homeria, sparaxis and freesia—that come back year after year with no special care. Lowe also has summer bulbs such as the lovely white *Zephyranthes candida*, which blooms furiously in August.

"I learned long ago not to tolerate prima donnas in my garden; they've got to hold their own," she says. Either they perform or they're replaced. "They all know fear," she says.

Lowe chooses plants that "cycle." She calls them perennials, but they are not the traditional herbaceous perennials of England and the East Coast. Her perennials—like the pentas, heliotrope, geraniums and begonias—bloom for a much longer time than do traditional perennials and are often somewhat shrubby. After they finish blooming, she cuts them back, and they start all over again. None dies completely to the ground in winter, as do herbaceous perennials, but most slow way down. The ones that need protection from the inland cold, she keeps against a south-facing wall or covers with spun Reemay horticultural fabric.

Garden Chores

Because Lowe's so-called perennials do so much flowering and growing, they need more frequent pruning and tidying up than do traditional kinds. In midsummer she trims many so they can come back into full bloom in the fall. She cuts back things such as the heliotrope, the Santa Barbara daisies and the daisylike euryops. She even cuts off about a third of the growth on her roses in midsummer.

In late August, even the bushy bougainvilleas growing in pots get cut back severely. Lowe has found that, if she properly prepares the garden in August by pruning and then fertilizing, the fall bloom will be nearly as nice as the spring.

Preferring that plants be open and airy, she works to keep the insides free of dead stems and leaves. If she has to sacrifice a few weeks of flowers in the name of neatness, she is willing to do so.

The garden has one last cleanup in late fall, which makes room for the emerging bulbs, which number in the hundreds. In spring, as soon as the bulbs finish blooming, she cuts back the foliage, a traditional garden no-no. In her garden, though, all but the daffodils bloom just as well the next year even if she immediately cuts off the foliage after bloom, before the foliage has time to wither and brown.

Lowe figures that she does 90 percent of the work in the garden between mid-September and the end of January, when it is cooler and the winter rains have begun or are on their way. She does much of her planting during that period, though she may have made her purchases in summer when they were in bloom. That is the only time of year one can find summer bloomers such as the zephyranthes. If they are flowering, Lowe usually trims the blooms off so the plants can bulk up for next year.

Summer is also when she finds two of her favorite summer heat lovers, the coleuslike iresine with its colorful leaves, and the firetail, or chenille plant, with its dramatic tassel flowers. Unavailable in fall, they are difficult to find even in spring.

The Miracle of Drip

Though Lowe often keeps her summer finds in their nursery containers, waiting until fall to plant, she can plant right in the middle of August if she chooses. How? Her whole garden is on drip irrigation. Making the change five years ago profoundly changed how she gardened. "I wouldn't be able to garden like this without it," she says.

Little spaghetti tubes run everywhere, but all are cleverly hidden by her and husband Dean. "We make it a game," she says. In summer, the drip runs for 10 minutes at a time, twice a day. In winter, between rains, it runs for only three to five minutes and but once a day.

Drip also allows Lowe to plant anywhere. "If I can imagine it, I can plant it," she says—so there are plants on top of birdhouses, in trees and in pots plopped here and there. Two champion hot-weather plants, the pink mandevilla and the blue clerodendrum, grow in drip-irrigated containers tucked into the garden beds.

Plants refrain from spreading wildly because they are not about to venture far from their little spots of moisture. Drip also allows Lowe to grow a greater variety of plants in her clay soil. Usually water has trouble soaking into clay soils, and when it finally does, the soil becomes too wet, causing root rot on some plants. With drip, water is metered so slowly that Lowe even gets away with not improving her soil.

Although clay is naturally rich, Lowe fertilizes every three months with a timed-release fertilizer, usually Osmocote. Occasionally she has to sprinkle the garden with water to activate the fertilizer and help it soak in.

Though most of her plants last for more than a season, she does grow a couple of short-lived plants, even though some break her tough-love rules. In the fall, then, she puts in delphiniums, foxgloves and Canterbury bells in the vicinity of the roses. She also sows seeds of several annuals, including linaria and Virginia stock, because they are so easy and surefire.

But pansies or snapdragons? They can't take the occasional sizzling hot winter day. "Summer lasts for more than six months," Lowe says. "So I just keep summery things going year-round."

WHEN VALLEY SUMMERS RUN COOL

Q: My zinnias are the prettiest ever—electric pinks and neon yellows—and almost four feet high. The problem is the leaves. They have white spots, almost like salt deposits. Today, when I picked some, all the leaves had it. Any suggestions?

—S.M., NORTHRIDGE

A: In cooler, coastal climates, powdery mildew is to be expected on zinnias, while in the warmer, drier valleys, it's almost unknown. But when summers are cooler than normal, mildew affects zinnias in the valleys, too.

In late summer, start applying one of the several fungicides (such as sulfur dust or Fungi-Fighter, also sold as Bayleton, made by Monterey Lawn and Garden). If mildew comes in autumn, there is no point trying to treat it, since the zinnias are almost finished for the season.

THE TRUTH ABOUT SWEET PEAS

Myths and legends surround the sowing and growing of sweet peas. Many were first spun in England when showing sweet pea blooms was almost a competitive sport, at the turn of the last century, with gardeners fiercely vying for flower show awards. That's where farfetched ideas such as pruning sweet peas to a single stem came from. One old English book advised digging a trench as deep as "the bottom button of your waistcoat" when you're standing in it.

As sweet peas have become popular in Southern California, our own myths have developed, and some of them are just as illogical, especially if you're only trying to grow a few flowers for the center of the dining room table.

Myth Number One: Sweet pea seeds must be sown before Labor Day.

This myth holds water only if you want flowers in time for the winter holidays. Planted any time in fall or winter, sweet peas will bloom, just later—and, actually, quite nicely.

This misinformation dates back to the early days of gardening in this state. In the 1940 classic *The Garden Beautiful in California* (Times Mirror), Ernest Braunton writes of August: "This is the best month for sowing sweet peas for winter blooms. If left until next month, they will not bloom until spring." Note that they will bloom, just later.

Another classic, *California Garden Flowers* by E.J. Wickson (Pacific Rural Press), this one from 1915, suggests planting early kinds in October for February bloom. "Or you can get a wealth of bloom on all varieties in May by sowing the seed in December and letting the early rains do the irrigating for you."

Seeds sown in early spring (January and February) will bloom, as long they are planted early enough so flowers can open "before the hot and dry weather sets in," according to Wickson, because sweet peas are a cool-season annual in Southern California.

As for blooming in time for the holidays, Renee Shepherd, of seed supplier Renee's Garden in Felton, California, suspects that only certain varieties will bloom in time if planted before Labor Day. Winter Elegance is one she thinks has a good chance.

The old books didn't specify varieties, but the old seed catalogs certainly did. I have a 1936 Germain's catalog from Los Angeles that touts its Winter Wonder Collection of frilly, winter-blooming Giant Spencer strains (for 50 cents, you could get "six different varieties, plus plant food tablets"!). I even have a few unopened packets of Giant Winter-Flowering Spencer Sweet Peas from 1957.

Myth Number Two: Frilly Spencer types from England are the best sweet peas.

Well, this may or may not be true, depending on where you live. Spencers have been the most requested kinds these last few years, but in Southern California they seem to do best grown near the coast, not in the inland areas. According to Pat Sherman, of seed supplier Fragrant Garden Nursery in Brookings, Oregon, regular Spencers bloom only when the day length is quite long, and by that time of year the inland valleys are often too hot.

However, the old-fashioned and Italian types, the Royal Family and Cuthbertson strains, and good old Winter Elegance all bloom when days are shorter, before the heat sets in. These are the good choices inland, Sherman says. Although the flowers are a little smaller and usually not ruffly, they are more fragrant, often powerfully so. "They can really perfume a room," says Shepherd.

Some new crosses from New Zealand, 'Cheri Amour' and 'North Shore', supposedly have the attributes of both groups—they're frilly and winter blooming.

Myth Number Three: Sweet pea seeds must be soaked overnight in a dish of water before planting.

Shepherd, for one, disagrees. It is too easy to forget and "oversoak" the seed, she says. She never soaks seed, and neither does Sherman, who must sprout too many seeds to lavish this kind of attention on them.

If seeds won't sprout, it may have nothing to do with whether they were soaked or not—the soil may be too dry or too wet. Braunton's old-time garden book gives this advice: Several days before planting thoroughly wet the soil to a depth of a couple of feet. Then sow the seed, and don't water again "until the plants are up an inch or two. This is how to grow the best sweet peas." In his book, Wickson concurs: Let "the hose run," sow seed a few days later and "let it be for several days."

It's hard—darn near impossible—for gardeners to sow seed and restrain themselves from watering. But if the soil was thoroughly watered to a depth of several feet before planting, there will be enough moisture to wick its way up to the seed to sprout it. You can experiment with other methods of watering, but the important points are not to sow seed in a dry soil, and not to keep it so wet that the seed rots.

If seeds still refuse to sprout for one reason or another (give them two weeks), simply plant more. Snails, slugs and cutworms are often the reason seeds don't seem to sprout—they do, but are immediately eaten. Bait for slugs and snails before you sow the seed, or sow it in little pots kept safely above ground. To avoid cutworm damage, the old gardening books suggest planting sweet peas in soil where nothing else has recently grown.

Meanwhile, Glenys Johnson, of Enchanting Sweet Peas in Sebastopol, California, a grower of cut sweet pea blooms and a supplier of seed, does soak seed before planting and is prepared to go one step further if they do not swell overnight. She has found a few varieties with extra-hard coats that she must nick or abrade so they absorb enough moisture to germinate.

Myth Number Four: Sweet pea seeds are best sown directly in the ground where they are to grow, not in pots for transplanting.

The practices of the professionals show you can start seed in small pots or directly in the ground. Either way, plant seed about an inch deep.

For her cut flower market, Johnson grows thousands of plants from seed—and sows them all in commercial cell packs that hold 50 seedlings apiece. Planted in regular potting soil, seedlings are then transplanted into the garden at about eight inches tall.

Sherman, who grows more than 3,000 plants each year, sows single seeds in two-inch plastic pots. She then transplants them into the garden, spacing the seedlings about eight inches apart.

Shepherd sows seed directly in the ground, spacing seeds only three to four inches apart.

Myth Number Five: Dig a trench as deep as "the bottom button of your waistcoat" when you're standing in it.

Okay, he's exaggerating. However, the importance of planting or transplanting sweet peas into deeply dug soil may not be complete fiction. The old books make quite a point of these plants needing excellent drainage. According to Braunton: "The best growers actually dig a trench three feet deep if in heavy soil, to get the perfect drainage needed. Those having favorable soils need not delve so deeply."

Three feet! It may not be necessary to get quite that carried away, but, Sherman says, "dig down two spades deep" when preparing a claylike soil for sweet peas.

In the old books, quantities of "well-rotted animal manure" are added to the soil, but this may be a little hard to come by nowadays. Being in farm country, Johnson has a friend who supplies her with aged turkey manure. Stay away from steer manure—it contains way too much salt. Use any good planting mix instead.

Don't forget to provide a six- to seven-foot fence, trellis or pole for peas to climb on. For maximum blooms, fertilize every two weeks once they are several feet tall, if it has not already been added. Shepherd uses fish emulsion and kelp fertilizer; Sherman uses Miracle-Gro or Peters.

Fact or Fiction: Constantly cutting sweet pea flowers keeps them blooming.

This is most definitely true. Allowing plants to make seedpods will quickly cut short their season. Gather flowers every day if you can, for the house or for friends. "You'll make someone extremely happy," says Shepherd.

Cut the stems when four or five of the flowers are open but two are still in bud. They don't last long in a vase. Pat Sherman has tried making them last with various treatments, none of which worked.

If stems are too short to cut, you can lengthen them "almost overnight," according to Johnson: Add blood meal and water it in.

Keep all seedpods picked off until mildew sets in. That's the sign that sweet peas are about to finish up and can be taken out. Save seed if you like, says Johnson, to sow next fall or winter.

Renee's Garden seeds are available at many nurseries; telephone 888.880.7228; on the web at www.reneesgarden.com.

Fragrant Garden Nursery, PO Box 4246, Brookings, OR 97415; on the web at www.fragrantgarden.com.

Enchanting Sweet Peas, 244 Florence Avenue, Sebastopol, CA 95472; telephone 800.371.0233; on the web at www.enchantingsweetpeas.com.

See Week 32 in 52 Weeks in the California Garden.

INVASION OF THE POPPY SNATCHERS

Q: For years we've had Iceland poppies in our Hancock Park garden. For the last two, though, the large buds that appear in the morning are bitten off by evening. We live across the street from a golf course with lots of squirrels. Could you offer any advice?

—P.P., Los Angeles

A: Several sources agree that squirrels seem to love Iceland poppy buds. To protect the buds, spray them with a ready-to-use hot-pepper (capsicum) solution, such as Get Away Squirrel and Raccoon or Hot Pepper Wax animal repellent. Once squirrels sample the treated buds, they'll probably stay away. Use it early in the season, before squirrels get set in their harvesting habits.

See Week 44 in 52 Weeks in the California Garden.

A LATE-SUMMER LILY

Q: A whole bunch of lilies are popping up in my yard. They flowered and died back in October, so I dug them up, separated them and replanted. Then I watered the dickens out of them. Now I read in a book that I should not be watering them because the bulbs are dormant in winter. Trouble is, most have already regrown their leaves. The book also said not to separate the bulbs, but I did, and there is no putting them back together. Should I be following the instructions in this book?

—B.L., STUDIO CITY

A: Toss that book out, because it's got it all wrong for California (as so many garden books published in the East do). You're probably growing the old-time California garden plant naked lady (*Amaryllis belladonna*), so named because the bulbs bloom in late summer with lilylike flowers, before leaves emerge.

A lot of us remember *Amaryllis belladonna* from our childhood: Just when everything else in the garden was exhausted from the long summer, suddenly these lovely big pink trumpet flowers would appear on stiff, two-foot stems. They'd grace even vacant lots filled with dead grasses.

The long, inch-wide leaves would follow after the flowers faded—the bulbs do their growing in winter. They are dormant in summer, when the leaves shrivel.

Less common in gardens now, they can still be found around many older homes. *Amaryllis belladonna* is a cast-iron plant for sunny or partly shaded spots: You can plant and forget. It can survive on rainfall alone, with no fertilizing, though it can tolerate some summer water. It is true, as with almost all bulbs, that once you separate a clump into individual bulbs, it may take a year or more to flower again while the bulbs recover from the loss of roots.

The lily in question could also be the closely related crinum lily, though these tend to flower later in fall. If the flower is attached to the stem by a long tube, it is a crinum. There are also crosses between the two, called amarcrinum, that have naked lady–like flowers on tall stems.

Crinums and amarcrinums, with pink, white or reddish flowers, tend to have leaves year-round, sometimes atop thick, short trunks. They appreciate some summer watering but can do without; the culture for all three is very similar, although the naked lady is the toughest.

See Week 33 in 52 Weeks in the California Garden.

THE MOST FRAGRANT FREESIA

Q: Do you know a source from which I might order the older, nonhybridized fragrant white freesia?

—S.F., SANTA MONICA

A: A lot of people remember freesias smelling stronger than they do today, but I suspect it's much the same as remembering our first date as being prettier or more handsome in retrospect. Most experts think that all freesias are powerfully fragrant, though they agree that single-flowered kinds are more fragrant than doubles and that white-flowered kinds may be the most fragrant.

At nurseries in the fall are bulbs (actually corms) of several single whites, including 'Matterhorn' and 'Tecolote White'. They are so fragrant, says Dan Davids, of Davids & Royston Bulb Company, a large bulb grower and wholesaler in Gardena, that "carrying a bouquet home in your car can be overpowering."

The freesia you may be thinking of is probably a species, or wild, freesia named *Freesia alba*, white with a yellow throat. "You never have to bend down to smell *Freesia alba*," says Hugh McDonald, owner of Neglected Bulbs in Berkeley, which sells seed-grown corms.

Another source is Jim Duggan Flower Nursery, which offers its catalog on the web. In spring its retail nursery, Encinitas Gardens, sells the bulbs blooming in pots.

September through November is the time to plant freesia corms. Bury them so they are covered by two and a half to three inches of soil and space them three to four inches apart in full sun, though one observer thinks that *Freesia alba* can tolerate a little shade.

Do not keep these bulbs too wet, at least until they sprout. Find places that stay fairly dry in summer and fall, that get less water than areas like rose beds. Such spots are at the edges of paths or where sprinklers don't reach. Another is in pots (which I let go bone-dry in summer). Planting in pots or beside paths also puts the fragrant freesias where you might catch a delightful whiff while they are in spring bloom.

Neglected Bulbs, PO Box 2768, Berkeley, CA 94702-0768; telephone 510.524.5149.
Jim Duggan Flower Nursery, 1452 Santa Fe Drive, Encinitas, CA 92024; telephone 760.943.1658; on the web at www.thebulbman.com.

STOWAWAY MOLD ON TULIPS

Q: I purchased tulip bulbs that had a residue of powder on them. I stored them in the refrigerator in their open mesh bag. Will this residue affect other produce? Is it harmful?

—B.S., HUNTINGTON BEACH

A: First, for those who might be wondering what the bulbs are doing in the fridge: To bloom well, tulips and a few other bulbs need to be cooled for six weeks before they are planted. The vegetable crisper is the place to keep them. Leave them loose, in their mesh or ventilated plastic bags, or keep them in paper bags.

Some surface mold can be found on the bulb skins, most often on those that have been packaged in the Netherlands—the source of almost all tulip bulbs—and, curiously, most often on red tulips. At harvest there the weather is sometimes wet and miserable, so the presence of mold is not surprising.

Dan Davids of Davids & Royston Bulb Company, a large bulb grower and wholesaler in Gardena, says if the refrigerated shipping containers were kept cool enough for the long boat ride, there should be no mold. If there is, simply wash and dry the bulbs before putting them in the vegetable crisper. The mold will not harm the bulbs, the produce or you.

Bulbs are never treated with anything once they are harvested, "period, end of story," according to Davids. Supermarket potatoes and apples have more chemicals on them than bulbs destined for the garden. The growers' nontreatment policy is also true for bulbs of edible plants such as onions, says Davids. "If you wanted, you could cook with the onion bulbs meant for planting."

TULIPS IN DUTCH

Q: All of my bulbs have grown and flowered, but not the tulips. When I dug up a few of the bulbs, I found they had turned into black mush. Any idea what went wrong?

—V.J., VALENCIA

A: The bulbs rotted, not an uncommon occurrence, especially in California, where tulips must be planted deep (up to eight inches) and sometimes in heavy soils that stay soggy for days. Next year, at planting time, try placing each bulb on an inch-thick cushion of washed builder's sand, placed in the bottom of the hole.

Many tulip fanciers swear by this technique. After a few years of adding sand to each hole, and then tilling the soil after the tulips come out, you end up with a sandier, more bulb-friendly soil as a bonus.

❧ ❧ ❧

Rose Parade

PICKING CHAMPIONS

So many roses to plant and so little room, what's a gardener to do? How does one choose a few when there are more varieties of roses than of any other garden plant? The choices include hundreds of hybrid teas and floribundas—the two most common categories, or classes, of rose. Then there are musk, Portland, Bourbon, China, polyantha, and all the different types of antique, heirloom or old roses.

Don't forget the descriptive class called ramblers and the shrub roses. And there are miniature roses and the new landscape roses, plus all those climbing roses.

It's simply overwhelming.

So I asked experts—gardeners from different climates who have grown several hundred, and even thousands, of kinds of roses—to name their favorites. Generally, they picked varieties that look good as blooming bushes in the garden, though they also named a few champion producers of cut flowers.

Where the gardeners live probably influenced their choices—a rose may thrive in the dry heat of an inland garden but be sickly by the beach. Only three varieties made more than one list—the climber 'Eden', the 1879 noisette 'Mme. Alfred Carriere' and the English rose named 'Mary Rose'. You probably couldn't go wrong planting these three!

Newer rose varieties made some lists, but as Edie O'Hair, who grows some 3,000 roses on her five acres in Temecula, puts it, "The longer one grows and knows roses, the more one appreciates the older ones."

Eden in Orange County

Beautrice Grow's garden in the warm hills above San Clemente includes many roses among an abundance of perennials and other flowers. This talented gardener loves the simple white ever-blooming floribunda 'Iceberg' and recommends it to new gardeners, who will find it "most forgiving," she says. "Even if you prune it poorly, it bounces right back."

Grow says the much fancier, many-petaled soft-pink English rose 'Mary Rose', after Henry VIII's famous flagship, "is one of the most gorgeous roses, and so vigorous." She keeps hers pruned into a small tree-shaped rose. As a bush it likes space, say, about six feet all around.

Though she hasn't grown it for long, 'Huntington's Hero' is another English rose she loves for its simple open shape and pale-buff to coral-pink flowers, tinged yellow in the middle.

On arbors she loves the 1985 'Eden', with its many-petaled soft-pink flowers, though she appreciates the deep-pink 1868 Bourbon rose 'Zephirine Drouhin', which has no thorns. "I don't have to be concerned when the children go running through the arbor," she says.

Royalty in the Inland Empire

Edie O'Hair of Temecula describes herself as a "mad, enthusiastic amateur." She is partial to older rose varieties and those colored cream or white. Her very favorite is the white-flowered climber 'Mme. Alfred Carriere', which she uses as a huge shrub, eight to nine feet tall by 10 feet across.

'Honor', with its masses of blooms and "honey fragrance," and the 1989 All-America Rose Selection named 'Class Act', with its heavy, sweet fragrance, are two of her favorite white hybrid teas. 'Etain' is a big rambler that she uses as a bank cover, having planted it at the top of a hill and letting it spill down. It has masses of flowers that are "a medley of copper, peach, pink and other warm tones," she says.

A hybrid tea from 1954, 'Lady Elgin' has well-shaped apricot flowers and nice fragrance. "All of the roses in my garden must have fragrance," she says. 'Betty Prior' is a floribunda she grows by the dozen because it is never without blooms, which, she says, "look like flocks of pink butterflies fluttering in a breeze."

Intrepid Climbers on the Palos Verdes Peninsula

Julie Heinsheimer, a Rolling Hills landscape designer who gardens on two and a half acres, has the room for some really big climbers. She first saw 'Mme. Alfred Carriere' covering the two-story cottage used as an office by famed gardener Vita Sackville-West at Sissinghhurst, England. Heinsheimer has since used this 1876 noisette at her home to cover a two-story chimney and the 20-foot-tall skeleton of a dead tree. Cream flowers with a pink blush open continuously.

The yellow Lady Banks' rose (*Rosa banksiae*) is a truly evergreen climber, though it blooms only in spring, when it is covered with little blossoms. Heinsheimer has it growing in a 25-foot-tall olive, which this rose fills to the top. "We have to do a lot of pruning every year to keep it in bounds," she says. Growing 30 feet in either direction along a low fence, 'New Dawn' is a big climber loaded with large pale-pink flowers that bloom mostly in spring. 'Altissimo' is a "fabulous climber, especially on a trellis," with blood-red single blooms and centers of golden stamens, "a fabulous combination."

A rose that blooms and blooms is the 1928 hybrid musk 'Felicia', with a "heavenly fragrance" and great clusters of peachy-salmon two-inch flowers. It grows to six feet "up and sideways," as Heinsheimer puts it.

Shades of Apricot in the South Bay

Sharon Van Enoo, a Torrance consulting rosarian for the American Rose Society, has grown at least 600 roses. About 300 roses are planted on her 50x100-foot lot, which is near the coast but out of the fog belt. "My motto is, if there's dirt showing, plant it, and, if possible, make it a rose," she says.

Van Enoo's favorites reflect a passion for apricot and peach. She is also very fond of the little-known and undervalued hybrid musk roses as well as the older but similar noisettes. 'Crepuscule', a noisette climber, has dainty flowers that combine copper with peach and apricot. "It never stops blooming," says Van Enoo. Its soft, relaxed canes make it easy to train, even up into the branches of a tree. "I'm crazy about the climber named 'Eden'," she says, "but the canes are thicker, and it's not as easily trained."

Even though it is a traditional hybrid tea, Van Enoo thinks 'Just Joey' is one of the best all-around garden roses, with its formal tea-rose blooms of apricot. 'Pure Poetry' is a floribunda with blooms that are a "wonderful, if somewhat odd, color"—yellowish with hints of peach and apricot.

Van Enoo loves English roses. Her favorite is 'Prospero', which makes a neat three-foot-round ball, covered with garnet-red flowers that look distinctly old-fashioned. For a smaller rose that grows to only two feet, she suggests the China rose named 'Irene Watts', with powerfully fragrant, light peachy-pink flowers of old-fashioned form. A new rose from Europe named 'Paul Bocuse' (after the five-star chef) has almost immediately moved to near the top of her list. A shrub rose, it makes a mound of good green foliage about four feet tall and wide, so it's a useful rose to plant in the garden with other perennials and shrubs. Its apricot flowers are old-fashioned in form.

Garden Party in Hancock Park

Behind landscape designer Judy M. Horton's 1910 home in the Hancock Park area is a tall arbor full of climbing roses, and two 12x33-foot beds of "roses, fruit trees and ephemerals."

'Mary Rose' is her idea of "what a rose should be," Horton says, "the quintessential rose." An airy six-foot shrub, it sports loads of old-fashioned, deep-dusty-pink blossoms that are "wonderfully fragrant."

If you're looking for a tough rose that's just about the perfect size for most gardens (three feet tall) and can even tolerate as little as a half-day of sun, Horton suggests the 1909 'Gruss an Aachen', with "creamy to pinky-white flowers." It looks a lot like the current crop of old-fashioned-appearing English roses, so much so that David Austin, rose heavyweight and developer of English roses, includes it in his book *English Roses* (Little, Brown, 1993).

'Erfurt' is a strong, spreading shrub rose that will grow eight feet wide but only three feet tall. The "only thing I don't like about this rose are the flowers," says Horton. "It's got great foliage and wonderful orange rose hips [the fruit], but the two-tone white and cherry-red flowers leave something to be desired." She grows it for the foliage, which one florist friend regularly comes over and cuts.

Though she uses them only in her cutting garden, she loves hybrid teas with really big flowers, such as 'Brandy', 'Garden Party', 'Mr. Lincoln' and 'Peace', to cut and bring into the house.

Partial to Polyanthas in Westwood

Avid gardener Sharon Milder grows more than 100 roses of all kinds, mostly in her front yard in Westwood. Of all the roses she has grown over the years, she is most impressed by the group known as polyanthas. "They have everything one wants in a rose, at least for those who garden near the coast," says Milder. While many roses in her garden get the orange-colored rust disease, these don't.

The four-foot-tall polyantha 'Marie Pavie', with blush-pink flowers, is her favorite. "Sometimes I think, 'Hello, why aren't the landscapers using this one?' It's just a stunning, tough plant, even better than Iceberg'," she says.

The 1884 'Perle d'Or', whose flower color is described as a soft golden-pink to buff, is another she adores. 'Mlle. Cecile Brunner', the shrub, not the climber, is another favorite polyantha. "Its flowers are a beautiful shade of pink, it blooms a lot, and it never gets diseases."

For a climber, she prefers 'Blush Noisette', another old-timer from 1817, part of the noisette clan. Milder says it has "absolutely the best fragrance, it's enchanting." This is a moderate grower that won't overwhelm a trellis or arbor. Like most of her other recommendations, it has small flowers but lots of them, because, she says, "I frankly love small flowers," preferring their grace to sheer size.

A Designer's Palette in Ventura County

Sandy Gaal grows more than 300 roses in Santa Paula and has recently started designing gardens. The Portland rose 'Marchesa Boccella' (also known as 'Jacques Cartier') tops her list, for the flower's full, many-petaled rosette form and its "incredible" fragrance. 'Excellenz von Schubert' is a huge, eight-foot-wide, cascading hybrid musk with the typically musky fragrance. It blooms a lot with clusters of lavender pom-poms.

'Yves Piaget' is one of the newish so-called romantica roses, with flowers that are modern hybrid tea in size and stature but with many more petals, so they also look old-fashioned. The flowers are a deep cerise pink; it is fragrant and blooms often. "Most of my favorite roses are old-fashioned or are English roses that look old-fashioned," says Gaal. Two of her favorite English roses are the many-petaled, medium-pink 'Gertrude Jekyll' and the black-red 'Tradescant'.

For landscaping, she loves a 1925-vintage hybrid musk rose named 'Cornelia', with light-pink flowers, described as exhibiting a "tug-of-war between lavender and brown" in one catalog. "It's very graceful, very healthy, and has nice dark green foliage," says Gaal. It can be used as a climber, but she grows it as a cascading six-foot-wide shrub.

A ROSE OF A DIFFERENT COLOR

Q: How is it possible that after three years a yellow rosebush can suddenly have burgundy-colored roses blooming? The nearest rosebush is about three feet away, and the new stems are coming from the bush itself, not up from the ground like a sucker.

—D.N., FULLERTON

A: It's not possible, says horticulturist and rose hybridizer Tom Carruth, of Weeks Roses in Upland. Those are suckers, sprouting from below the graft, from what is called the rootstock. Anything that sprouts from below the graft, whether the graft is above or below ground, is a sucker.

Many roses are grafted onto the roots of a different variety, most often a 100-year-old variety named 'Dr. Huey'. It is 'Dr. Huey' that has the velvety red blooms of medium size, on strong upright growth that is somewhat "climby." This growth must be coming from the roots, not the grafted or budded plant on top. You might also notice that the leaves on the suckers mildew easily, another characteristic of 'Dr. Huey'.

Snap these suckers off with a quick jerk. Cut suckers tend to return with a vengeance. Remove them as quickly as possible so they do not overwhelm the top growth—the variety you want to keep. As new sprouts arise, immediately snap off any coming from below the graft.

It's not uncommon to see roses in gardens that have been overwhelmed by the vigorous 'Dr. Huey' rootstock so that is all that remains. Carruth notes this is one reason roses are increasingly being grown "on their own roots," not grafted to a different rootstock.

FRECKLE-FACE FLOWERS

Q: Why does my normally white 'John F. Kennedy' rose sometimes get pink polka dots?

—M.M., PICO RIVERA

A: It's similar to people getting freckles. According to rosarian Joe Brown, of Weeks Roses in Upland, at certain times of the year and in certain weather, light-colored roses develop reddish spots. It happens not only to white rose blossoms but to light pinks and lavenders as well.

Spots may be caused by dew or moisture sitting on the petals when the sun is intense, as is often the case in the fall. The drops cause the pigments, even those normally not visible, to intensify in that spot—like a freckle—to protect the tissue from the sunlight. You could call it a kind of rose sunburn. The dots seem most likely to appear when there are sudden fluctuations in the weather, such as cool nights followed by brilliant Santa Ana–winds days.

Avoid the problem, says Brown, by picking roses when the buds are about one-third open, early in the day before the sun hits them. The spots are most noticeable on fully opened rose blossoms that are several days old.

HOLES IN ROSE LEAVES

Q: For the last few years my roses have been riddled with little holes. Someone said it was rose slugs. What can I do to stop them?

—S.M., WEST LOS ANGELES

A: Rose "slugs" are actually larvae of the sawfly, a bee and wasp relative. Early in the rose season, the small, green, quarter-inch-long larvae skeletonize dot-sized areas, munching bigger and bigger holes in leaves as they grow. They spend winter becoming adults in the ground, then lay eggs on edges of leaves in early spring.

Nonchemical controls include neem (such as Safer BioNeem) and insecticidal soap spray. One rose gardener has been able to control them with simple horticultural oil sprays (such as Safe-T-Side or SunSpray Ultra-Fine), if she sprays early in spring and then every two weeks until early summer.

However, many serious rose growers believe that carbaryl (Sevin) works best on these chewing insects, also killing those hiding in the ground. This insecticide is highly toxic to earthworms, bees and fish, though. The systemic Orthene is another poison said to offer some control.

PREVENTING ROSE DISEASES

Q: Spring's relatively cool temperatures and high humidity can cause major fungus problems with my rosebushes. Got any suggestions?

—J.S., LOS FELIZ

A: Rust and mildew are often epidemic following a cool, overcast spring. Sometime in early winter—after roses have been pruned but before they leaf out—is the time to prevent a repeat. "People are reluctant to do anything in winter when they can't actually see the disease," says chemist Tommy Cairns, author of *All About Roses* (Ortho Books, 1999). Yet after-the-fact cures are often ineffective or short-lived.

In January, pick off last year's leaves and rake all leaves off the ground. Send them to the dump, not the compost pile. Soak the bare canes and the ground with environmentally friendly dormant oil and sulfur sprays (available at nurseries). This helps keep last year's diseases from infecting this year's roses.

After roses begin to grow, Cairns says, Funginex (made by Ortho) does a fair job preventing rust and mildew—if applied before diseases show and reapplied at intervals suggested on label directions. Make sure to spray the undersides of leaves, which is where orange rust fungus grows.

Clair Martin III, curator of the Rose Garden at the Huntington Botanical Gardens in San Marino and author of 100 *Old Roses for the American Garden* (Workman Publishing, 1999), is also a big believer in garden cleanup and dormant sprays during the dormant season. "We try to prevent disease, not cure it," he says. During the growing season, he says, "we do nothing."

On already infected bushes, pick off rust-infested leaves. Rust is one disease that makes rose fanciers particularly desperate. In her nursery's newsletter, Mary Lou Heard, of Heard's Country Gardens in Westminster, related a most radical control for rust, recommended to her by an old nurseryman: Set the ground on fire.

Burning a little shredded newspaper or excelsior under a bush kills rust spores on the undersides of leaves, she says. The quick fire may kill a few leaves, but most are unharmed because they are moist and green. Still, she keeps the garden hose handy just in case. "It really does get rid of the rust," she says. It sounds like a desperate measure to me.

Heard's Country Gardens, 14391 Edwards, Westminster, CA 92683; telephone 714.496.2444; on the web at www.heardsgardens.com.
The Rose Garden at the Huntington Botanical Gardens, 1151 Oxford Road, San Marino, CA 91108; telephone 626.405.2141; on the web at www.huntington.org.

CLIMBERS TAKE A POWDER

Q: We're currently plagued by a white powder on our climbing roses. We've tried dozens of sprays and a fertilizer that's supposed to protect them, but it's an endless struggle. Any suggestions?

—M.P., LOS ANGELES

A: You are describing powdery mildew. Some roses are more prone to mildew,

---

BAKING SODA CURE FOR POWDERY MILDEW

water
1 1/2 tablespoons baking soda
1 tablespoon canola oil
1 tablespoon insecticidal soap
1 tablespoon vinegar

To one cup water, add baking soda, canola oil and insecticidal soap.
Add vinegar, then enough additional water to make a one-gallon solution. Spray on foliage.

and on those kinds it can be prevented with Funginex—if you apply it before you see any signs.

For very large shrubs or on climbers that are difficult to spray, chemist and rose expert Tommy Cairns recommends Fungi-Fighter (also sold as Bayleton). A systemic, poured on the soil at the base of the plant, it is taken up by the roots and distributed throughout the plant to the leaves. It can also be sprayed. Be sure to reapply it at the intervals suggested on the label.

Fungicides like these won't do much good once powdery mildew takes hold, but natural sulfur products kill actively growing mildew on contact. These can be mixed with water and sprayed, or dusted directly on plants.

After much experimenting, Cairns came up with a homemade baking soda formula that, sprayed on foliage, quickly knocks powdery mildew down. Diseases usually reappear, though, and plants will need spraying again. Don't use baking soda or sulfur sprays when temperatures exceed 75 or 80 degrees—leaves can burn.

If roses consistently mildew, try growing other rose varieties touted as being more disease resistant. Or relocate the roses. It is said that stagnant air often brings on mildew, so finding a breezy, sunny spot should help.

CPR FOR CUT FLOWERS

Q: What is wrong with my roses? They grow and bloom well, but when I put them in vases, they do not open all the way but die partly closed.

—C.L., CHATSWORTH

To help prolong the life of cut flowers, recut the stems underwater.

A: To open properly, cut roses need to keep growing, and so require water and nutrients. To assure a ready supply of both, follow this advice:

Cut early in the morning or late in the evening with sharp shears. Immediately put the stems in a pail of warm (110 degree) water. Bring it indoors and cut the stems again, this time making the cuts underwater. This prevents little bubbles of air from blocking the water uptake.

Put a commercial preservative in a vase of water, or add a quarter teaspoon household bleach and one and a half teaspoons sugar to each quart of water. Or use a nondiet, citrus-flavored carbonated drink, such as 7-Up. Any of these provide nutrients and prevent bacteria from blocking uptake.

If you don't use a preservative, change the water every day.

Flowering Shrubs

HELP FOR CAMELLIAS

Q: I hope you can help all of us who have camellias that suffer from brown blight. Mine have increasingly shown blight, dropping buds, sticky blossoms or dried brown buds or failing to blossom at all.

—T.E., HAWTHORNE

A: You are actually describing a number of camellia ailments, though most gardeners tend to blame them all on a disease called camellia petal blight. According to Tom Nuccio, of Nuccio's Nurseries in Altadena, longtime camellia specialty growers, the dropping of buds can be varietal—some kinds, such as 'Pink Perfection', do it, others don't. Or it can be brought on by the weather—Santa Ana winds or rain.

Some camellias bullnose: The petals stick together, the buds look wet and shiny, and the flowers don't open. Overhead watering with sprinklers can be a cause, or it may be the variety or weather.

Dried brown buds can also be varietal or cultural. It usually happens on plants that are not happy with their care or environment. Flowers that turn brown may just be old or getting too much sun. This often happens on plants that have outgrown their shady location and now grow in the sun.

If the flowers become heavy with water and turn to mush (try rubbing the petal between your fingers), and the veins in the petals get darker, only then do you have camellia petal blight. According to Art McCain, a University of California

For healthy camellia blooms, keep spent flowers picked up
and renew mulch each year.

Cooperative Extension plant pathologist, there really are no sensible chemical controls, despite the fact that some books recommend PCNB, which must be applied to the ground in winter, or benomyl, which must be sprayed on the flowers "nearly every day." See Nuccio's suggestions in the next answer.

Nuccio's Nurseries, PO Box 6060 (3555 Chaney Trail), Altadena, CA 91003; telephone 626.794.3383.

THE BROWNING OF CAMELLIAS

Q: I have white, pink and red camellias. The red lasts longest, turning brown only at the end of bloom. But the white, a beautiful flower, turns brown almost as soon as it opens. Is there any way of preventing this?

—P.B., PACIFIC PALISADES

A: Variable weather causes most browning, though some varieties are more susceptible than others. Some whites, especially 'Conrad Hilton', have a tendency to turn brown, Tom Nuccio says. 'Silver Waves' is one large white with wavy petals that does well near the coast and doesn't brown; 'Purity' is another older variety to try.

Browning could also be petal blight, brought on by days of rainy weather. Drizzly "mushroom weather" encourages small, cup-shape mushrooms that shoot spores up onto the flowers. Infected flowers become not only brown but mushy. When the weather dries out a little, the blight usually doesn't appear on subsequent flowers. In other words, the disease spreads from mushroom to flower only when it's releasing spores, usually following rainy periods.

The mushrooms grow on fallen, blighted flowers from the previous year, so the only control is to rake them up and send them to the dump. Nuccio suggests spreading a fresh, inch-thick mulch around the plants (but not directly at the bases). Use wood chips, shredded bark or some other organic mulch. However, the spores can drift in from someone else's camellias, so even this isn't foolproof. The smaller-flowered sasanqua camellias, incidentally, don't get camellia petal blight.

ALL BUDS AND NO BLOOMS

Q: I have a well-established camellia facing north in my back yard. Every year it produces hundreds of buds, but they never bloom. For the 10 years we've lived here, they have never opened up—they just drop. Can you help?

—C.L., GLENDALE

A: This regularly happens to some camellias near the coast, but in Glendale the problem probably has to do with the variety, especially considering the age of the plant. Jim Nuccio, of Nuccio's Nurseries, says that a number of years ago several popular varieties, including a red named 'Eureka', had this failing—the buds never open, just fall off.

If you have one of these varieties, you have two choices: Keep it and enjoy it as a handsome, green nonflowering shrub that tolerates the lack of sun on the north side of the house, or cut it almost to the ground and graft another, floriferous variety to it. Get a how-to book on grafting to do that.

Near the coast this often happens to camellias with full, many-petaled flowers, such as 'Nuccio's Gem'. The flowers start to open, but moisture in the air causes the petals to stick together, and the buds abort. Sprinklers hitting the buds, or rain, can also keep the buds from fully opening.

BRUNFELSIA BLOOMED YESTERDAY,
BUT NOT TODAY

Q: I bought a plant at a swap meet called yesterday-today-and-tomorrow. It was in bloom but hasn't flowered since. Help!

—F.B., LOS ANGELES

A: Like many shrubs, *Brunfelsia pauciflora* 'Floribunda' blooms once a year, in spring and early summer. In colder areas it may lose most of its leaves in winter.

Brunfelsias, blooming along with late camellias, look similar and like similar conditions—some shade, moisture and a slightly acid soil. In time they make a 10-foot-tall shrub, usually taller than wide, with handsome, glossy leaves.

The common name comes from the way the flowers change color, starting out purple, changing to lavender and finally to white, although there are other kinds of brunfelsias. Be assured it will bloom again next spring.

UNSOLVED MYSTERY: GARDENIAS

Q: My 'Mystery' gardenia forms flower buds, but just as they mature to the point of opening, they drop. Why do they fall off?

—R.P., SIMI VALLEY

A: There are several possibilities, according to Kevin Naylor, of Monrovia Nursery Company, a large wholesale grower:

• Nearly invisible bud mites. Other than using a 20X hand lens to spot them, the only clue is that the scales of the flower bud turn brown or black at the tips. Carbaryl (Sevin) will control the mites, but it is extremely toxic to bees and earthworms, so use it carefully. It also might result in an increase in spider mites. A rather radical but nonchemical control is to pick off and destroy all the buds and hope the next crop will be clean and pest-free.

• A deficiency of micronutrients, such as magnesium or manganese. Use a liquid fertilizer, such as Peters 20-20-20, that contains micronutrients, and drench the plant so some is taken in by the foliage as well as the roots. Follow the label instructions carefully—you don't want to use too much and burn the foliage.

• Soil that is not acidic enough. Gardenias like heat, sun and acid soil. In winter—if the plant is small enough—dig it up, improve the soil with organic amendments, and replant. Alkaline soils also tend to tie up micronutrients, so alkaline soils and nutrient deficiencies are often linked.

• Weather that is too hot or too cool, or roots that have been damaged from overwatering or root rot.

See Week 26 of 52 Weeks in the California Garden.

LILAC FEVER

It seems that lilacs do grow, and flower, in Southern California. I once mentioned in a column that I had never seen a handsome, healthy lilac outside of the chilly high desert or Descanso Gardens (its Lilac Grove has a nice collection of lilac cultivars), which is situated inland in La Cañada Flintridge in a cool canyon bottom dotted with oaks.

"Perhaps someone will send me a snapshot of his or her lilacs, and I'll become a believer," I goaded. "Until then, I'll continue to think that lilacs look great beside a granite doorstep in New Hampshire but are a poor choice next to a decomposed granite path in Southern California."

Donna Potts from South Pasadena answered my challenge: "I have a great lilac in my typical California garden (no decomposed granite path, though). I do not know the specific variety, but they have a delightful fragrance."

She sent photos of a bush in full bloom, and peeking over the garage behind was the top of a palm tree, so I knew these photos hadn't been surreptitiously taken in New Hampshire. The pictures she enclosed were very pretty, but South Pasadena's not *that* far from Descanso Gardens.

However, another letter was from a reader in Rancho Palos Verdes. E.A. Trabin wrote that they've had lilacs blooming in their garden for the last 15 years. The Palos Verdes Peninsula is a long way from Descanso, a completely different, coastal climate. Another photo came from the Turski family in Venice, also a coastal community, of a very young plant in bloom.

From Valencia, in the Santa Clarita Valley, Pete Colato wrote: "Read your article whilst sitting in the garden admiring the neighbor's lilacs in full flower. Having lived in the East, I am well acquainted with lilacs, and these are as beautiful as any back there." He sent photos of lilacs hanging over the neighbor's fence.

More photos came from Larry and Helen Merken in Chatsworth, of a bush nearly as tall as their chimney in full flower. And from West Covina, Ruth Midyett sent photos of a big, handsome 25-year-old bush. Photos piled in from Glendora, Reseda and Thousand Oaks.

And Nancy Lewis, who lives in Arcadia near the Arboretum of Los Angeles County, sent a photo of a lilac, the original Descanso hybrid 'Lavender Lady', covered with blossoms. Of all the lilacs, these hybrids are supposed to do best in Southern California. Other Descanso hybrids for mild climates include 'White Chiffon', 'Spring in Descanso', 'Mrs. Forrest K. Smith', 'Descanso Giant', 'Sylvan Beauty', 'Pride of the Guild' and 'King of Descanso'. I suspect that most of the lilacs in the photos I received were 'Lavender Lady'—since it is the most common at nurseries—or one of these others.

Descanso Gardens Weighs In

Descanso Gardens, of course, was quick to comment. Rudy Schaffer, volunteer curator of the lilac collection, has many suggestions on how to make the most of lilacs in Southern California:

• To get flowers on the mild-climate lilacs such as 'Lavender Lady', stop watering after September 15, and let them live on rainfall alone. (This applies only to plants that have been in the ground for two or three years.) This drying out forces dormancy, which makes for good flowers. Resume watering when the first leaf or flower buds begin to open in spring. For this reason, if you're planting a new lilac, don't put it near lawns or shrubs that need irrigation in winter.

• As lilacs finish blooming, cut off the old flower spikes so seedpods can't form. If they do, they'll cause the lilac to bloom poorly the next year.

• Prune and thin plants older than three years when they finish blooming.

Pruning also enhances flowering. Begin the pruning by taking out twiggy growth. Then prune out any growth sprouting from the ground that is thinner than a pencil. Also prune out a few of the oldest, tallest canes that sprout from the ground, those that are three to four inches thick or more. This will keep the plant from growing too tall (so you are no longer able to smell the flowers), while encouraging the young, vigorous canes that will make more flowers. Don't prune after June 30.

• Fertilize plants about mid-May with a 10-10-10 or similar type fertilizer, and then put a thin mulch around the plants to conserve summer moisture and keep the roots cool. Fertilize one last time with a 6-10-10 (if you want more growth) or 0-10-10 mixture or something similar in late June. Don't fertilize after June 30.

Descanso Gardens offers lilac fanciers handouts on planting and caring for lilacs in Southern California.

I guess I'm now a believer, and the clincher came from information provided by Monrovia Nursery Company. I had always assumed that this wholesale grower raised its lilacs at its Oregon facility. But the nursery grows its lilacs in Azusa.

The Lilac Grove at Descanso Gardens, 1418 Descanso Drive, La Cañada Flintridge; telephone 818.952.4401; on the web at www.descanso.com.

A LILAC IN DISTRESS

Q: I have a large, old lilac but it doesn't bloom much and needs pruning. Can you tell me how?

—M.J., RESEDA

A: You seem to be another gardener who has succeeded in growing lilacs in Southern California. Lilacs need cold winters to thrive, but lilac fancier Joel Margaretten, who has grown lilacs in mild Beverly Hills and more recently had 50,000 bushes growing on 80 acres in the Leona Valley (which borders the high desert near Palmdale but in the hills), says the real secret is to make them go dry from late October until March to force dormancy.

During that period, he even suggests covering the ground around the lilac with sheet plastic to keep the plant dry if it rains a lot. Planting them on hillsides or on mounded soil also keeps them dry enough if they are not watered during fall and winter. Begin watering deeply but infrequently in March. This might get your lilac blooming.

Ordinarily, in places where lilacs grow easily they need little pruning, and pinching them back is not a good idea since flowers come on the previous year's growth. Remove suckers from around the base, and cut out dead wood. To renovate very overgrown plants, Margaretten says, remove all the suckers from outside of about a four-foot circle with a sharp spade when the plant is dormant, then cut the other canes to about a foot off the ground. In summer, cut out all but a dozen or so canes that are growing strongly. It will take two years for the plant to regrow and begin blooming again.

❦ ❦ ❦

Tropicals: Trouble in Paradise

PRINCESS FLOWER DIARIES

Q: My princess plant does not appear to grow, although it has some flowers. What are its food and watering needs?

—N.P., Tarzana

A: Princess flower (*Tibouchina urvilleana*) has simple needs, normally growing to become a lanky 10 to 18 feet tall. This Brazilian shrub likes moderate watering, warmth and to be kept out of constant or strong breezes. It also likes a slightly acid soil, and this may be the problem if you garden in a highly alkaline soil. Alkaline soils reduce the availability of some nutrients necessary for growth.

Changing the pH of a soil (the measure of alkalinity or acidity) can be done over time. Start by mulching the soil with acidic materials such as pine needles, ground bark (*not* bark chunks) or cocoa bean hulls. Working gypsum and soil sulfur into the soil will also help; follow label directions.

Fertilize in spring with an acidic fertilizer (such as those used for azaleas and camellias) and then lightly after each cycle of bloom. Once the plant starts to grow, pinch the new growth to force the plant to branch and become more bushy. Prune more heavily each spring.

Another option is to replant the princess flower in a raised bed or mound where the soil has been heavily amended with acidic materials, such as ground bark or peat moss. Early spring is a good time of year to move warmth-loving subtropicals like this, as long as they haven't grown too big.

A PASSION FOR PASSIFLORAS

It is a summer evening, and there are only two empty folding chairs left at the packed meeting of the Culver City Garden Club. The crowd is there to hear member Jorge Ochoa talk about passion flowers, those amazingly complicated, almost-hypnotic blooms that fascinate gardeners and nongardeners alike. "No one knows the passiflora like Jorge," says one member.

Next to ordinary flowers like daisies, passion flowers look as if they're from another planet. Viewed from above, their intricate and symmetrical construction resembles a fanciful Indian mandala, and they seem to radiate some kind of cosmic energy. The name comes from the sacred symbolism seen in the flower's parts, which reminded the 17th-century Spanish discoverers of the Passion of Christ. This is a very metaphysical flower.

At the meeting, Ochoa displays some of the more unusual kinds of vines on two long tables pushed together. He has also brought along some of the many products made from the fruit or flowers. "I wanted people to know they weren't just pretty flowers," says this major fan of the genus.

Ochoa has boxes of herbal remedies—dried flowers and leaves—used by some as mild sedatives. A few people even believe the plant to be aphrodisiacal, perhaps misunderstanding what the *passion* in passion flower refers to. The plant's flowers are also used in a number of herbal hair products, including shampoo and hair spray. In the tropics, the fruit, or *granadilla*, is found in many foods.

Scattered around the meeting room are cut flowers, which Ochoa has brought from his home in South-Central Los Angeles. He invites everyone to take a flower or two home, apologizing for the fact that most passion flowers stay open for only a day and will be wilted by morning.

At his family's home on Compton Avenue, passion flower vines grow on every fence and wall and completely canopy the front yard. Born in Jalisco, Mexico, Ochoa has lived in this neighborhood since he was nine. He discovered passion flowers at a sister-in-law's home in Culver City, but he found his second variety in his own neighborhood and a third a few blocks away.

Visiting the Arboretum of Los Angeles County in Arcadia to observe more, he found that his collection of three was larger than its collection of one. The arboretum librarian did find him an authoritative book. *Passion Flowers*, by John Vanderplank (MIT Press, 2000), is the current edition.

This intense interest in passion flowers led him to study horticulture for two years at Long Beach City College and Cal Poly Pomona. When he had to choose a plant for a particular project, he always picked a passiflora. For plant anatomy class, he'd slice up a passiflora. For tissue culture class, he'd clone a passiflora. "I majored in passion vines," he says, "with a minor in plant pathology." He now works for the Los Angeles Department of Parks and Recreation.

He's still compiling his "bible" on passifloras, a binder many inches thick with research papers and notes. He's searched every site on the web, read every book. His aim is to know all he can about the genus—and to grow as many as he can lay his hands on.

Passiflora is native mostly to the cooler, wetter parts of Central and South

America—which is why they tend to do better in the less-hot areas of Southern California, away from the inland valleys. There are isolated species scattered around the world—in Africa, Australia, on our own East Coast and even one in nearby Baja. Of the approximately 500 kinds, Ochoa has managed to collect about 60, "with 20 in the mail." Only a few are available at nurseries, so he grows most from seeds that he gets from the Passiflora Society International seed bank.

Ochoa's interest is only in the species passifloras, the wild, unhybridized kinds. "I prefer their natural beauty," he says. He does grow one hybrid—the dramatic, frilly cultivar named 'Incense', whose flowers are among the most beautiful. This perennial can take cold weather and has two-inch, egg-shaped tasty edible fruit.

Some of the most common passion flower vines sucker badly. Suckers are sprouts from the roots that pop up all over the garden, even on the other side of sidewalks and paving. Ochoa suggests growing only kinds that don't have this tendency. Of course, growing them in pots will keep the roots contained—passion flower vines do great in containers and will even tolerate indoor conditions.

Passiflora caerulea is the most common passion vine (seen even on the sides of freeways), and it suckers badly. Though it is the source of sweet *granadilla*, used in many foodstuffs, it can become a real pest and has given all passion fruits a bad name.

Because most passion flower vines are large, they need something to clamber on—a trellis or a fence (they quickly cover chain link), where they can provide shade or a background for the garden. Twisting tendrils hold them fast.

Many plants can grow to 30 feet long if allowed. Ochoa cuts his back a little every year, just to keep them in bounds and to remove dead growth. Cutting them back hard, he cautions, can be fatal to the plants.

Most like full sun, but some will grow in shade. He waters once a week or more but only fertilizes once a year, in spring. The plants prefer humid weather and temperatures that are not extreme. They do better in plain, unimproved, fast-draining alkaline dirt and do not like amended soils. It may take two years for them to start flowering heavily or to produce fruit.

Many leaves have nectar glands on them that may appear to be a pest problem. However, he says, the glands are thought to be a defense mechanism. The sweet stuff secreted by these glands attracts ants, which chase off pests. If you see ants on your vines, don't be alarmed—in this rare case, they're actually helping with the pest control.

Don't worry too much about culture, though—Ochoa says, "No passiflora is hard to grow."

Passiflora Society International, c/o Butterfly World, 3600 Sample Road, Coconut Creek, FL 33073; on the web at www.passiflora.org.

CATERPILLARS DINE ON PASSION VINE

Q: Last year I planted a passion flower vine. At the end of summer caterpillars were stripping the vine of all foliage, so I sprayed with *Bt*. I then realized the caterpillars were the larvae of a beautiful butterfly. If I allow the caterpillars to munch on my vine, will it die or will it regrow?

—L.P., WESTCHESTER

A: That beautiful butterfly is a Gulf fritillary, easily identified by the orange monarch-like coloring of the wings, with distinctive metallic markings underneath. Although native to Latin America, it has been here a long time. It feeds exclusively on passion vines, apparently only on *Passiflora caerulea,* the kind with soft, five-lobed leaves, not on the thicker, three-lobed garden hybrids.

The caterpillars can pretty much defoliate a passion vine, but I have never seen them kill one. The vines always rebound, usually growing faster than the caterpillars eat them, though just barely. And because the butterflies do not wander far

---

OTHERWORLDLY FLOWERS

Passion-flower enthusiast Jorge Ochoa here selects a few choice passion vines to consider.

Passiflora actinia (also sold as *Passiflora phoenicea* or as 'Ruby Glow'): Dramatic, flaring flowers, right out of a sci-fi movie, have a circular mass of slim filaments that are striped purple and white. Ochoa highly recommends this Brazilian vine to neophytes because it "doesn't get too big" (although it covers his front yard) and it tolerates cold.

Passiflora coriacea: The bizarre Bolivian bat wing passion flower vine is also grown for its foliage, which is an odd diamond shape that looks like a leaf only in that it's green.

Passiflora serratifolia: Bearing spectacular flowers with very frilly filaments, this one grows right through Southern California winters and tops out at 10 to 15 feet.

Passiflora trifasciata: Ochoa also suggests this one for beginners. Growing in complete shade, it stays quite small, under eight feet. Its spectacular leaves look like dinosaur tracks, colored burgundy and green on top and purple underneath. The flowers are very small, as is the fruit.

These two in Ochoa's garden enchanted me.

Passiflora foetida and *Passiflora manicata*: The former has amazing feathery green bracts around the flowers, like a moss rose or the old-fashioned flower called love-in-a-mist. The latter is a striking scarlet color. Neither suckers.

Caterpillars of pretty Gulf fritillary dine exclusively on passion vines.

from the vine, it is well worth growing just to keep them in the garden. I used to grow one in the side yard where its skeletonized remains were out of sight. I even got edible fruit off the poor thing. You do want to be careful where you plant this one, since it can become a real pest, seeding and suckering. Some gardeners grow it in containers.

Although the biological *Bt* (*Bacillus thuringiensis*) is one of the safest controls around, it must be used wisely. Spray indiscriminately, and the larvae of the lovely monarch or mourning cloak will die right along with the caterpillars you're after. Make sure to spray only the plant under attack and only when there is no breeze to blow it onto unintended targets.

MEXICAN HELICONIAS

Q: I finally made my first trip to Hawaii and was impressed by the heliconias, those most tropical of flowers. I heard they could be grown here, but when I tried to find one, people thought I was crazy or had never heard of them. What's the scoop, and where can I get some?

—J.G., CAMARILLO

A: Though the 12-foot-tall *Heliconia schiedeana* (pronounced "shay-de-ANN-a") has been grown here for years, most kinds are far too tropical, even when planted on warm, frost-free slopes. However, Gary Hammer, of Desert-to-Jungle Nursery in Montebello, has brought some new kinds from the more temperate areas of southern Mexico and Central America. He says they are extremely hardy and tough and will even survive most winters in the San Fernando Valley. His associate, Del Pace, thinks the plants are hardy easily to 27 degrees.

The new species come from mountain forests, growing near the 3,000-to-

4,000-foot altitude, so they actually prefer cooler temperatures. It is too warm for them to grow in more tropical Florida, Hammer says, but they "thrive and bloom here, not merely hang on." Because these heliconias come from mountain forests, they require partial to fairly deep shade, except for right along the coast, where they can take morning sun.

But for the tropical look, you can't go wrong. When actor Jeff Goldblum requested a jungle look for his garden, designer Robert Cornell says he ordered "a truckload of heliconias" from Hammer. Note that it is the bracts of the plants that are decorative. Because they are not true flowers but modified leaves—similar to the red "petals" on a poinsettia—they last a long time, though tiny true flowers briefly appear inside.

The new kinds of heliconias have bracts colored yellow, pink, magenta, red or mustard orange. The pink one, *Heliconia spisa*, is Hammer's favorite because it grows to only six feet and does well even in a container.

Many species reach 12 feet and more, growing to the height of big bananas, which they vaguely resemble. Like bananas, heliconias need to be grown in a protected spot, or wind will shred their leaves. They also need lots of water: "They are not drought resistant!" says Hammer.

Heliconia aficionado and attorney David Lloyd has been growing Hammer's heliconias in his protected north San Diego County garden and finds them the toughest of the 250 or so kinds he's experimented with—and so far the only ones to bloom. He currently has about 30 to 40 varieties in the ground that look promising.

His favorite from Hammer's selection is *Heliconia angusta* (*Heliconia citrina*), with clear yellow bracts and wind-resistant leaves. Growing from three to five feet tall, it's the one a beginner should start with, Lloyd says.

Don't expect to see blooms from nursery plants for at least two years. If you are interested in the more tropical varieties for a greenhouse or indoors, contact mail-order specialist Aloha Tropicals in Vista.

Desert-to-Jungle Nursery, 211 West Beverly Boulevard, Montebello; telephone 323.722.3976. Retail nurseries can order from Hammer's wholesale-only Glendale Paradise Nursery.
Aloha Tropicals, 1247 Browning Court, Vista, CA 92083; telephone 760.941.0920; on the web at www.alohatropicals.com.

PLUMERIAS FROM HAWAII

Q: Do plumerias grow in full sun? I live in the Pomona Valley.
—S.M., CLAREMONT

A: To bloom well, plumerias must grow in at least half-day sun; a full day is

Tropical plumerias will grow and flower in Southern California.

preferable. According to wholesale grower Marilynn Cohen, who grows 50 types of Hawaiian hybrids, they do very well in the Pomona and San Gabriel valleys (San Gabriel Nursery in San Gabriel in is one of her biggest customers), as well as in the Los Angeles Basin and Orange County. Only in such places as Phoenix or Palm Springs do they need a little afternoon protection from the sun. She adds that in shady areas, they may get spider mites and thrips.

Plumerias need a warm, sunny spot, against a south or west-facing wall, for instance, or on a pool deck, where there is reflected heat. In your area, however, they may also need protection from occasional frost.

They are usually grown in pots because they need a fast-draining, porous soil and because they do not have a big root system. In containers, they can be moved to a safe spot if frost is predicted, and the soil can be kept dry in winter when they are dormant (resume watering when they begin to leaf out in spring).

They will grow in the ground but may rot in wet winter soils, and in the ground, protecting them from frost becomes a much bigger job.

A 'KONA' HIBISCUS

Q: Do some hibiscus lose their leaves in winter? This is the second time I've planted 'Kona' hibiscus, and it is losing its leaves again.

—R.C., LOS ANGELES

A: Although there is a deciduous hibiscus called rose of Sharon (*Hibiscus syriacus*), that's not what you're growing. The tropical hibiscus (*Hibiscus rosa-sinensis*)—grown all over Southern California—should not lose its leaves, though some leaf drop is typical in winter.

The two most likely causes are too much shade and too much water. Hibiscus want full, hot sun, moderate water and good drainage. If the plant is in a chilly, shaded spot, it will lose leaves, and if the soil is cool and damp all the time, ditto. It sounds like your hibiscus is planted in a bad spot or in a heavy clay soil.

According to one hibiscus grower, however, young hibiscus may falter in cooler weather, especially in heavy, wet soils where their roots are not getting enough oxygen, and the leaves will defoliate from the inside of the plant out. Don't be too hasty to take the plant out; instead, wait and see if it adjusts to its new home with time. Hibiscus are one of our more reliable flowering shrubs, though nowadays they are often covered with the giant whitefly.

🐝 🐝 🐝

The Urban Forest

CORAL TREES, THE LOS ANGELES CITY TREE

Q: I have noticed that all the coral trees near the Beverly Hills Hotel flower. I have three of these trees of the same size, planted about 10 years ago and regularly

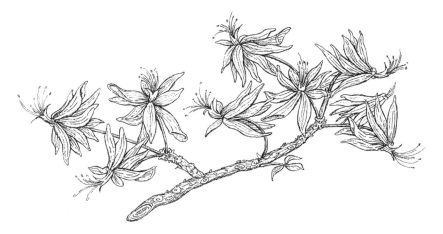

The coral tree, Los Angeles' city tree, produces its bright red blooms on new growth; it flowers best if pruned at the right times, and not too often.

cut back, and am still waiting for flowers. What could be the problem?

—E.N., BEVERLY HILLS

A: Cutting back a coral tree (*Erythrina caffra*) each year will keep it from flowering, because all the growth that makes flowers is being removed. It is possible to thin them, leaving some of this flowering wood, but even doing this greatly reduces flowering.

If they must be pruned, do it right after they flower (or when they would flower if they could, usually in March). All that pruning you are doing indicates the trees are too big for their spot in the garden. Maybe a smaller flowering tree would be a better choice.

Too much water and fertilizer, as when they're planted in a lawn or in a heavy clay soil, also can stop them from flowering (all they do is grow new leaves). The best-looking coral trees I've seen, small, compact and covered with flowers, grow on an unirrigated, rocky slope in Malibu. This is one tree that shouldn't be watered or pampered in any way, at least in summer.

ORNAMENTAL PEACHES

Q: I live about 10 blocks from the beach and would like to plant the peaches that grow at Cal State Long Beach. Would these work?

—N.I., LONG BEACH

A: According to grounds manager Jeff Riggs, the flowering peach at Cal State Long Beach is *Prunus persica* 'Helen Borchers'. It is signature tree for the campus, where every year nearly 3,000 of them send out their large pure pink blossoms around commencement time. The campus is inland a bit, in Sunset Zone 22; however, the tree will grow right up to the beach, in Zone 24, according to the Sunset *Western Garden Book* (Sunset Publishing), though it may leaf out oddly in spring. Ornamental flowering peaches are generally more adaptable than are their fruiting cousins.

REMOVING SUCKERS

Q: A semidwarf plum tree is planted in a four-foot raised planter at the back of my yard. It has been sending up suckers at its base and now down below in the grass area. Can anything be done to prevent or control this?

—J.B., LAKE FOREST

A: Plums of all kinds, edible and ornamental, are notorious for suckering. So are olives, mayten trees, Chinese and other elms, willows and a few others. Trees that start sending up suckers are usually under some kind of stress. Perhaps the roots, which are close to the surface, have been damaged, by lawnmowers or by digging.

To remove suckers from the roots or trunk, cut them off at the collar—look closely and you will see a little collar-like swelling on the bark where the sucker is attached. This is where pruning cuts should be made on trees, not flush with the root, branch or trunk, as is often suggested, but a bit back from it. A cut here will heal quickly and surely. Cover the wound with tree paint or wound dressing (sold at nurseries), and the suckering may stop.

There is also a chemical approach. Monterey Lawn and Garden Products makes a product called Sucker-Stopper RTU, a plant-growth regulator that comes in spray bottles. After pruning the suckers off, spray the cuts with Sucker-Stopper, and they shouldn't return for a year, according to the manufacturer. Or spray the trunk or roots where suckers reoccur, before new ones sprout. Sucker-Stopper can also be used on apples, citrus, olives and woody ornamentals, but do not spray it on flower buds or leaves. Read and follow label directions.

CONTROLLING FRUITING OLIVES

Q: I have an annual problem with the tremendous amount of olives that fall from two trees, causing much extra heavy labor and, of course, a source of carpet staining when crushed olives are tracked into the house. Do you know of any way we might keep trees from bearing fruit?

—G.P., SIMI VALLEY

A: Nurseries sell fruit eliminator sprays, such as Florel. This product, which contains ethephon, prevents the formation of fruit, according to the manufacturer, Monterey Lawn and Garden, on many plants, including flowering pear, olive, liquidambar and sycamore—trees that bloom all at once. It must be sprayed onto the flowers when the plant is in mid- to full bloom. Timing is critical because any flowers that aren't sprayed will make fruit. Follow all directions carefully, using three ounces per gallon of water, and wash the spray off car paint or any glossy painted surface.

The trick is to make sure that the spray reaches the flowers, which is not too difficult on an olive since it is a fairly short tree. A good hose-end sprayer should do the trick. If the tree is too tall, this is a job best done by professional spray applicators.

Some arborists believe that the products made to prevent olives can damage trees and may cause their eventual decline.

Another reader from Garden Grove asked how to prevent the purplish-red, berry-size fruit on eugenias. If the eugenias bloom all at once, Florel will work, but if they bloom off and on, as they often do, it will affect only those flowers that happen to be blooming.

PRUNING PALMS

Q: Our palm trees drop their tiny black fruit in such numbers that daily sweeping of a long stairway is necessary. Is there a product to inhibit flowering and fruiting such as exists for olive trees?

—H.F., Los Angeles

A: Not really. No chemicals will work. If those products damage olive trees, they may also damage palms. None of the growth regulators that might prevent flowering are registered for use on palms. Try simply cutting off the bloom spikes as soon as they poke out with a pole-mounted pruning saw, if you can reach them.

OAK ORDINANCES

Q: We've had a volunteer oak tree (we did not plant it) growing in our front yard for three years, and it is now one and a half inches in diameter at the base and 12 to 15 feet tall. The problem is that it is only 15 inches away from the house. My husband fears that it will become a problem as it grows. Can I prune or transplant it? If not, am I allowed to remove it? I've heard there are strict ordinances regarding oaks.

—M.M., Burbank

A: It's almost impossible to move a volunteer oak that size. Oaks have small but very deep root systems. You can try—in late fall and winter—but don't be too hopeful. It would be much easier to start a new oak from an acorn.

Pruning will not help the problem because of its close proximity to the house. In gardens, the coast live oak—the most common and probably the oak you describe—grow very fast and get very large.

Many communities are trying to protect native oaks, perhaps the most significant California tree and certainly one of the most majestic. Ordinances typically cover the evergreen coast live oak, mesa oak and scrub oak as well as the deciduous valley oak and black oak.

Most ordinances don't cover young oaks, however. The Los Angeles County ordinance (governing unincorporated county areas, but used by some cities as well) regulates oaks with a diameter of more than eight inches, measured four and a half feet above the ground. On oaks larger than this, limbs larger than two inches in diameter cannot be removed without a permit (unless the branch is dead). Permits are also required if you plan to build near an oak, pave or trench within five feet of the drip line (the area below the very perimeter of the tree's foliage), or spray with toxic chemicals.

To get a permit for unincorporated Los Angeles County areas, call the Department of Regional Planning Land Development Coordinating Center. The permit process is not cheap. A permit for one oak at a single-family residence is about

$502. Since this volunteer oak is clearly in the wrong place, I'd remove it quickly and plant another in a more appropriate spot.

Los Angeles County Department of Regional Planning Land Development Coordinating Center; telephone 213.974.6411; on the web at planning.co.la.ca.us.

ROOTS IN A LAWN

Q: I have a 10-year-old birch tree in the front lawn, and the roots are surfacing through the grass. What's happening?

—A.R., REDLANDS

A: Birch trees are notorious for their surface roots, and after 10 years they're bound to have many, especially in a lawn in which most of the moisture is near the surface—lawns are typically watered frequently and not deeply. Roots tend to grow best where moisture most often is.

Since birches aren't very big trees, have the surface roots removed and then try watering deeply to encourage deep rooting. This irrigation (maybe once a week in your area) would be in addition to watering the lawn. Make sure the water soaks several feet into the ground. However, the tree would probably make new surface roots in short order, so you might not want to bother with the expense of doing this.

I've never thought birches are a good choice in West Coast lawns, though they are often planted there. In the East, frequent rainfall helps make the trees deeper rooted. They also get aphids and often have brown leaf tips because of the salts in our water.

Trees and lawns are seldom compatible (with the possible exception of the well-behaved mayten). It's healthier to grow shrubs and ground covers under trees, not lawn, so that is the best solution: Take the lawn out from under the tree, and plant things that don't need to be watered so often. Suggestions: abutilon, acanthus, ajuga, Japanese anemone, bergenia, bletilla, brunfelsia, camellia, campanula, coral bells, corydalis, some kids of geranium (_Geranium_ 'Biokovo' is great under trees), lamium, liriope and the dwarf 'Cream de Mint' pittosporum.

FLOWER COMPETITION

Q: I have a problem with my front flower bed, where there are a jillion trees. I have managed to get grass (St. Augustine), bushes and shrubs to grow in the dense shade, but azaleas die in less than two weeks, impatiens grow no higher than five inches and I cannot find an honest-to-goodness flower that will put up with this perpetual shade. Any suggestions?

—M.Z., CANOGA PARK

A: If impatiens won't grow, shade is not the problem, but tree roots—I suspect you'll find roots everywhere you dig. They are sucking the soil dry so no flower can become established. Try this: Use a sharpened spade and dig up the top few inches of soil, remove all the smaller roots (this won't hurt most garden trees), and mix in bagged organic amendments. The exact amount will depend on your soil type.

Install sprinklers so you can keep new flowers moist. Contractors often double up the sprinklers under trees to make sure there's sufficient water for everything. For instance, instead of six sprinklers, they install 12 that overlap. Make sure sprinklers never wet the trunks of trees; this can cause rot and eventually even their death.

You may never get azaleas to grow in this situation. Bedding begonias and impatiens will, though—try the more interesting New Guinea impatiens with the colored foliage. You could also plant cineraria, cyclamen, forget-me-not, foxglove and primrose in the fall for winter and spring color, or coleus and caladium in summer, though they are grown for colorful foliage, not "honest-to-goodness" flowers.

Where it's shadiest, try clivia, which, notes one expert, "will grow in a cave" and tolerates root competition—although the big orange flowers bloom only once in spring.

PRUNING INVASIVE ROOTS

Q: When we landscaped our back yard 45 years ago, we planted a row of liquidambar to remind us the maples of the Northeast. Now their roots are ruining everything, including a brick patio and the pipes underground. Can you tell us any way to stop or slow down the roots, short of killing the trees?

—R.S., VALLEY VILLAGE

A: Liquidambars have extensive root systems. In a clay soil, many roots grow near the surface (because roots need to breathe, and air doesn't penetrate very deeply in a clay soil). Shallow watering (as for a lawn) also encourages shallow roots. It's not at all surprising that they're lifting paving and disrupting sewer pipes. But it would probably be cheaper to redo the paving and have the pipes reamed and cleaned regularly than to remove the trees.

Roots can be pruned just like the tops of trees. However, root pruning is tricky work, says Bob Hansen, a Santa Monica consulting arborist; you don't want to weaken the tree or cause it to topple. It's not a job for the homeowner or for inexperienced tree crews. Call in a consulting arborist.

Once the roots are pruned, a 12- or even 24-inch-deep root barrier at the edge of the paving will protect the patio for quite a while, especially from mature trees like yours.

CALLING IN A TREE DOCTOR

Q: About 12 years ago we purchased a beautifully shaped, healthy-looking liquidambar tree. This year, I noticed that a lot of leaves were yellow-green on one side of the tree. It is still well shaped except that the very top branches did not develop leaves. What can be done to help it grow leaves on top? Is there such as thing as a tree doctor?

—M.S., FULLERTON

A: This is a job for a consulting arborist, a "tree doctor" who is trained to look at a tree and its surroundings and tell you what's actually wrong. You can find members of the American Society of Consulting Arborists on its web site.

Consulting arborist Bob Hansen has seen similar problems. One liquidambar was also doing poorly on only one side and wasn't leafing out on top, he says. It turned out that a trench had been dug for a sprinkler line on one side of the tree, severing some of the roots. He also relates the time he went to a garden where a row of big liquidambars was dying. A trench had been dug for electrical lighting along one side, and all the roots had been cut. Ironically, the lights were to illumine the liquidambars, but the whole row died just after installation.

Hansen says that if he gets the chance, before work is done, he tells electrical contractors and plumbers to think of roots as high-voltage or gas lines. "You wouldn't cut through a two-inch gas line, would you?" he asks them. "So don't cut through roots. Tunnel under them."

American Society of Consulting Arborists is on the web at www.asca-consultants.org.

What Can I Put Here?

❦ ❦

Landscape Solutions for Special Situations

GARDENERS ARE QUICK TO DISCOVER which plants they like and which they don't. What takes time is figuring out how and where to use them. Many a gardener has asked where to grow this or that plant, and many asked what they could grow in a particular spot, having had difficulty in the past.

What to grow in the shade, in wind or in poorly drained soils is a very practical matter, as are landscaping considerations when you have lively dogs, a swimming pool or neighbors who can peer into your back yard. If you want to create a whole new landscape, how do you put all the individual elements together in a workable, enjoyable scheme? In this chapter we'll also throw in how to use plants with exceptionally handsome foliage to really liven up a garden.

Getting plants placed just right might be the ultimate challenge in gardening. I know, I'm still working on it. And just when you think it's all working perfectly, something changes—a power pole suddenly appears when the big avocado tree is taken out—and it's back to square one.

🌿 🌿 🌿

Covering New Ground

GARDEN BASICS

Q: We're moving to a new house with an empty back yard in Culver City. We're also expecting our first child, so we will be strapped for cash and energy. Do you have any guidelines on dealing with a back yard of dirt? My husband wants to "just throw out some grass seed."

—C.H., CULVER CITY

A: With a child on the way and a lot of ground to cover, your husband's idea is a good one. Children are the best reason for a lawn. For areas that don't get too hot, a tall fescue lawn grass, such as 'Marathon' or 'Medallion', is probably the best choice. Sow the seed in fall or early spring. For hotter inland areas, consider Bermuda grass or St. Augustine.

Before planting the lawn, invest in soil amendments or planting mix (available at nurseries). Improving the soil texture will make everything, from weeding to watering, easier later on. Because the lawn will need to be watered, sprinklers would be nice, though you can always use a portable sprinkler and add an underground system later.

If the budget allows, break up the lawn with paths or patios and save a good, sunny place for vegetables. Teaching children how to grow their own vegetables is one of the joys of parenthood—childhood is when many of us first got the bug. If you have the room, plant fruit trees—a lemon is a good choice since every good cook needs one.

Consider planting a shade tree right away, since it takes so long for them to grow, and your child will need a place to hang a swing or build a tree house. My grandfather planted a California live oak in my parents' yard the day I was born, and its growth kept up with mine, so it was always the perfect size for climbing or building forts. I did something similar with my kids.

The simplest way to choose a tree is to walk the neighborhood and pick out the ones whose texture, shape and size you like. This way you know how they will look after a few years and that they thrive in your neighborhood. Take small branches to a good nursery and find out their names. Look up your choices in the Sunset *Western Garden Book* (Sunset Publishing). Be careful not to plant fast, weedy ones, or too many, or kinds that will get too big for the property. Site them carefully—not too close to the house or shading the yard, although shading the house is an energy-saving idea. Site them on the south-facing side of the house, not on the north side. This is all neatly explained in "Smart Planting for the New Urban Forest: A Guide to Planting Trees Around Your Home," put out by the TreePeople and the Los Angeles Department of Water and Power. Quite useful, it also includes a good list of trees, all illustrated, for Southern California.

Once your trees are in, don't let grass grow close to the bases—not only will it affect the health of the trees and shrubs, but it is difficult to grow in their shade anyway. Keep the lawn at least five feet away, preferably even farther, mulching the area instead with fallen leaves or shredded bark (not chunky bark, which harbors bugs and weeds).

As for other plants, you can take your time finding ones you like. Avoid completely surrounding the house with plants. This is what is called foundation planting, an awkward and dated scheme. Ditto along the fence. Seeing parts of the house or garden walls keeps the garden from looking hemmed in, so it appears larger.

But start with the lawn. You can always dig out parts for future plantings. At least the dirt and mud will be covered, and the kids will have a place to play. Once the kids are grown, you might want to plant something more interesting that requires fewer resources to stay alive. When the last of our three kids moved out, we took out the front lawn entirely and left only a tiny patch in back, replacing it with flowering shrubs and perennials and some sunny new vegetable beds.

―――――

"Smart Planting for the New Urban Forest: A Guide to Planting Trees Around Your Home" is available on the web at www.treepeople.org.

FOR THE DOGS

Q: We are planning to landscape our back yard, which is also home to our exuberant 90-pound dog. We want to install a sod lawn, shrubs and ground cover that will withstand the dog's digging and chewing. What do you recommend? Please, no cactus, and don't tell us to get rid of the dog—she's a member of our family.

—M.B., GLENDALE

A: Dogs and gardens can get along, but it requires a lot of effort. Years ago, for its April 1987 issue, *Sunset* magazine surveyed readers, veterinarians and even dog psychiatrists for solutions. Noting that dogs are creatures of habit who tend to follow the same routes, this classic article suggested letting the animal establish paths and areas around the perimeter of the garden where it can make its rounds, and then planting around these. Training (the article had some good tips), combined with tall raised beds or low fences, can keep the pooch out of the pansies or potato patch.

Dogs hate prickles, but you don't have to go so far as to plant cactus. Use roses, mahonia and junipers as barriers to more delicate parts of the garden. Also, dogs are less likely to run into such vining ground covers as ivy and vinca. Obviously stiff plants are tougher than soft plants.

As for a lawn, John Rector, an agronomist formerly with Pacific Sod, recommends 'El Toro' zoysia, a fast-growing, spreading grass developed by the University of California. Or consider a hybrid Bermuda such as 'Tifgreen'. Rector suggests seeding one of the tall fescues on top of the zoysia to hide the zoysia's long dormancy (two to three months each winter).

With two black Labs that "act like wild horses" in his back yard, landscape architect Michael Lombardi, of Pamela Burton & Co. in Santa Monica, tried Rector's suggestion, planting an 'El Toro' sod lawn in September and overseeding it with 'Medallion' fescue in November. The lawn of his Lakewood garden hangs tough—resisting claws and recovering quickly from holes and spots.

In his somewhat coastal climate, Lombardi says, 'El Toro' zoysia never goes completely dormant but does slow down. In summer it is an aggressive, fast-growing grass. Contain and control it with an edging and regular mowing and maintenance.

FROM LAWN TO MEADOWLAND

Lots of people have wondered if it is possible to replace that monotonous, consumptive contrivance called a lawn. After all, that bright green swath is a carry-over from wetter English and East Coast gardens. To keep it going in California's climate requires water, fertilizer and a weekly mow-and-blow by noisy, polluting machines.

Grass guru John Greenlee, having literally written the book on the subject, *The Encyclopedia of Ornamental Grasses* (Rodale, 1992), is convinced that no-mow meadows of natural grasses and sedges are an excellent option. At this point, nothing yet rivals an ordinary grass lawn for covering ground inexpensively. Seed and sod are readily available and relatively low cost, and just about anyone can care for a grass lawn. But horticulturist Greenlee has planted a number of what he calls "natural lawns," which he hopes will someday rival lawns in popularity.

His Greenlee Nursery in Pomona supplied the plants for the meadow at the Norton Simon Museum in Pasadena and for smaller meadows in a number of residential gardens, including one in Huntington Beach by San Diego landscape architect Raymond Hansen. "Greenlee's meadow plants have a soft and natural quality that isn't found in other landscape forms," Hansen says. "And hopefully they'll have

---

A FEW GOOD SEDGES

- Baltimore sedge *(Carex senta)*: Virtually identical to *Carex retroflexa* but slightly neater.
- Cajun sedge *(Carex retroflexa texensis)*: Medium green, tolerates shade, more yellow green in full sun.
- California meadow sedge *(Carex pansa)*: Dark green, tolerates half-day shade.
- Pennsylvania sedge *(Carex pennsylvanica pacificum)*: Dark green, best in sandy, well-drained soils.
- Texas meadow sedge *(Carex perdentata)*: Yellow green, tolerates shade and needs half-day shade in the desert.

lower maintenance requirements as well."

Greenlee's interest in no-mow lawns was piqued on a trip. "We were in this meadow in the Chiricahua Mountains in southeast Arizona," he says. "We were looking at these short little carexes [sedges] that were still green after all the grasses had dried out and turned brown, thinking, 'Nobody's mowing it, nobody's watering it, but it looks great. So why not make a lawn out of this?'"

Sedges look very much like grasses; however, they seldom or never require mowing and need no fertilizer, and native kinds make do with little water. Most have gracefully arching blades that "feel acceptable between your toes," according to Greenlee, though they are slightly stiffer with edges that are a little sharper.

And that's what he's been experimenting with ever since. Although Greenlee's sedge meadows have yet to stand the test of time as grass lawns have, he has experimented enough to have a list of favorite lawn sedges. They grow low—three to six inches—so they are easily walked on. They "hold the meadow together," according to Greenlee. And they can actually be mown like a lawn for a tidy look, though they seldom get as dense as lawn grasses.

Greenlee plants from little plugs spaced about 12 to 18 inches apart. He mows most of the sedges about twice a year, once to remove flower spikes before they mature into seed.

A key part of establishing such a meadow, or sedge lawn, Greenlee says, is killing absolutely all the creeping lawn grasses, such as Bermuda and Kikuyu, before planting. They cannot be allowed to become enmeshed in the new meadow.

Plant one or two types of these low growers and you could call it a lawn, mowing it now and again. Mix other sedges and true grasses of varying height, texture and color to get a more varied meadow look. "That's when the fun begins," says Greenlee. "I plant South African and other Mediterranean bulbs that pop up in it, and wild violets or veronicas that creep through it."

He sometimes leaves little "divots" where he plants annual flowers in their seasons. You can plant all sorts of things in a meadow and rearrange it constantly so you can, in effect, garden in your lawn. "With a meadow, you can break down the barrier between the lawn and the flower bed," Greenlee says. "It's a brave new world."

Before one gets too excited about the meadow concept, remember that this is a brand-new idea. Although Greenlee supplies a few retail nurseries, sedges and some other crucial meadow components are in limited supply, at least until there is more demand. But so were the first microwave ovens.

LOW-MAINTENANCE CURB PLANTINGS

Q: As a new homeowner, I am learning to cope with a lawn for the first time, but I find it pretty boring. I'm trying to come up with a prettier and more environmentally friendly yet relatively low-maintenance solution for my curb strips, like a wildflower seed mix for a mini-wildflower field. Do you think this would work?
—A.B., NORTHRIDGE

A: Though people grow all sorts of things, from gazanias to vegetables, in parkways, only turf grasses are legal. There are good reasons: It makes it feasible to open car doors, reduces the work of cleaning up litter and dog droppings, and doesn't block the view of motorists. It also lends neighborhoods a unifying look.

Now that you're properly forewarned—yes, you could grow wildflowers there. In spring they would be lovely for a few weeks. But the seed can only be sown in fall, and you must prepare the soil as laboriously as you would for a vegetable or flower garden. Wildflowers are never as tough as weeds, and you can bet there are plenty of weed seeds lying in the soil.

The other problem with wildflowers is that they are annuals: They die in spring. The ground would be barren all summer and well into fall. The California poppy is the one wildflower that lingers longer, even behaving like a perennial, but it looks worse each season. So you would need to start fresh each autumn. The truth is, wildflowers are best planted in less conspicuous places than a parkway. They're great on hillsides or used here and there in garden beds.

A better plan for a parkway might be to grow drought-resistant, low-growing perennial grasslike plants that you either don't mow or mow very high, like the one mentioned above. There are tough, spreading sedges, even one with gray foliage, and there are a number of grasses that would also do well, including the native elymus and various fescues and muhlenbergias. Another candidate is buffalo grass, with a kind of funky look if it isn't mowed. It's available as seed and even as sod.

Such a scheme might put the lowest-growing grasses, such as the buffalo grass, near the curb. Near the sidewalk you could grow taller grasses, even a few low, drought-resistant shrubs or ground covers. This would be quite graceful, wouldn't require weekly mowing and wouldn't need much water after the first year or two. And it wouldn't impede car doors or be too hard to clean up. What the neighbors might think is a different story.

See Week 48 in 52 Weeks in the California Garden.

GOING NATIVE

During fall and winter, California's golden hillsides turn green as seeds sprout and leaves plump—a sign that the rains have returned and we can begin planting California's native flora in our gardens. The planting window is long enough—from mid-October to at least mid-February—to allow for projects big or small. Plant an entire back-yard habitat or just a few representative species to remind you of that last hike in the hills.

In my own garden, I cannot imagine spring without the native iris that make parts of the yard look like the Mendocino coast or autumn without the zauschnerias that brighten my entry path like they do the highway to Big Bear.

Put in just a few of the appropriate species, and you might awake one morn-

---

LISTS OF TOP 10 TROUBLE-FREE NATIVE PLANTS

VENTURA COUNTY	LOS ANGELES COUNTY	RIVERSIDE COUNTY	ORANGE COUNTY
MATILIJA NURSERY, MOORPARK	THEODORE PAYNE FOUNDATION, SUN VALLEY	PLANTS FOR DRY PLACES NURSERY, LAKE ELSINORE	TREE OF LIFE NURSERY, SAN JUAN CAPISTRANO

VENTURA COUNTY — MATILIJA NURSERY, MOORPARK
- *Salvia clevelandii*
- matilija poppy
- *Salvia apiana*
- *Iris douglasiana* and relatives
- monkey flower (*Mimulus aurantiacus longiflorus*)
- deer grass (*Muhlenbergia rigens*)
- *Heuchera maxima* and hybrids
- island bush snapdragon (*Galvezia speciosa*)
- blue-eyed grass (*Sisyrinchium bellum*)
- ceanothus

LOS ANGELES COUNTY — THEODORE PAYNE FOUNDATION, SUN VALLEY
- matilija poppy
- *Salvia apiana*
- ceanothus
- manzanita
- island bush poppy (*Dendromecon harfordii*)
- woolly blue curls (*Trichostema lanatum*)
- flannel bush (*Fremontodendron*)
- *Iris douglasiana* and relatives
- monkey flower (*Mimulus longiflorus*)
- coyote brush

RIVERSIDE COUNTY — PLANTS FOR DRY PLACES NURSERY, LAKE ELSINORE
- matilija poppy
- toyon
- *Ceanothus* 'Dark Star'
- deer grass (*Muhlenbergia rigens*)
- *Penstemon spectabilis*
- flannel bush (*Fremontodendron*)
- *Salvia clevelandii*
- manzanita
- desert willow (*Chilopsis linearis*)
- sugar bush (*Rhus ovata*)

ORANGE COUNTY — TREE OF LIFE NURSERY, SAN JUAN CAPISTRANO
- toyon
- lemonade berry (*Rhus integrifolia*)
- ceanothus
- manzanita
- *Salvia clevelandii*
- California fuchsia (*Zauschneria californica*)
- coast live oak
- California sycamore
- *Stipa* species
- deer grass (*Muhlenbergia rigens*)

ing to find quail scurrying for cover or see your first pygmy blue butterfly. If you live too far inside the city to attract much wildlife, native plants can still bring wild smells into your back yard. A single sage, such as *Salvia clevelandii*, will perfume an entire yard, especially on a warm morning.

Many natives may be tough, surviving on sun-baked hillsides in wretched soil, but they also are pretty enough to vie with any exotic for a gardener's attention. The native coral bells, for instance, the toyon, with its bright-red winter berries, the flaming, fall-blooming California fuchsia—all are handsome plants.

But native plants have a reputation for being difficult to grow in a garden setting. I've killed quite a few myself. So I asked a number of leading natives nurserypeople, from different parts of Southern California, for their lists of 10 tough, trouble-free native plants. Take a look at the list from the nursery closest to you, or in a similar area, to find the plants best suited to your garden.

Of his list, Mike Evans, of Tree of Life Nursery in coastal San Juan Capistrano, says, "You could plant a whole garden using just these 10 plants and have a real nice look." Bob Sussman, of Matilija Nursery in Moorpark, says about his Top 10: "All of these are difficult to kill if they are planted properly," and at the right time.

Inland gardeners will find that there are many natives they can't grow—note that the selection of popular natives at Plants for Dry Places, in the Menifee Valley in Riverside County, is quite different from the others. The nursery's Susan Frommer says many California native plants hail from coastal areas and will burn in inland locations or freeze in winter.

For instance, most ceanothus, says Elizabeth Schwartz, of the Theodore Payne Foundation in Sun Valley, are coastal and have big, thin leaves, including 'Concha', 'Frosty Blue' and 'Yankee Pt.'. The few that do well inland, such as *Ceanothus crassifolius*, have small, leathery leaves that do not sunburn. Manzanitas (*Arctostaphylos*) generally do better inland; some favorites include 'Howard McMinn', 'James West', 'Sentinel' and 'Lester Roundtree'.

Frommer suggests inland gardeners look to the desert to find plants such as the desert willow (*Chilopsis linearis*) or even those native to the deserts of the Southwest, such as autumn sage (*Salvia greggii*) or Mexican marigolds. She also suggests that inland gardeners begin planting natives later in the year, in late November, and stop sooner.

Natives planted in the fall or winter need just a little water their first summer and even less in following summers—it is summer irrigation that is often fatal to natives. Watering about once a month is right in that first summer, although even that little bit could kill a few of the most persnickety native plants, such as the glorious fremontodendron. And how much water a native needs depends a lot on where you live. Inland gardeners have to water much more often.

Where you plant certain natives in your garden often determines their fates. For plants native to dry hillsides, a flat, irrigated garden—which may lack drainage and therefore be constantly moist—is sure death.

Matilija Nursery, 8225 Waters Road, Moorpark, CA 93021; telephone 805.523.8604; on the web at www.matilijanursery.com.
Theodore Payne Foundation, 10459 Tuxford Street, Sun Valley, CA 91352-2126; telephone 818.768.1802; on the web at www.theodorepayne.org.
Plants for Dry Places, 25735 Garbani Road, Menifee Valley, CA 92584; telephone 909.679.6612.
Tree of Life Nursery, PO Box 635 (33201 Ortega Highway), San Juan Capistrano, CA 92693; telephone 949.728.0685; on the web at www.treeoflifenursery.com.
See Week 45 in 52 Weeks in the California Garden.

SOIL PREPARATION FOR NATIVES

Q: You talk about amending the soil for planting, but when I went to the Theodore Payne Foundation to purchase native plants, they told me not to amend the soil. Should I do it anyway?

—S.B., WEST LOS ANGELES

A: It would be convenient if the question on amending the soil were as simple as do or don't. It depends on what kind of soil you garden in.

Amending the soil pertains usually to flower and vegetable beds and those other intensively cultivated parts of the garden. These plants do a lot of growing, flowering and fruiting and really use up a soil quickly.

Native plants, as well as many shrubs and trees that eventually grow large, seem to do best in unamended, undisturbed soil, recent scientific experiments suggest, but there are some notable exceptions.

For most plants, avoid amending only the soil in the planting hole. This creates an artificial, often impenetrable "interface" between native soil and amended soil. It is like putting the new plant in a bathtub, or a container, with no drainage holes. The first rain or irrigation will fill the hole with water. While many common garden plants will survive this, natives tend not to.

Roots will want to circle around in that amended soil inside the hole, as they do in a container, and not venture out into unamended garden soil. Big shrubs and trees need to get their roots out into the surrounding soil if they are going to support themselves and not topple or strangle. You can't make a big enough planting hole to do them any good.

When you plant, refill the hole with crumbled native soil, breaking up all the clods. You can amend the top few inches to make it easier for water to soak in, but that often isn't necessary.

What you can do—and may have to, in some cases—is amend the soil over the whole area, say to a depth of four to eight inches, or even deeper. This will be necessary with heavy clay soils (where native plants, other than grasses, don't naturally grow), and on extensively graded lots and hillsides where no topsoil remains. Mike Evans, of Tree of Life Nursery in San Juan Capistrano, points out that there is nothing resembling real soil around many new Orange County hillside homes. It was carted off or shoved aside during development. The new gardener finds only lifeless, mineral soils. In these cases the entire garden must be improved, and it's probably best to first have the soil tested to know exactly how. Improving the existing soil is better than bringing in so-called topsoil, which may come with its own problems, like horrific weeds or chemicals, or which may be little better than the original soil.

You can also cover the ground to a depth of several inches with a degradable organic mulch, such as leaves, partially decomposed compost or wood chips from a tree trimmer, keeping this mulch away from the very bases of the plants. As these decay, they slowly improve the soil, and they should be renewed from time to time. Bark, gravel and lawn clippings *won't* work as soil-building mulches.

As a very general rule: Don't amend the soil for natives or for trees and shrubs on typical urban and suburban lots; amend just those beds that will be dug and planted frequently. On hillsides, get the soil tested.

USING COLORFUL FOLIAGE

In Southern California, some leaves color up briefly before they fall or get blown away by autumn's Santa Ana winds. During a good year, places like Pomona, Pasadena and the San Fernando Valley resemble Vermont. Well, almost.

But big deal. While we might not have the fiery fall colors of the East—flame red, orange or gold—in our climate we can grow plants that sport colorful foliage all year long. Gray, silver, lime, chartreuse, maroon, purple and bronze—we've got hues that turn a Grinch-green monotony into a complex, compelling garden with a well-developed sense of space, depth and brightness.

It could be said that silver and gray plants broke the color barrier since they were the first nongreen plants to make their debuts in many landscapes. Los Angeles garden designer Christine Rosmini, whose sophisticated gardens have appeared in countless magazines, uses gray foliage to make a garden's edges seem more distant. "Gray plants look like they are far away, part of the misty background," she says. They make a garden look bigger than it actually is.

Gray and silvery plants also reflect light at night and glow in the moonlight. Gardens just don't look the same without their shimmer and glow.

Variegated or golden leaves and light green or lime kinds brighten dark, shaded areas. Pasadena landscape architect Shirley Kerins uses lime and light green foliage to keep shady areas from feeling "like the dark woods with wolves all about." Even in the sun, they stand out.

Jan Smithen, a lecturer and teacher of the popular Fanatic Gardeners class at the Arboretum of Los Angeles County in Arcadia, is "in love with lime-colored plants," for the contrast the greenish-yellow color provides when mixed with somber greens. Laguna Beach garden designer Christin Fusano includes a few variegated plants in every garden scheme because they "really brighten places up."

Plants with purplish or bronzy leaves have the opposite effect. They are "like shadows" and recede from sight, adding depth to plantings, says Rosmini. Smithen favors bronzy and purplish foliage because other colors—"except perhaps yellow," she notes—look great against these dark shades, and they help "marry other colors together."

Rosmini doesn't stop with just one shade of green, gold, bronze or silver. She says she uses "lots of colors that are closely related but not the same"—six different shades of bronze foliage, for instance, not just one. She thinks these delicate shadings give garden plantings an "opalescent" depth.

Kerins, referring to the plant sales at the Huntington Botanical Gardens (which she has organized in the past), says that silver was the most popular for years, and then burgundy and lime green became hot colors.

Following, these four experienced gardeners suggest specific plants and how to use their colored foliage to great effect:

Silvers and Grays

In her own garden, Kerins grows a lavender named 'Fred Boutin' because, unlike other lavenders, which get too big and tend to collapse, this one stays dense and tight for years. She likes to combine several kinds of silver, so next to this lavender she grows the silvery and sticky *Salvia discolor* and the shimmery *Helichrysum* 'Icicles'.

One way of dealing with the rampant growth of many silver or gray plants is to whack them back. This doesn't work on all kinds—lavenders and the common licorice plant will likely die after heavy pruning. However, Smithen grows the honey bush (*Melianthus major*), with its big, silvery, serrated leaves, and cuts it to the ground twice a year, once at rose-pruning time in January and again in midsummer. "My garden is really tiny, so I have to keep things in bounds," she explains. Otherwise, this very elegant, though slightly smelly, perennial grows 10 to 12 feet tall.

For a brilliant silvery sheen that looks almost metallic, you can't beat the bold but sometimes hard-to-grow silver sword (*Astelia nervosa*), according to Rosmini. She also lauds the equally scarce *Acacia iteaphylla*, which makes a misty blue-gray shrub about eight feet tall. Blooming twice a year, it is powerfully fragrant.

As a designer, Rosmini points out that the most useful plants with colorful foliage are not the most exciting. *Pittosporum crassifolium* 'Compactum' may be short on drama, for instance, but makes a dense permanent shrub that tops out at a manageable four feet tall by six across. A refined plant with leaves with a soft gray sheen, on the excitement scale it's only a notch above 'Glacier' ivy, also a favorite of Rosmini's. She uses this reliable ivy, with its gray-green leaves marked with white, to landscape impossibly shady spots, which it "really brightens," she says.

Light, Bright Greens

For light green, a small Australian shrub named *Westringia* 'Morning Light' is a trouper, according to Rosmini. Growing to only several feet high and across, it has small variegated leaves that seem to glow—especially when backlit by the sun.

Helichrysum petiolare 'Limelight' is the classic lime-leaved plant for partial shade, but don't expect it to last very long. It has long, trailing branches that need to be cut back after a few years, which will probably kill the plant. Easily replaceable, it is so useful at brightening that this fault can be forgiven.

Similar in color is Kerins' "absolute favorite," a seed-grown columbine named 'Woodside'. She's also fond of spotted ligularia for its yellow dots that look like spots of dappled sunlight in a shady bed. A pulmonaria named 'Spilt Milk' will grow in deep shade and has neat white markings. Kerins couldn't resist growing this next to a dark brown or burgundy ajuga named 'Chocolate Chip'. Another fun brightener is the golden breath of heaven shrub, *Coleonema* 'Sunset Gold'. "It demands shade and moisture," says Smithen, but makes a soft, pretty lime-green shrub about two feet tall. "It's one of those plants you want to pet." Try it with azaleas, she suggests.

Two sturdy shrubs with variegated foliage are on Fusano's list, including lily-of-the-valley shrub, *Pieris japonica* 'Variegata', which needs filtered light and an acidic soil, and "the only euonymus I'll use in a garden," *Euonymus japonicus* 'Microphylla Variegata'. The oh-so-common euonymus are often described as cast-iron plants.

Fusano's favorite, however, is the yellow-green oregano named 'Jim Best', which is "really not for culinary use," though it might be found in the herb section at nurseries. She uses this spreading plant's bright-golden foliage in the gaps between steppingstones.

Purplish Hues

Of late, all sorts of new plants with purplish foliage have appeared at nurseries, from the purple-leaved coral bells to the burgundy-leaved loropetalums, also called fringe flowers. Their leaves may be described as mahogany, purple, red, wine, maroon, burgundy and other colors, but most are a similar dark shade of green suffused with purple.

A favorite of Fusano's is *Loropetalum chinense* 'Sizzling Pink'. Rosmini finds loropetalums useful and versatile, too. "They'll spill over a bank or grow up against a hot south-facing wall," she says. Rosmini also loves the feathery texture of purple-leaved fennel and the wispyness of purple fountain grass (*Pennisetum setaceum* 'Rubrum'). Billowy and soft, it makes a great contrast for other plants. It is extremely easy to grow and it doesn't seed about like the weedy green fountain grass.

This burgundy hue can even be found in the leaves of trees, such as the Eastern redbud 'Forest Pansy', which is "just a delight," according to Rosmini. A favorite of Smithen's is the purple-leaved smoke tree (*Cotinus* 'Purpureus'), only she keeps it a small shrub by pruning it back every year to an 18-inch-tall trunk. Even though her garden is small, she managed to fit two of these into its confines, a measure of its worth.

Smithen's "absolute favorite," however, is the red-foliage grape (*Vitus vinifera* 'Purpurea'). She grows two. One is on a trellis with a red 'Altissimo' rose, and the other grows with a purple clematis. To keep them in bounds, they are pruned hard each year as if they were growing in a vineyard.

A burgundy-leaved chervil (*Anthriscus*) is one of Kerins' favorites. Named 'Ravenswood', it is short, lacy and so dark that "it would look like a black hole," she notes, without something to set it off. She grows it with the variegated Bowles' golden grass, another good choice for semishade.

And for reddish foliage that almost approaches autumn's hot colors, Kerins likes some of the newer nandinas and barberries with descriptive names like 'Firepower' and 'Ring of Fire'. These have colorful foliage all year long, but in the chill of fall and winter, the colors are especially bright.

FIRE SAFETY VS. ENERGY SAVINGS

Q: I'm in a quandary. The Department of Water and Power says to plant shade trees close to the house; the Fire Department says not to plant them closer than 30 feet from the house. In addition, the two departments contradict each other in that many xeriscape plants are flammable. I challenge you to show us plants that are drought resistant and fireproof.

—G.S., MALIBU

A: If you live in a fire-prone area, surrounded by brush, the Fire Department is right: Protecting your home from brush fires outweighs the energy savings trees might provide by keeping the house cool.

In fire areas, the way you design your plantings is more important than what you plant, so you can use drought-resistant things, even natives, if they are spaced properly and kept neat. No plant is "fireproof." Even the old standby ice plant has been found to spread brush fires because so much dead matter accumulates under the leaves.

The basic idea of firescaping is that "available fuel," or plant material, is gradually reduced the closer you get to the house. Nearest the house, then, low-growing plants would be irrigated, although there is some evidence that native oak trees and citrus, at least, are quite good at resisting fire. A little farther out, plantings are low growing, though taller plants may be mixed in as long as they are spaced properly.

On the hillsides, the current thinking advocates retaining much of the native vegetation—removing all the native vegetation destabilizes hillsides and may cause slippage or serious erosion. Plants are thinned out so they are not close together and cleaned up of dead branches and litter.

In typical gardens, away from brush-fire danger, shading the house to reduce the cooling load takes precedence, as is using as little water as is feasible. "Smart Planting for the New Urban Forest: A Guide to Planting Trees Around Your Home," put out by the TreePeople and the Los Angeles Department of Water and Power, is one of the better guides. It explains how to site trees for lower energy use, lists a number that do well here (with illustrations) and spells out exactly how trees should be planted to assure longevity.

Find firescaping ideas and recommended plants on the web at cecalaveras.ucdavis.edu/land.htm, www.firesafe.com/firescape.html and www.firesafecouncil.org/landscaping.html.
"Smart Planting for the New Urban Forest: A Guide to Planting Trees Around Your Home" is available on the web at www.treepeople.org.
See Week 48 in 52 Weeks in the California Garden.

NO-SLIDE HILLSIDES

Q: I live on a hillside and am concerned about all the slopes that have slid in past years. Right now my slope is covered with ivy. Should I plant something else that might better hold the hill together?

—R.F., WOODLAND HILLS

A: Prevention of catastrophic landslides—like those that occur during wet winters in a few Southern California areas—has more to do with the geology, or how the slope is engineered, than with plants. If you're concerned, consult an environmental or soils engineer.

By breaking the force of the raindrops and holding the surface of the soil together, plants do play a limited role in maintaining hillsides, says Claremont landscape architect Bob Perry, also a professor in the landscape architecture department at Cal Poly Pomona and the author of several excellent books on plants for the West, including *Landscape Plants for Western Regions* (Land Design Publishing, 1992).

Two of the best soil binders on large hillsides, Perry says, are ivy (English or Algerian) and Hall's honeysuckle (*Lonicera japonica* 'Halliana'), although they are aggressive and somewhat weedy. On big slopes, he uses the honeysuckle with the lavender-flowered *Lantana montevidensis.* Both need to be cut back severely on occasion to keep them from accumulating too much dead growth underneath.

To keep hillsides from looking monotonous, says Perry, plant the ground covers mentioned with trees, shrubs or billowy, spreading plants such as *Jasminum mesnyi* or the yellow Lady Banks' rose. Perry sometimes mixes in common periwinkle (*Vinca*), which is less aggressive but grows better in wetter or shadier spots.

On a steep hillside, the worst thing you can do is "plant ice plant and water a lot," Perry says. Ice plant is not a very tenacious ground cover. An equally bad idea, he says, is "cutting away at the toe of the slope with poorly made retaining walls to try and gain more space." It's also important to prevent water runoff from a garden situated above a slope.

On smaller slopes, plant natives, such as coyote brush and manzanita, and exotics.

BEFORE THE REMODEL

Up through the construction debris—the sawdust, the bent nails and the bits of stucco and concrete—came the fall-blooming crocuses, like some floral phoenix rising from the dust and dirt laid down by remodeling. We had just finished remodeling and adding on to our home, and the garden had suffered, mostly from neglect, during the three months of construction. As if to remind us that they were still there, up came the crocuses between the front stepping stones.

Remodeling tends to be an all-consuming project, even when someone else is doing the work. If you're not at Home Depot buying light fixtures or bathroom sinks, you're lying awake at night trying to figure out what color the grout should be or whether the pocket door to the dining area should be three or four feet wide.

Because the addition would be to the north side of the house and shade the garden in winter, we tried to keep it low. This is something architects seldom consider, but gardeners should. These kinds of decisions are best made early on in the planning, as it's much easier to avoid too much shade than it is to garden in it. To make sure our addition would not be too tall, we put up a pole the height of the addition's roof to find where its shadow would fall, before plans were finalized.

We also made sure the addition wrapped in an L-shape around an existing tree, which lightly shaded a patio. It takes too long to grow new shade trees, so it's wise to save the ones you already have. We even made it part of the new kitchen by

Some autumn-blooming crocus manage to bloom though
the sawdust, nails and bits of plaster of a remodel.

putting a clear skylight in, so we could look up into its flowering branches (and check the weather).

The skylight helps bring the garden indoors, another thing to consider in the planning process. Remodels don't have to destroy a garden, and gardens shouldn't have to play second fiddle to the house. If you're going to use a landscape designer, have him or her sit in on the early stages of planning.

The contractor was very careful of the garden. He cut only a 10-foot-wide swath for scaffolding and materials, so most of the garden was unhurt. And there was still plenty of garden. My wife and I spend a lot of time outdoors, so we didn't fill the yard with house, as is too often the case in California. When I see these remodels, I ask myself, "Why live in this glorious climate if you can't be outdoors?"

To make the loss of garden space less noticeable, I had let (cleverly, I think) some shrubs next to the house grow way too big. Then at the last moment, I took them out and substituted a room addition! It wasn't exactly a seamless switch, but one week there were big, bland shrubs and the next, new rooms. We hardly noticed the change. Of course, we added only about 250 square feet, but that was enough to make quite a difference. Conversely, we subtracted only about 250 square feet from the garden.

When the work outdoors was done, I was a bit surprised at how much debris ended up on the soil. I think the contractor was a bit surprised at the pile I made one weekend—for him to cart off—of soil left over from the foundation excavation and soil contaminated with paint and stucco. I did not want to discover little shards of broken glass, rusty nails and sharp metal stucco lath as I dug in the garden.

The building crew had taken most of it away, but a lot had gotten spread out on top of the old garden soil, raising its level to an unacceptable height while concealing all sorts of debris that probably wouldn't do the garden any good. In this day of city-supplied trash cans, getting rid of excess rubbish is no longer a matter of putting it out on the curb in boxes and bags.

Still, it is impossible to get rid of everything. How do all those bits of stucco and concrete affect the soil? To find out, I called soil scientist Garn Wallace, of Wallace Laboratories in El Segundo, a soil consulting and testing firm.

I should have called him earlier, because his first piece of advice would have saved me a lot of digging and sifting: Put plastic around the walls to catch the excess stucco and concrete. Failing this, he says, you'll have remove the top two inches of soil near the building along with the debris.

Both concrete and stucco secrete chemicals that make a soil extremely alkaline. Stucco has a pH of 10 to 12. Luckily, a good rainy season or lots of irrigations will leach much of this out of the soil in a year's time, so the soil ends up with a pH of about 7.7. A new concrete foundation, however, will make the soil right next to it too alkaline for azaleas or camellias for a few years. A simple way to check the alkalinity, says Wallace, is to pour a little battery acid or even vinegar on the soil. If it fizzes, the soil is still too alkaline.

To aid the leaching process, he suggests adding some gypsum and soil amendments to speed drainage. I followed this directive.

I had already followed his other advice—keep all concrete and stucco mixer washings, even paint residue, out of the garden. Pigments in paints are toxic to plants, even if the paints themselves are not. In older homes, it's very important to keep any chips of old lead-based paint out of the garden. Lead, a poisonous heavy metal, is not biodegradable and builds up in urban soils, becoming a lasting threat.

With a little forethought and some careful cleanup, there's no reason a garden can't emerge healthy and unscathed after a home remodel.

PLANTING POOLSIDE

Q: Which plants are less likely to be affected by chlorine water splashing from a swimming pool?

—A.P., MALIBU

A: All plants are affected. "Plant them anyway, and don't worry," says Cleo Baldon, of Cleo Baldon & Associates in Venice, garden designer of some of the most exciting, elegant pools in Southern California. In her book, *Reflections on the Pool* (Rizzoli, 1997), there are 40 gorgeous pools by several designers, and every one of them has plants growing right up to the water's edge (usually in raised beds) and even hanging over it.

In her own garden, Baldon has asparagus fern and spider plant dripping into the pool, and, she says, "They get splashed a lot." Leaves touching the water die, but the rest of the plant is fine.

In short, most plants will grow near a pool; all will be damaged by splashing water, but they'll keep growing.

West Los Angeles gardener Linda Estrin has a veritable botanic garden growing around her pool, full of truly exciting, unusual plants, many of them drought resistant. Only the standard four-foot walkway, if that, separates the plants and water's edge, and since she has children, the plants do get splashed. She has lost a few plants to chlorine—when the pool service accidentally purged the filter into the garden beds and during the Northridge earthquake, when much of the pool water sloshed out—but the garden continues to thrive.

For pools, bigger concerns should focus on choosing benign plants, without spines or sharp leaves, and those that are not messy. Baldon, though, takes issue with the latter because she enjoys the look of fallen leaves on the water's surface. "A Guide to Plant Selection," in the Sunset *Western Garden Book* (Sunset Publishing), lists tidy plants to use near swimming pools.

❦ ❦ ❦

Creature Comforts

GARDENS FOR WILDLIFE

In Long Beach, the wildlife garden of Tina and Jim Vince builds like an ocean swell: Plants favored by birds and butterflies rise from the back yard to the eaves of the house and above, before crashing over the house and into the front yard, spilling greenery across the sidewalk and into the street. It's a wild froth of a garden that is as much for animals and insects as it is for the Vinces. And, on the off chance you can't figure out why it looks this way, a small sign in the front yard proclaims: Official Backyard Wildlife Habitat.

In California, 1,249 gardens are officially certified by the National Wildlife Federation as wildlife habitats, gardens where creatures of various kinds can find food, water, shelter and safety, maybe even a place to rear their young. A garden can be a small window box in the city or a big property that encompasses acres. The $15 certificate is a bit like an honorary diploma, in that it doesn't protect the creatures or the garden or entitle the owners to anything special, except the little sign, which costs an additional $15.

Much of the planted habitat in the Vince garden is in the front yard of their small city lot. The 20 or so feet between the street and their 80-year-old bungalow is stuffed with plants such as tall, lacy anise, chewed here and there—fodder for the larvae of the spectacular swallowtail butterfly. Several other kinds of butterflies flit from flower to flower on colorful lantana and pentas.

Hummingbirds with iridescent ruby-colored throats are attracted to the various tubular flowers, especially those of the honeysuckle that threatens to overwhelm the house and the bright-red *Lobelia laxiflora* from Mexico.

In the back yard are several bird feeders and a variety of birdbaths. "Birds actually line up to use this one," Tina Vince says, pointing to a shallow dish filled with water and a few pebbles. This is surprising because it sits right on the ground, which makes birds easier prey for cats.

The garden didn't get this way overnight. "It wasn't like we got up one morning and said, 'Let's build a garden for wildlife,'" Tina explains. After raising four children, the couple began replacing the lawn with plants that birds like, because they like birds.

It's trash collection day when I visit, but over the hydraulic noises of the garbage trucks, all the birds in the garden can be heard. I can pick out the cooing of doves (and see one spying on me from its eye-level nest by the back door), the copycat songs of mockingbirds, screeches from jays and the chatter of kinglets searching for bugs in the birch trees. Other calls I do not recognize—the Vince garden is haven to some unusual birds, such as the little hermit thrush and the black-masked, bright-yellow Townsend's warbler. There are so many interesting birds that a friend, wildlife photographer Peter Knapp, has taken a number of prize shots of birds here.

Not just birds and butterflies visit. A small pond filled with aquatic plants in the back is regularly ravaged by raccoons. "But it bounces right back," Tina says. In a wildlife habitat garden, creatures come first. As hard as it might be for some of us to accept, those devilish raccoons are wildlife, too.

In Riverside, creatures that do not grace city gardens—rabbits, coyotes, quail—make a different, wilder kind of Backyard Wildlife Habitat. On the two-and-a-quarter-acre property of Nan and Bob Simonsen, red-tailed hawks nest, squirrels abound and skunks make their presence known. "We don't often see the skunks, but we can sure smell them," says Nan. Bob has even seen the kittens of a bobcat.

Part of her garden is elegant and formal, filled with roses and iris, but it is the wild half of the property she most likes, as much for the animals as the plants. Planted with tough native plants, this garden has paths more akin to trails, and, incredibly, a natural spring-fed stream, bustling with frogs and dragonflies. "I love having movement in the garden," says Nan Simonsen, who finds that wildlife animates a garden.

When they bought their home many years ago, they knew immediately what to do with all the land. "While we were still in escrow, Bob said, 'Let's make this a park,'" says Nan, who teaches gardening at a community college and at the UC Riverside Botanic Garden. And that's exactly what they did, planting mostly native trees and shrubs while preserving and augmenting the stream bed and its plantings of willows and other riparian plants.

While some native plants, such as the spectacular flannel bushes (*Fremontodendron*) and the clambering morning glory, are mostly for show, many were chosen for their value as a food source: native oak, toyon, manzanita, ceanothus, gooseberry, elderberry, buckwheat and verbena. Even the prickly opuntia cactus has fruit relished by birds.

"I'm all right with nibbled leaves," says Nan, who, like Tina Vince, actually selects plants that she knows will be eaten and would never think to spray for pests. Other plants, such as the wild roses, provide habitat, a place for birds to hide and nest.

Even dead plants can be useful. Biologists say that snags (what they call dead trees) provide perches, shelter, cover and lots of bugs for food and may be more important to wildlife even than live trees.

In their Riverside garden, the Simonsens have let several dead willows remain for this reason. The Vinces, in their more citified Long Beach garden, have not trimmed the dead branches from an old avocado. It was on one of its ghostly gray limbs that Tina first saw a rare Cooper's hawk—quite a sight for city folk.

Backyard Wildlife Habitat information is available though the National Wildlife Federation Backyard Habitat Program, 11100 Wildlife Center, Reston, VA 20190; telephone 703.438.6586; on the web at www.nwf.org.

BIRDS FLOCK TO A BIRDBATH

You wouldn't think that where you put a birdbath would make all that much difference. When ours was in front, it was tucked under a climbing rose next to a small eucalyptus. It seemed like a good spot and, in fact, looked very quaint.

A nearly tame scrub jay frequently came to bathe, so vigorously that we had to refill it every day. Most of the time, though, the bath just sat there, not attracting birds the way I had intended. Birdbaths are said to attract more birds, and more variety, than even bird feeders.

Then I moved the bath to the back yard and positioned it as wildlife experts suggest. Soon it was as crowded as Venice Beach on a hot summer day. Not all the time, of course, but often enough. And it was now visible from the patio, so I could watch my fine-feathered visitors.

Birds feel a lot safer bathing if there are no dense plants where cats might hide, though they do appreciate tree and shrub branches they can flee to.

Mockingbirds were the first to discover the new locale. This was no surprise, though, since they are as cocky and commonplace as scrub jays—and equally fervent bathers.

Then a flock of sparrows spotted the birdbath. There were five fat sparrows splashing up a storm, with a few more waiting their turns in the bushes. Enter a mockingbird, who waded in and, as the sparrows sat patiently on the edge, showed them just whose bath this was. Before taking his leave, he shook himself off, and they all ducked and flinched like children getting splashed at a public pool.

When they hopped back in, glistening droplets flew everywhere. They got the ground so wet that I decided I had better plant things that enjoy moisture at the base of the birdbath. In the front yard, it had never seen such activity.

Next came a lone warbler with a touch of yellow on its rump, one of those birds that are always moving. "Active flittings" is how Roger Tory Peterson describes warbler behavior in *A Field Guide to Western Birds* (Houghton Mifflin, 1998). This new visitor stayed for weeks.

A flock of yellowish bushtits, each about as big as a golf ball and nearly as round, arrived next, though I only saw them drinking the bathwater. They stayed for a while, darting through the bushes eating all sorts of bugs.

This was an unforeseen benefit, and reason alone to attract birds to your garden. In the front yard, the bath had been surrounded by tough, drought-tolerant plants, which have few pests. In back, it was near several pest-plagued shrub roses, under a lemon tree with its share of aphids, scale and whiteflies. Once the birds showed up to bathe, they stuck around and ate whatever bugs they could find, cleaning up the lemon and the roses. Birds can be valuable allies in the gardener's battle against bugs and weeds.

Though they might sometimes eat good bugs along with bad, for the most part they eat those stationary, sucking insects that infest plants. Birds with more needle-like bills eat insects; those with shorter, stockier bills eat weed seeds. Birds will also eat the seed you sow, along with the weed seeds, so protect new sowings with netting.

Experts on wild birds have come up with some recommendations on how to lure birds into the garden.

• Place the bath where it can be easily seen from the sky, so birds flying overhead can spot it.

• Put it in a sunny spot. Think of how popular a shady Venice Beach would be.

• Mount it about three feet high (this is usually how those with pedestals come). If you must keep a birdbath on the ground, place it at least six feet away from where cats can lurk, like little lions waiting to pounce.

• Place it near some trees or big shrubs where birds can perch to dry off or to flee. Plants should be three to six feet away. If these plants are prickly or thorny, like my roses and lemon happened to be, cats are less likely to climb them.

• Keep low plants around the base of the bath so cats can't hide. In our birdbath's new location, birds can see in all directions, and refuge is a quick, upward flight—the perfect situation.

• Keep the water no deeper than an inch, though ours is somewhat deeper in the middle and the birds don't seem to mind. In fact, that's where the bigger birds bathe. Scrub off algae that forms in old baths.

As for the bath itself: Its edges should be wide and curved for the birds' feet, not narrow or sharply angled. Its bottom should not be too sloped or slippery. Ours is a very old bath, a concrete charmer that belonged to my grandfather. My mother had it next, and after it fell over in the Loma Prieta earthquake up north, she carefully patched it back together with concrete cement, which added to its patina.

Then my wife and I brought it south and had to patch it again when it fell over in the Northridge earthquake. By now it looks a couple hundred years old, though it dates from the 1940s. I suspect that the birds like that it's old and weathered.

I did make one mistake in setting it up the second time. I put it on newly tilled and planted soil. Then I noticed it leaning like the tower of Pisa. And like that fabled tower, I had to re-engineer the ground underneath it, setting it on a layer of stomped-down gravel and sand. Now it's quite stable.

The jay still uses (and empties) the bath. But in its new location, many other birds do too, now that they have a clear, bird's-eye view of the garden and any cats it might harbor.

EASY-CARE PONDS

Q: How much work is involved in the maintenance of a pond with a few gold-fish and a minimum of plant life? My wife wants a pond but doesn't want to spend hours maintaining the thing. Would you install an above-ground filter or not? We are not into koi.

—T.C., LOS ANGELES

A: For most of the year, few things in the garden are easier to care for than a pond. Building it may be another story (a flexible liner makes installation easier), but you won't need that filter you mentioned. Only ponds packed with koi need fil-ters.

Plants act as natural filters (that's why they're part of the planned recycling system for the first manned trip to Mars), so you really don't want a "minimum of plant life." Without plants, ponds get dirty and filled with algae.

To prevent green algae–filled water, 75 percent of the water's surface should be covered by plants like water lilies. Lilies and other aquatic plants with floating leaves, including water snowflake and water poppy, are the easiest to care for because they grow at reasonable rates. Many aquatics, especially those called bog plants, such as water iris and azure pickerel, require more work because they grow so fast and must be divided often.

Once a year, in late winter or very early spring, water lilies need to be divided and repotted, and that is a lot of work. Because they are grown in pots or tubs inside the pond—in ordinary clay soil—they must be lifted out, and they are very heavy and very messy.

Other than this big job, ponds pretty much take care of themselves, if you have a balance of fish, such as goldfish, pond snails and plants. Pond snails can live only in water (they do not plague the garden), and all are scavengers, eating decay-ing vegetation and algae.

See Week 30 in 52 Weeks in the California Garden.

❦ ❦ ❦

Too Dark and Too Damp

SEVERAL DEGREES OF SHADE

As trees mature and houses top two stories, gardens are becoming increasingly dark in many Southern California neighborhoods. Shadows creep across the landscape, and there is less of that precious full sun that plants are so fond of. Nurseries, getting wind of this trend, label more and more plants: Sun/Part Shade. This, of course, suggests that the plant can grow in either situation, though in many cases it's not true.

Most plants want a full day of sun, from sunup to sundown. Any less, and their growth is weak and floppy, they may not flower, and they are often prone to pests and diseases. If your garden has become shady, forget about roses and tomatoes and a thousand other sun-loving plants. But don't abandon hope. There are plants that grow well in shade, though first you must determine what kind of shade you have.

Deep, Dark Shade

Is the shade in your garden deep and dark, even gloomy, as shade is under a ficus tree or an evergreen magnolia or under the wide eaves of a house? Architecture sometimes conspires against gardening. Says Los Angeles landscape designer Chris Rosmini: "Architects sometimes add little nooks and crannies and say, 'Hey, that's a wonderful place for plants.' But it's like gardening in a closet." The choice of plants that will grow in such a situation or under a big, dense tree is extremely limited. Ask anyone trying to grow something under an avocado tree. Even weeds won't sprout.

DARK-SHADE PLANTS

- acanthus
- aspidistra
- bromeliad, some, e.g., *Billbergia nutans*
- clivia
- English ivy
- lady palm (*Rhapis*)
- lily turf (*Liriope*)
- maidenhair, mother and sword ferns
- monstera
- philodendron
- *Ruscus hypoglossum*
- spider plant (*Chlorophytum*)

Not enough light may be only half the problem. A plant may also be competing with tree roots, so it must be able to survive on the dry side, making do with whatever moisture the tree doesn't take. When planting under trees, don't plant right up to the base of the trunk. For the health of the tree, leave a little breathing room around the trunk, an unplanted circle of several feet.

Bold, orange-flowered clivia are the unchallenged champions in deep shade. They'll even grow under an avocado. Pale-yellow clivia are now available, for those with more modest color schemes. For a little more variety, Rosmini says, use the variegated English ivies, such as 'Glacier', as a ground cover in dark areas, perhaps punctuated by tufts of the grasslike white-striped 'Silver Dragon' liriope.

The gold-and-white markings on variegated plants look especially good in the shade, and often these plants do better out of the sun. "They're bright points of light in dark places, pretty even if they don't flower," she says.

Light Shade

There are several degrees of light shade. The shaded ground under a tree can be an excellent growing environment, if it is open and high, letting in speckled sunlight from above and scattered light from the sides. Lots of plants thrive in this light shade environment, which some call dappled shade or filtered sun. Lighten the shade of a dense tree by pruning out entire branches and twiggy growth. This technique, called lacing, allows more light for plants growing underneath without destroying the cooling canopy of the tree.

Consider yourself "blessed," says Laguna Beach landscape architect Jana Ruzicka, if you have this kind of light shade. "In Southern California, it is such a relief from the hot sun, and you can grow so many beautiful plants in it," she says. Many plants actually prefer light shade over direct sun, especially inland, where the sun is more intense. She mentions princess flower (*Tibouchina*) as one plant that does fine in full sun near the coast but needs light shade inland, in places like Tustin.

In one lightly shaded area in a Pacific Palisades garden, Colleen Holmes, a San Fernando Valley landscape designer and contractor, put in a classic planting of azaleas, baby's tears, cannas, ferns, foxgloves and white impatiens. This grouping is nearly foolproof in light-to-medium shade, yet it provides a variety of heights, leaf sizes and textures. The color scheme is simple white and pink.

If you're feeling more ambitious, try what landscape architect Mark Beall did in his own Silver Lake garden. He has found that many tropical, or tropical-looking, plants thrive in shade. Around his shadowy patio, he mixes the tropicals with more traditional temperate-climate shade plants. His hillside garden, however, is essentially frost-free.

In the darker areas he mixes the big-leaved monstera and *Philodendron selloum* with mother ferns, ligularia, ajuga and *Aristea ecklonii*, an iris relative with small, true-blue flowers. He's found that the Brazilian plume flower (*Justicia carnea*) blooms bright pink in complete shade. Shrimp plants (*Justicia brandegeana*) and some bromeliads (*Billbergia*, in particular) also reliably bloom in the shade.

One visit to Beall's garden proves it's quite possible to plant a fascinating palette—a garden to please any plant lover—even without sun.

It's also possible to have an English-inspired garden of lavish perennials and small shrubs. Much of Rosmini's garden near Mt. Washington in Los Angeles grows in the shade of large trees on a north-facing slope, but she manages full-blown English-inspired borders. In the shade, she grows things such as the stunning green-flowered shrimp plant (*Justicia brandegeana* 'Chartreuse'), variegated grasses and sedges, and golden wandering Jew (*Tradescantia albiflora* 'Aurea'). The latter she found at a Huntington Botanical Gardens plant sale, and it makes a sturdy, shady

---

LIGHT-SHADE PLANTS

- abutilon
- ajuga
- *Allium triquetrum*
- aluminum plant (*Pilea cadierei*)
- angel's trumpet (*Brugmansia*)
- *Aquilegia formosa*
- *Aristea ecklonii*
- azalea, some
- begonia
- bergenia
- Boston ivy
- Brazilian plume flower (*Justicia carnea*)
- calla lily
- camellia
- campanula
- *Cestrum elegans*
- *Cissus*, various
- coral bells
- *Corydalis nobilis*
- crinum lily
- epidendrum orchid

- *Eupatorium sordidum*
- fern, many
- foxglove
- *Francoa ramosa*
- fuchsia
- *Geranium macrorrhizum*
- *Geranium maderense* and *Geranium canariense*
- ginger
- *Helichrysum petiolare* 'Limelight'
- *Heliotropium* 'Alba'
- hellebore
- *Impatiens olivari*
- native iris
- Japanese anemone
- ligularia
- mahonia
- meadow rue (*Thalictrum*)
- mondo grass
- *Pittosporum tobira*,

- some varieties
- *Plectranthus argentatus*
- *Rehmannia elata*
- ribbon bush (*Hypoestes aristata*)
- *Salvia chiapensis*
- schefflera
- sedge, many (*Carex*)
- shrimp plant (*Justicia brandegeana*)
- Spanish bluebell (*Scilla hispanica*)
- spotted nettle (*Lamium*)
- star jasmine
- strawberry begonia (*Saxifraga stolonifera*)
- wandering Jew (*Tradescantia*)
- yesterday-today-and-tomorrow (*Brunfelsia*)

ground cover of surprising color.

Francoa ramosa and *Rehmannia elata*, with their tall flower spikes, are favorite perennials, as are *Corydalis nobilis*, coral bells and several true geraniums. The purple-leaved coral bells seem to need shade, and two of her favorite geraniums are the ferny *Geranium maderense* and *Geranium canariense*. Maroon-flowered hellebores and ajuga grow near the bushy but hard-to-find *Eupatorium sordidum*, with its maroon-tinged leaves and ageratumlike flowers.

Ruzicka's gardens are full of interesting plants that thrive in light shade. Some of her favorites include the fast-spreading strawberry begonia (*Saxifraga stolonifera*); the hard-to-find *Oxalis regnellii*, which looks like our native wood sorrel; some of the sedges, including the native Berkeley sedge (*Carex tumulicola*), and the native red-flowered columbine (*Aquilegia formosa*).

The shade found on the north side of a house or wall is still another story, a kind of light shade where the garden is in shadow, but nothing blocks the light coming from overhead. Although plants may never get any direct sun, plenty of scattered light comes from the sky. Here, for instance, is the favored place to grow camellias, and there are many other choices.

Many of the plants mentioned above grow here as well. So do many azaleas and the camellialike shrub yesterday-today-and-tomorrow (*Brunfelsia*), with its fascinating flowers that open purple and fade to lavender and finally to white. Several kinds of the substantial shrub *Pittosporum tobira* grow in north shade or even darker areas, though most get quite large. One sold as 'Wheeler's Dwarf' can grow to six feet tall by eight feet across, hardly dwarf. The variegated variety also gets huge, but the colorful dwarf variety named 'Cream de Mint' seems to top out as a very manageable three-to-four-foot shrub.

Several vines, such as star jasmine, Boston ivy and some *Cissus*, grow in shade, even on the north wall of a house.

Shade, Then Sun

An entirely different situation is where plants are in sun for part of the year and shade for the rest, or in shade half the day, in sun the rest. This can be tricky, but some plants can stand the dramatic seasonal, or hourly, changes. Venice designer and gardener Barry Campion managed to find a handful of plants to grow in a border near a pool that was shaded all winter but warm and sunny in summer. She mixed bushy cestrum, abutilon, towering angel's trumpet and yesterday-today-and-tomorrow with smaller pentas, white tulbaghia, valerian and a sun-tolerant fuchsia named 'Gartenmeister Bonstedt'.

Although shade that turns suddenly to blazing sun may be the most difficult situation to plan for, many plants are up to the challenge. And while those Sun/Part

Shade nursery tags are a bit misleading, there is quite a selection of plants that will grow well in one of the many kinds of shade.

VINES FOR THE NORTH SIDE

Q: We live in Venice about a mile inland and have been considering the 'Zephirine Drouhin' climbing roses for the north wall of our house. It's described as being shade tolerant. Do you think this rose would work on this wall? If not, what would you recommend as a good flowering climbing plant for a north wall?

—G.T., VENICE

A: I grew the oddly colored 'Zephirine' several miles from the coast, and it did poorly. Torrance resident Sharon Van Enoo, consulting rosarian for the American Rose Society, says it "mildews badly" near the coast and isn't a particularly good rose anywhere in Southern California. The Rose Garden at the Huntington Botanical Gardens took its out, but you can still see 'Zephirine Drouhin' growing as shrubs at Descanso Gardens, in La Cañada Flintridge.

Few roses bloom in shade. According to Van Enoo, only a group called noisettes stands a chance, as does our own native rose, *Rosa californica*. Other vines are better choices.

Randy Baldwin, of the wholesale nursery San Marcos Growers in Santa Barbara, offers the names of some other clinging or climbing north wall candidates. Getting good foliage is easy, he says; it's getting flowers that's tricky. Most climbers for north walls are known and grown for their foliage, such as the several kinds of grape ivy (*Cissus*) and Boston ivy and Virginia creeper (*Parthenocissus*). *Cissus antarctica*, *Cissus rhombifolia* and *Cissus striata* all grow well in shade, but the flowers are almost invisible. *Parthenocissus henryana* has nicely colored burgundy foliage but is deciduous in winter.

"Flowering plants prefer at least some sun," says Baldwin. Two common viney plants for a north wall are the white-flowered star jasmine (*Trachelospermum*) and potato vine (*Solanum jasminoides*). The waxlike *Hoya carnosa* will definitely flower in north shade, and, if it's bright and warm enough, so should stephanotis, though both are a little spare looking.

Hibbertia vine, with yellow flowers, is recommended for shade, but it tends to get thrips and mites. Though hard to find and sensitive to cold, bleeding heart glorybower (*Clerodendrum thomsoniae*) and *Pandorea jasminoides* should flower on a north wall, as should the violet trumpet vine (*Clytostoma callistegioides*, formerly named *Bignonia violacea*). *Clematis armandii*, *Lonicera confusa* and *Sollya parviflora* are three more. Violet, vanilla-scented *Distictis laxiflora* does "tolerably well," according to Baldwin.

All of these should also grow in bright or dappled shade or the north side of buildings. Your local nursery will likely order the more exotic vines; San Marcos Growers, which has a very useful web site loaded with information, is one source.

San Marcos Growers is on the web at www.smgrowers.com.

WHERE DRAINAGE IS POOR

Q: I have a brick planter in front of my house that is about a foot high with concrete underneath. It apparently has very poor drainage. Can you recommend any perennials that are hardy enough to withstand soil that does not drain well?
—W.M., SHERMAN OAKS

A: There are some plants that are not as fussy about drainage as others, but I suggest fixing the drainage problem. Remove the soil and break up the bottom of the planter with a 60-pound electric pavement breaker. This doesn't require a compressor and can be rented at most rental yards. Or drill down through the bottom or in through the sides near the base, using a heavy-duty drill and large masonry bit. Refill the planter with good potting mix, mixed with about one-third garden soil.

If you would rather try planting things that don't need good drainage, here are a few. Many are grown for their foliage, not their flowers. Elephant ear (*Alocasia*) and calla lily take wet soils, as do many grasses, sedges and bamboos. The variegated acorus, which looks like stiff grass, is quite handsome and will grow in a bog. Many ferns can tolerate wet soils, as can some species of iris, such as the Louisiana iris. *Lobelia cardinalis* and the mimulus sold as a summer bedding plant at nurseries can't be kept wet enough in the garden, so they are probably a good bet. Japanese anemones also have a chance.

Garden designer and teacher Phil Chandler, in his *Reference Lists of Ornamental Plants for Southern California Gardens*, suggests good old agapanthus and daylilies, acanthus, ajuga, crinum lily, geum, ligularia, *Ranunculus repens* and *Viola odorata*.

Reference Lists of Ornamental Plants for Southern California Gardens *is available through the Southern California Horticultural Society, PO Box 41080, Los Angeles, CA 90041-0080; on web at www.socahort.org.*

❧ ❧ ❧

Privacy Issues

SHRUBS FOR THE PROPERTY LINE

Q: Our neighbor removed some 30-year-old Italian cypresses because they were pushing a fence over and dirtying his swimming pool, which is only three feet from the property line. Now we have no privacy or protection from Santa Ana winds. He has agreed to plant a replacement. Can you recommend something that can grow in a space only two feet wide, without invasive roots, is fast, low maintenance, evergreen and tall enough to block a second-story view?

—S.B., BEVERLY HILLS

A: Well, that's a tall order. Few plants are as tall, narrow and dense as an Italian cypress. Though it can be a little messy when it is that old, a replacement is going to be hard to find. It will take a while to fill its shoes, especially when it comes to blocking wind.

Del Mar designer Linda Chisari has used *Podocarpus macrophyllus* in situations similar to yours. San Diego landscape architect Raymond Hansen comments that it is "soft and fluffy and clean for sure." Not as stiff or dense as a cypress, it does block views and temper winds. Hansen notes that in a five-gallon can it is already six feet tall (it can grow to 50 feet), that it is easily clipped into a hedge or kept narrow and natural-looking, and that it is tough and trouble-free.

Sometimes called the yew pine for its similarity to English yew, the classic European hedge plant, this Chinese native grows anywhere in Southern California except the coldest parts of the high desert. It's as close as you'll get to the do-everything, Swiss Army knife plant you are searching for.

Tall bamboos might do the trick but pose their own set of problems, and eugenias are always a possibility, now that the leaf-deforming psyllid is less of a problem. Other options can be found in "A Guide to Plant Selection" in the Sunset *Western Garden Book* (Sunset Publishing).

THE ULTIMATE HEDGE: BAMBOO

It's every homeowners' nightmare—the modest house next door becomes a two-story, lot-filling monster after an ambitious remodel. Or a three-story apartment suddenly springs up where that little bungalow used to be—every one of its windows looking down into your back yard.

Quickly now, what do you do? Sell? Remodel?

A number of homeowners have opted for bamboo—and not a diaphanous screen of the little 10-foot-tall stuff, but a solid wall of 50-foot-high timber bamboo, planted as a linear, lot-defining forest. Overkill? Maybe, because many homeowners then have to top the bamboo at a more manageable 20 or 30 feet. But it sure does the job.

Giant timber bamboo (*Bambusa oldhamii*) encircles one Santa Monica garden designed by landscape architect Pamela Burton, of Pamela Burton & Co., making it so private and so quiet that one is unaware of the busy world beyond. The owner thinks it's not that the bamboo blocks sound, but that the gentle rustling of its leaves masks the urban squeaks and rattles. It certainly blocks any views of neighboring properties and even disguises the conspicuous power pole at the rear of the lot.

Bamboo creates an otherworldly place even for children in this garden: A secret path snakes though the canes on its way to a sandbox. Timber bamboo might as well be giant sequoias, as far as children are concerned.

In nearby Mar Vista, landscape architect Katherine Spitz, of Katherine Spitz Associates in Marina del Rey, has been living with timber bamboo since 1986. She thinks it's "fabulous." It screens out everything—even the two-story apartment behind her—and it is still growing in a neat, hedgelike row less than 30 inches wide. She admits, however, that its extensive root system makes gardening difficult within about 20 feet. She does almost nothing for the bamboo—she hardly even waters—but the Los Angeles Department of Water and Power does top the grove at about 40 feet to keep it out of the power lines.

According to landscape architect Randall Williams, manager of Southern California Edison's tree compliance program, bamboo is second only to palm trees as the utility's least favorite plant because it must be cut back so often. He strongly suggests "not planting the big ones under power lines." Timber bamboo quickly shoots up and gets between the lines, causing them to slap together in winds, which, he says, can short out neighborhood power.

Even though giant timber bamboo may grow taller than need be for privacy, it is often planted because it makes for instant coverage, available to landscape professionals in full-grown clumps, in big, 24-inch wooden boxes. When a three-story remodel suddenly sprung up next to avid gardener Ruth Borun's Brentwood home, she needed privacy for her garden "right away." She had a contractor order a dozen 24-inch boxes of timber bamboo, planting the clumps so they almost touched!

"I've been carefully planting things for the last 30 years so the garden would be peaceful and private. In a few months the privacy was gone. All I could see was the three-story white remodel towering over the garden," Borun says.

Bamboos can only be grown from divisions, so they are often hard to find and usually expensive. They are seldom found in anything smaller than a five-gallon nursery can, which might cost $50. Timber bamboo in 24-inch boxes can cost $350 a pop. "My husband won't need to buy me birthday presents for a very long time," says Borun.

Not everyone appreciates timber bamboo as a screen, especially neighbors, it would seem. "Good fences may make good neighbors," says one, "but a stand of bamboo does not. Eight years ago our neighbors planted a stand of giant bamboo. Ever since then I have had to clean out the gutters every three months. Our side yard is impossible for growing because of the quantity of debris the bamboo drops. Ironically, the bamboo has very few leaves on the lower levels, so it provides no practical privacy."

Timber bamboo, though tall and fairly easy to get, may not be the best choice. "It is good, but it really doesn't make the best screen," says Timothy Phillips, former director of horticulture at Quail Botanical Gardens in Encinitas, home to the largest West Coast bamboo collection. For one thing, it may not have any leaves or side branches at eye level or near the ground. Indeed, most are planted in front of eight-foot fences.

For best tall bamboo, Phillips nominates the scarce painted bamboo (*Bambusa vulgaris vittata*). Growing very upright, it gets to 30 feet, with golden culms (what bamboo stems are called) streaked with what look like drips of green paint.

Another tall bamboo is *Bambusa membranacea*, which can get to 60 feet in the

SCREENING PATIOS AND BALCONIES

Two running bamboos—black bamboo (*Phyllostachys nigra*) and the common golden bamboo (*Phyllostachys aurea*)—make soft upright screens for a patio or balcony. Two more elegant and lovely container plants I cannot think of. Almost all small or midsize bamboos do great in containers, especially some of the more rambunctious kinds that run amok in the ground.

Plant them in 18- to 24-inch-diameter pots, or in half wooden barrels. Growing in pots, bamboos are dwarfed a bit, but if they do get too tall, shorten by pruning off the tops.

You can bring bamboo inside for an occasional visit, but it is an outdoor plant. Even outdoors, bamboo prefers full sun, though there are kinds that tolerate shade, such as the small Himalayan blue bamboo (*Himalayacalamus hookerianum*).

right situation. It makes loose clumps of culms that grow straight as arrows. Still another big one, but with purple-black canes, is the Timor bamboo (*Bambusa lako*), which grows reasonably straight to 30 and even 60 feet tall.

For shorter screens, Phillips suggests the various types of *Bambusa multiplex*. Commonly called hedge bamboos, they typically grow to 25 feet, still tall enough to make good screens. There are several decorative kinds, including 'Alphonse Karr', which has bright golden yellow canes with green vertical stripes, and 'Silverstripe', which has some white-striped leaves and culms.

George Shor, editor of the newsletter for the American Bamboo Society, which maintains the collection at Quail Botanical Gardens, recommends other good bamboos for screening. His favorite is the weaver's bamboo (*Bambusa textilis*), so-called because fibers from the thin-walled culms are used for weaving mats in Asia. It makes very tight clumps of culms that grow nice and straight to a height of 40 feet. "It's great in tight places," he says. The punting pole bamboo (*Bambusa tuloides*) is a straight, tall bamboo, growing to 50 feet, that makes extra-dense clumps.

For shorter bamboos, Shor suggests the hedge bamboos, including *Bambusa multiplex* 'Golden Goddess' and 'Fernleaf', which top out at 10 feet. Even though these gracefully arch outward, he says they makes good screens. Hedge bamboos are usually available at nurseries. The American Bamboo Society puts out a source list of 300-plus bamboos.

All of the bamboos suggested so far are clumping kinds, which more or less stay in one spot. The other type, called running bamboo, sends its creeping rhizomes outward, sometimes great distances. Horror stories about bamboo running amok have given all bamboos an undeserved bad reputation. It is said runners can

---

BANISHING BAMBOO

While the American Bamboo Society's mission is promoting bamboo, it does have a solution for getting rid of unwanted stands: Starve them. Cut the bamboo to the ground. Break off new shoots as they appear, or paint them with the herbicide Roundup. Plants allowed to make new leaves will manufacture food for the roots, and you will end up at square one. Sever any roots to an existing stand—say, the one in the neighbor's yard—that might be supplying food. This will keep the herbicide from killing their bamboo. Keep at it, and in time the roots will die. Unfortunately, there are no faster or easier solutions.

be controlled with a buried, sloping barrier, which forces the aggressive rhizomes up and over so they can be spotted and lopped off. But nothing easily contains them.

The very pretty black bamboo (*Phyllostachys nigra*) is a runner that needs either a lot of room or some kind of containment. Common golden bamboo (*Phyllostachys aurea*) is another yard-eater.

With clumping bamboos there are no such worries. They are not maintenance-free, however. The inner culms in old clumps begin to die out in time and must be pruned out to make room for new, vigorous shoots. Some clumps get so thick that it's nearly impossible to cut out the old culms. Bamboo fanciers use high-powered electric reciprocating saws (such as a Sawzall) to get between the dense culms.

Bamboos are really big grasses, and, like lawns, they love water and fertilizer. Give them both to grow; withhold both to slow them down. They also need the mineral silica, which they use to make those sturdy canes. Leaf litter left as a mulch recycles the silica to the bamboo. Cart the litter away, however, and silica will need to be added. The leaf litter is actually quite decorative, and, once clumps settle in, new shoots will burst through it with amazing speed. You'll have a grove in no time.

American Bamboo Society, 2655 Ellentown Road, La Jolla, CA 92037; on the web at
    www.bamboo.org/abs.
The bamboo collection at Quail Botanical Gardens, 230 Quail Gardens Drive, Encinitas, CA 92023;
    telephone 760.436.3036; on the web at www.qbgardens.com.

❦ ❦ ❦

Choosing the Right Tree

THE POWER POLE COVER-UP: EPISODE ONE

Imagine my surprise at finding a telephone pole in my back yard—although I am partly to blame for its sudden appearance. When our new neighbors mentioned that they couldn't grow anything in their back yard, I pointed at the huge old avocado back by the fence. The tree covered most of their tiny yard and part of mine as well. Nothing could grow in its dense shade—except for some clivias on our side of the fence.

To add insult to injury, it produced only a handful of avocados each year. Down it came.

I shed no tears over its disappearance, but I was surprised to discover that it had hidden a utility pole in the corner of their yard. I had been vaguely aware of its existence but had had no idea how many additional lines the cable and phone companies had been stringing on it. Suddenly the pole was the central feature of my garden.

How could I hide this thing? I started to wonder. I decided to call a few garden designers to see what planting choices they could offer.

Landscape architect Rick Fisher, of Toyon Design in Altadena, said that in his own yard he's covered the pole with morning glories, which is "real unpopular" with the utility companies since they have to cut them off about twice a year. Morning glories had been my wife's first thought. However, Santa Barbara landscape architect Owen Dell said, "The worst thing you can do is plant a vine on it. It drives the utility companies crazy, and it draws attention to the pole."

In clients' gardens, Fisher has used Nichol's willow-leafed peppermint (*Eucalyptus nicholii*). "What you want is an upright, lacy tree about 30 feet tall that will soften the pole and draw the eye away from it," Fisher said. This graceful 30- to 40-foot eucalyptus with furrowed, reddish-brown bark filled the bill.

Actually, several small eucalyptus would have worked. Another was *Eucalyptus sideroxylon* 'Rosea', with deeply furrowed bark the color of a creosote-covered utility pole. Though the tree ranges from 20 feet to 80 feet, most I'd seen were narrow and not too tall. I liked the idea of the bark color being similar to the pole's.

If I followed the advice of Claremont landscape architect Bob Perry and planted two trees in front of the pole, the pole would appear to be the third trunk in a little grove of eucalyptus. As all design students know, three of anything is aesthetically better than one or two.

I also liked the fact that eucalyptus is fast growing.

Fisher had also used the shoestring acacia (*Acacia stenophylla*), another fast-growing, graceful 30-footer, but it is an even filmier tree, with long (to 16 inches!), narrow leaves and a droopy habit. This would cast virtually no shade, and the pole would be visible behind it. It wouldn't conceal so much as veil.

However, as Bill Evans, the distinguished tree expert and landscape architect for the several Disney theme parks, pointed out, "You don't have to obliterate the pole, just give the eye something else to rest on."

So pole hiders don't have to be dense. If I wanted dense, an Italian cypress in front of the pole would hide it but probably wouldn't look that great. A little obvious, it would make such a strong statement that the eye would be drawn to the pole right away. Anyone would know that I was trying to hide it, none too successfully. Wires would seem to be sprouting from its top.

Evans has introduced a group of evergreen trees new to this country but native to Japan. They were found during a long search for evergreens hardy enough to survive at Disney World in Orlando, Florida, which gets colder than it does here. In Tokyo, they are the backbone for Disney's park. One of these, the Japanese blueberry tree (*Elaeocarpus decipiens*), is fast and upright to 30 feet. Wholesale grower Monrovia Nursery Company is now raising it (the company has an exhaustive web site). It would do a fine job of pole concealment, said Evans.

Perry also suggested sweetshade (*Hymenosporum flavum*), an underutilized Australian tree. It looks a bit like a pittosporum, with shiny, dark-green leaves and yellow flowers that smell of orange blossoms. Growing upright to 30 feet, but slowly, it is not dense and looks nice planted in small groves.

Fisher also brought up another point: Plant the tree too far from the pole and it won't effectively hide it; plant it too close and the utility companies will behead it.

Landscape architect Gordon Kurtis of Los Angeles suggested several trees that are "vertical, evergreen, fast and cheap," including the madrone-like Brisbane box (*Lophostemon confertus*, formerly *Tristania conferta*) and the bottle tree (*Brachychiton populneus*), which is tough enough for the low desert.

The obvious choice, Kurtis said, is the cajeput tree (*Melaleuca quinquenervia*, sometimes sold as *Melaleuca leucadendra*), because it is as upright as a birch and a better choice for Southern California. It grows to 30 feet and will obscure a pole. Its thick, spongy bark is its biggest attraction. Its cousin, the flaxleaf paperbark (*Melaleuca linariifolia*), is not as vertical but is a little more elegant. It also has spongy bark and looks like a puffy white cloud when it is in bloom.

Pittosporum undulatum, *Podocarpus gracilior* and *Prunus caroliniana* are all fast, classic screening trees that need some regular pruning to keep them from spreading too much, but they will screen a pole. Two of these are what Dell called "trees

---

LANDSCAPE PROFESSIONALS' LIST OF POLE-HIDING TREES

- Brisbane box (*Lophostemon confertus*, formerly *Tristania conferta*)
- cajeput tree (*Melaleuca quinquenervia*)
- *Eucalyptus sideroxylon* 'Rosea'
- flaxleaf paperbark (*Melaleuca linariifolia*)
- Japanese blueberry tree (*Elaeocarpus decipiens*)
- Nichol's willow-leafed peppermint (*Eucalyptus nicholii*)
- *Podocarpus gracilior*
- shoestring acacia (*Acacia stenophylla*)
- sweetshade (*Hymenosporum flavum*)

with a lower-case *t*," or treelike shrubs, as opposed to "trees with a capital *T*," which get really big. To that list he added the native mountain mahogany (*Cerocarpus betuloides*), which is what hides the pole in his yard.

Big shrubs like these are not a bad idea. "Sometimes you don't have to put the tree right next to the pole," Dell said. "All you have to do is put the tree or shrub somewhere between where you sit and the pole. That might be only partway out into the garden, but the canopy will still block the view." This struck me as a good idea—then the tree won't interfere with the wires on the pole, and the utility company will leave it alone.

He also suggested "making the garden really beautiful so the eye doesn't go to the pole." To my mind, I had already done that, but my eye still went to the pole. And I already had a *Melaleuca linariifolia* in back. Given the other choices, I began to think a eucalyptus might be my best option.

However, choosing a tree is a huge decision with lasting effect, so I decided to keep an open mind for a while. In the meantime, I thought I might plant a morning glory at the pole's base. If the utility company wanted to complain, they certainly knew where to find me. I had a few complaints of my own, about ugly, messy-looking poles.

Monrovia Nursery Company is on the web at www.monrovia.com.

THE POWER POLE COVER-UP: EPISODE TWO

In the weeks following Episode One's appearance in the newspaper, I thought for sure I'd hear from my utility company, the Department of Water and Power, about my plans to hide its pole. Instead I heard from Southern California Edison.

Landscape architect Randall Williams, manager of Edison's tree compliance program, voiced concern that some of the trees recommended by the landscape professionals were too big (though none grew taller than 35 feet, the height of the average pole). He had some fascinating information from the other side of this plantsperson-versus-power-company scuffle.

For instance, Edison has about 1.5 million poles, of which 1.2 million have trees growing under the wires. Only about 30 percent of those are in back yards, Williams said. The utility trims 740,000 trees each year to keep them out of the power lines, which costs about $28 million, "even though we don't own any of these trees," he said. (However, poles and lines are usually inside a power company easement through back yards.)

Edison maintains an inventory of trees growing near power poles, enabling Williams' department to determine which trees need pruning most often and which cause the most trouble.

Palm trees are far and away the biggest troublemakers, which came as a surprise to me because they can barely be called "trees." But chances are good that any time there is an electrical outage in your neighborhood, it was caused by flying palm fronds. According to Williams, Edison cleans up palms that are as many as eight blocks from the power lines. During Santa Ana winds, he said, "old fronds become like airfoils and fly for blocks," knocking down lines.

A palm can't be pruned, just tidied up. Cut off the top and it dies. You may have seen some of these topless palms around town—that look is reason enough to keep palms well away from utility lines.

Also included in Edison's inventory of problem trees is, not surprisingly, the blue gum eucalyptus (*Eucalyptus globulus*), but also the red gum (*Eucalyptus camaldulensis*) and the popular silver dollar gum (*Eucalyptus polyanthemos*). Many people buy the silver dollar type because it looks so good in a nursery can with its nearly round silvery leaves. But it quickly grows to as high as 60 feet tall.

I did have eucalyptus on my pole-hiding list, but much shorter kinds. Even Edison has small eucalyptus on its list of acceptable trees.

Ash and poplars are other troublemakers.

One problem plant, the giant timber bamboo, had been suggested by one of the designers. Edison has about 200 *Bambusa oldhamii* growing under power lines in

---

THE UTILITY COMPANY'S LIST OF POLE-HIDING TREES

Following is Southern California Edison's list of acceptable trees to plant within 15 feet of a power pole. Note that many of these "trees" are simply big shrubs.

- blue palo verde (*Ceridium floridum*)
- bronze loquat (*Eriobotrya deflexa*)
- citrus
- coral gum (*Eucalyptus torquata*)
- crape myrtle (*Lagerstroemia indica*)
- desert willow (*Chilopsis linearis*)
- flowering plum (*Prunus cerasifera*)
- Japanese black pine (*Pinus thunbergii*)
- Japanese maple (*Acer palmatum*)
- mayten (*Maytenus boaria*)
- New Zealand Christmas tree (*Metrosideros excelsus*)
- orchid tree (*Bauhinia blakeana*)
- peppermint tree (*Agonis flexuosa*)
- persimmon
- *Raphiolepis* 'Majestic Beauty'
- red-flowering gum (*Eucalyptus ficifolia*)
- redbud (*Cercis occidentalis*)
- strawberry tree (*Arbutus unedo*)
- toyon (*Heteromeles arbutifolia*)
- *Xylosma congestum*

Many small trees will help hide a utility pole, but don't plant one so close that
the utility company must prune it into an awkward shape.

its inventory, which is more giant bamboo than I thought grew in all of Southern
California. It's a major problem because each new shoot promptly grows up into the
lines (they can grow to 50 feet), so Edison must check them frequently.

Ideally, Edison would like to prune trees near its poles only every five years,
though the utility ends up pruning many every three years and a few more frequently than that. There are about 1,400 power outages every year caused by trees,
and only a little less than half of those occur during storms. Outages, it turns out,
can be caused by trees bumping or rubbing against power lines.

If branches wear through the lines' insulation, trees can carry voltage to the
ground, causing circuit breakers to trip, shutting off a neighborhood's power.
Williams also mentioned that trees touching power lines can carry dangerous voltage in certain weather conditions, so children should never be allowed to climb or
build forts in trees close to lines.

It's Williams' job to try to reduce these tree-related problems, and it often
puts him in the oddly uncomfortable situation, for a landscape architect, of having
to have a tree topped or taken out. Edison would prefer trees within 15 feet of the
pole to be only 20 feet tall, and even from 15 to 65 feet from the pole, the company prefers trees that grow to only 40 feet tall.

Williams was kind enough to put together a list of acceptable trees to plant
near power lines. Naturally, none grows as tall as a typical pole, but as noted in
Episode One, there are places and ways to position trees so that even short ones
can block the view of a pole.

Unfortunately, I was still staring at the ugly pole in my back yard, trying to
decide what to plant to hide it. After hearing the other side's point of view, I decided to try to keep my final choice well away from the power lines, but I wasn't sure

I could live with this 20-foot, or even 40-foot, height restriction.

A city filled with nothing but 20-foot trees that don't even get up to the roof peak on the average house would be a pretty plain place. And it's already hard enough to find spots for trees on the typical urban property. Plant and pole would just have to learn to get along in my garden.

THE POWER POLE COVER-UP:
EPISODE THREE

In my quest to hide the utility pole in my back yard, I had armed myself with lists of trees from designers and another from the utility company. Now it was time to go see some of these trees in person. I wanted to look at as many as I could, in the ground and in nursery containers. Choosing a tree is the biggest decision a gardener gets to make.

Visits to various Southern California arboretums turned up most as mature trees, so I could see what they would eventually look like. Finding them at nurseries was much more difficult, because few nurseries carry many trees these days, thanks to the cost of land.

I fell back on an old favorite, John Boething's Treeland Nursery in Woodland Hills. I'd heard it's been there since 1952, when nurseries were spacious and filled with trees for the new suburbs. Treeland has some 25 acres devoted to trees in containers of various kinds.

The valley air was warm and dry as I drove up, and the mountains were crystal clear in the distance. You enter the nursery on a dirt road and park under old California sycamores. It was a fine fall day with golden grasses, oaks and wild walnuts turning bright colors on the hillside behind the nursery. Does anyone still wonder why fall is such a great season for gardening?

There were rows and rows of trees in big wooden boxes and in extra-large plastic containers. A boxed sour gum, or tupelo (*Nyssa sylvatica*), was turning bright red by the sign on a weathered wood building that read: Information. This is where I met experienced gardener and nurseryman (and former stockbroker) Bill Schoenbeck.

He took a look at my short list of finalists and took me around to look at each, offering valuable advice, such as how big he has seen them become or how well they do in my neighborhood of West Los Angeles, where he had lived for many years. Naturally, many of Boething's trees do best in the Valley.

My short list included Australian willow (*Geijera parviflora*), shoestring acacia (*Acacia stenophylla*), peppermint tree (*Agonis flexuosa*), sweetshade (*Hymenosporum flavum*) and willow pittosporum (*Pittosporum phillyreoides*). Treeland was the only retail nursery I had called that had all five. They were all short trees, growing to less than 25 or 30 feet tall (the height of a power pole), and all were lacy, several even weeping in form, like a willow.

I had been convinced by Randall Williams, of Southern California Edison's tree compliance program, that I really didn't want to grow something that would end up in the power lines, where the power company (Los Angeles Department of Water and Power, in my case) would have to top or mangle the tree to keep it out of the lines.

I also wanted the tree to be reasonably fast-growing but more or less permanent (often fast-growing trees are short-lived). I did not want to wait for a shrub to grow tall enough to be called a tree. And I ruled out temporary fixes, such as planting something at the power pole's base, maybe ivy or morning glories, which one power company person had called a "lineman's nightmare."

So I was down to a short list of interesting trees that would probably look good in my back yard next to two citrus, not too far from my flaxleaf paperbark (*Melaleuca linariifolia*). These might not be the best choices in all back yards, but they seemed right for mine.

Schoenbeck, however, added another one, *Podocarpus henkelii*, a slow-growing, vertical tree with drooping foliage. It is rapidly becoming a trendy tree among designers, and for good reason. After looking at a few spectacular specimens, though, I decided it was a little too exotic-looking for my garden and was perhaps better used as a property-line screen.

Luckily, my wife was along to help make this weighty decision. I tend to look at plants in their nursery cans when deciding which to plant and then find a place for them in the garden. She can visualize them in the garden.

TREELAND NURSERY'S LIST OF SMALL TREES

Boething Treeland Nursery's landscape designer John Bates and nurseryman Bill Schoenbeck came up with this list.

- Australian willow (*Geijera parviflora*)
- carrot wood (*Cupaniopsis anacardioides*, or *Cupania*)
- mayten (*Maytenus boaria*)
- peppermint tree (*Agonis flexuosa*)
- *Podocarpus henkelii*

- *Rhus lancea*
- water gum (*Tristaniopsis laurina*, formerly *Tristania laurina*)
- willow pittosporum (*Pittosporum phillyreoides*)

I really liked the acacia with its incredibly long but thin leaves (and will probably find a place for it elsewhere in the garden), and the sweetshade with its shrublike foliage and fragrant flowers. The willow pittosporum won out.

It didn't look that great in a nursery can, but its dark, willowy foliage, thin and slightly twisted, would make a fine foil for the broader citrus leaves nearby. The deal was clinched when Schoenbeck showed me a photo of it in landscape architect Bob Perry's *Landscape Plants for Western Regions* (Land Design Publishing, 1992). A graceful tree indeed, which would shame the power pole into the background. "That's the one I would have picked," said Schoenbeck, as the tree was delivered by cart to my car.

Getting a 15-gallon-size tree home was no problem, as long as no one followed too close behind on the drive back to West Los Angeles. The tree stood almost 11 feet tall in its container, so it stuck out of the trunk a good seven feet. Nurseryman Justin Winston helped me load it and wrapped black plastic bags around the foliage to keep the leaves from getting windburn or blowing off. I secured the trunk lid, used a rag to cushion the lid where it hit the tree and tied a bright-red flag to the tree's tip to make my precious load legal.

We also loaded two tall, sturdy wood stakes, so I would be able to properly support the rather spindly 15-gallon pittosporum once it was in the ground. I was planting it in the fall, and while that's the best time to be planting trees, it is also the season of the Santa Ana winds.

Safely home, I placed the skinny tree to one side of the power pole, about six feet away. It had already rained, so digging a big hole was easy. I was careful not to dig it too deep, because trees do better if they are on solid, undisturbed soil that won't settle with time. I added nothing to the backfill, because trees do best without soil amendments. I did mix a little slow-acting organic fertilizer into the soil.

I untangled a few roots that might have become constricting, although the tree was not the least bit root-bound (a problem when trees sit too long in containers). I watered the hole when it was half-full, then filled it the rest of the way with soil, lightly packing it down.

I cut off the stake that came with the tree, and then drove my two sturdy stakes about 14 inches away from, and on either side of, the trunk, taking care not to impale the root ball. I found where the trunk was most flexible and used plastic ties between each stake and the trunk so the trunk could sway gently in the breezes (which makes it stronger, like flexing one's muscles). The tree looked great in its new spot and happy to be there.

A few days afterward it rained, another good reason to plant in the fall. Nothing waters in a new plant so gently or so thoroughly.

In established neighborhoods such as mine, you don't often get the chance to plant a tree. If anything, there are already too many to leave much sun for vegetables and flowers. But it's a deeply satisfying experience when you follow all the tree-planting rules and the tree actually seems happy and vibrant, once you cut it from its stake and it's swaying in the gentle offshore autumn breezes.

Proper planting practices should also make the tree grow fast, so it would be hiding that power pole in no time.

Boething Treeland Nursery, 23475 Long Valley Road, Woodland Hills, CA 91367; telephone 818.883.1222.

SRO FOR SMALL TREES

Q: Can you think of a small evergreen (or nearly evergreen) tree to plant in a little area? I'm hoping to find something without invasive roots but more interesting than the usual carrot wood, Brazilian pepper, oleander or crape myrtle.

—S.B., WEST HILLS

A: After talking with several experts—Thousand Oaks landscape architect Ken Smith, who wrote the excellent *Western Home Landscaping* (HP Books, 1978), landscape architect Bob Perry, author of *Landscape Plants for Western Regions* (Land Design Publishing, 1992), and UC Cooperative Extension specialist Donald H. Hodel, who wrote *Exceptional Trees of Los Angeles* (California Arboretum Foundation, 1988)—I can recommend some good small trees.

Because no tree is perfect, look each up in the Sunset *Western Garden Book* (Sunset Publishing) or in Perry's encyclopedic reference to make sure it's right for your situation and to confirm that it grows in your area. None of these should be unusually messy or have invasive roots.

For really small spaces, consider *Raphiolepis* 'Majestic Beauty' or pineapple guava (*Feijoa sellowiana*), which are both big shrubs trained and sold as small trees. Most of these other trees are about 25 feet tall at maturity, perfect for small gardens.

Several small willowlike trees make elegant, draping backgrounds, including Australian willow (*Geijera parviflora*), *Podocarpus gracilior* and the peppermint tree (*Agonis flexuosa*), though this last willowlike tree is not hardy in the San Fernando Valley.

The very trim water gum (*Tristaniopsis laurina*, formerly *Tristania laurina*) looks a little like a cross between a eucalyptus and a madrone, but grows to only about 10 to 15 feet tall in that many years. For a very formal, dense look, consider the small kinds of evergreen magnolia, such as the dwarf 'Little Gem' or compact 'Saint Mary'. Bronze loquats (*Eriobotrya deflexa*) also have big leaves, but the effect is coarser. Carolina laurel cherry (*Prunus caroliniana*) makes a dense, formal, glossy-leaved small tree.

For a completely different, spare look, consider the architectural palo verdes, *Cercidium* and *Parkinsonia*. Both are deciduous. Although their hardiness is in doubt in the San Fernando Valley, other spectacular flowering trees stay on the small side, including the narrow and upright firewheel tree (*Stenocarpus sinuatus*), trumpet tree (*Tabebuia*), red-flowering and coral gums (*Eucalyptus ficifolia* and *Eucalyptus torquata*) and the spectacular gold-medallion tree (*Cassia leptophylla*). Several species of the orchid tree (*Bauhinia*) thrive in the Valley, and the elegant fringe tree (*Chionanthus retusus*) flowers heavily inland.

Although common, crape myrtles (*Lagerstroemia indica*) are one of the best small flowering trees for the Valley; don't scratch them off the list. Coastal gardeners often can't grow certain varieties because they mildew so badly. Even inland, look for the mildew-resistant varieties, such as 'Muskogee' or 'Natchez'.

Chitalpa (*Chitalpa tashkentensis*) is a fast-growing, tough, deciduous tree that grows only to about 30 feet. The Chinese pistache (*Pistacia chinensis*) is another small-to-medium deciduous tree that turns flaming orange in fall in the Valley and other colder areas. Redbuds are handsome small deciduous trees, especially *Cercis canadensis*, or the variety with burgundy leaves named 'Forest Pansy'.

You could also try sweet bay (*Laurus nobilis*) and use the leaves in cooking, or the strawberry tree, *Arbutus unedo* or *Arbutus* 'Marina'. Both are slow, reasonably small and strikingly handsome with deep-green leaves, the latter with reddish bark.

Be sure to check each candidate in references and in person at botanic gardens, and carefully weigh the pros and cons.

TREES FOR THE WINDY COAST

Q: We're looking for a tree for our front yard, where we get a lot of "house-directed" wind. Previous trees in that spot have blown down, produced prominent ground-level roots or had so many droppings that they killed the grass. What's a good choice?

—B.B., HUNTINGTON BEACH

A: Most of the trees listed above are sturdy, but the New Zealand Christmas tree (*Metrosideros excelsus*) is one tree that can really take your ocean wind, even salt spray if it has to. In New Zealand it grows right at the ocean's edge.

Vaguely bottlebrush-like in appearance, it is much softer and fuller—a really lovely tree—with wider leaves and bristly scarlet flowers in summer (Christmastime in New Zealand, hence the common name). It grows to only 20 or 25 feet and is slow, adding about one and a half feet of growth a year. It looks best (and is strongest) as a multitrunked tree.

It can grow in lawns but is happier with little or no irrigation if planted in heavy clay soil. It's not very messy and needs little pruning. Frost tender, it doesn't do well inland, but you can see handsome old specimens in many beach-side parks, including along the bluffs in Santa Monica. Recently a slew of very handsome metrosideros cultivars, most large shrubs, have appeared at nurseries.

For smallish windproof beach-side trees, Bill Long, at Coastal Zone Nursery in Malibu, also suggests the native Catalina ironwood (*Lyonothamnus*), which abhors irrigation and clay soils but looks handsome planted in small groves; the fast primrose tree (*Lagunaria*); the shrubby, slow-to-become-a-tree *Melaleuca nesophila*; twisted, or Hollywood, juniper; various leptospermums, and the boring but speedy, tough-as-nails myoporum. Red-flowering gum (*Eucalyptus ficifolia*) is a spectacular small tree for the coast when in full flower. All these trees are evergreen.

What the Heck Does That Mean?

Garden Jargon

I F A GARDENER MENTIONS that he plans to deadhead this weekend and another says she's potting up, what exactly is going on? Gardeners have their own vocabulary, words that may not even be in the dictionary. Even if they are, they have other meanings unique to the world of growing things.

allée *n* [French] : swath of lawn, path or road with overhanging trees on each side; a classy device to focus attention in grand gardens.

amendment *n* : any material added to a soil that improves drainage, aeration and tilth; usually an organic material or mix of materials, such as ground bark and peat moss. Gypsum is an example of an amendment that chemically improves soils. Amendments may have nutrient value but should not be confused with fertilizer or potting mix.

annual *n* : plant that lives for only one season and propagates itself by setting seed.

bed *n* : area in a garden where certain plants are grown (as in a bed of roses) and that typically requires more than ordinary work, so unlike the piece of furniture designed for repose.

bedding out *v* : setting out and planting bedding plants.

bedding plant *n* : plant sold by nurseries that is meant to be planted in quantity, to live for only one season and then be taken out; usually refers to annuals but may include perennials that are grown for only a season.

bolt *v* : to stop making leaves and suddenly send up a seed stalk (as when lettuce bolts and turns bitter).

border *n* : narrow bed that borders a lawn, patio or path. Usually of perennials (as in a perennial border, the classic English contrivance in which perennials are massed together in tiers).

botanical name *n* : proper Latin scientific name; used to denote plant classification. Necessary for accurate identification because many plants share common names. Italicized in text.

broadcast *v* : to scatter seed.

bud *n* : flower, leaf or branch that has yet to develop.

bud union *n* : bulge at the base of a plant that has been grafted or budded onto the rootstock of another. Many roses, citrus and deciduous fruit trees have bud unions.

chill *n* : hours of chilling (usually defined as temperatures below 45 degrees) required by plants that originate in cold climates, to flower, fruit or grow.

compost *n* : organic material, usually clippings, fallen leaves and other healthy garden debris, that is left, or made, to rot, usually in a pile. In England, compost can also be any potting soil or amendments. This confusion has spread to the United States, where many organic products are called composts, although commercial composts, which usually contain rock dust and other nutrients, are more like fertilizers than amendments.

compost *v* : to make compost.

cross *n* : plant with dissimilar parents.

crown *n* : base of a plant, where roots meet the stem. A critical area susceptible to water-induced diseases. Many gardeners plant so the crown is a little higher than the surrounding soil so it does not remain too wet. Mulches should be kept clear of the crown.

cultivar *n* : selected plant variety found in gardens and nurseries (a "cultivated variety"); usually propagated by cuttings so it is identical to its parents. In text, appears in single quotation marks, as in *Pittosporum tobira* 'Wheeler's Dwarf'.

cut back *v* : to remove the dead or unsightly foliage on perennials in winter.

cutting *n* : section of stem (usually several inches of the tip) that has been cut off. In propagation, its lower leaves are removed, and it is partly buried in sand so it will form roots.

deadhead *v* : to remove spent flowers from plants to promote more bloom. Some gardeners do this manually, creating a kind of mini shear by pressing a thumbnail grown long enough against a forefinger.

dibble *n* : small tool used for transplanting or pricking out seedlings.

die back, die down *v* : tendency of foliage on many herbaceous perennials to die completely to the ground each fall or winter. Dead foliage can safely be cut off and in many cases must be. Completely new foliage and stems regrow in spring.

disbud *v* : to remove buds from flower clusters so the remaining flowers grow larger. Gardeners often remove the largest central bud from floribunda roses so the rest makes a larger spray.

divide *v* : to separate clumps of plants into smaller, plantable pieces. Some perennials require dividing, as their centers grow old and die or stop flowering.

double dig *v* : to prepare soil in vegetable beds and perennial borders in the following manner: First, remove a row of soil (reserving it for the last row), then loosen and add amendments to the soil underneath. Turn the upper soil from the next row, amend it, and put it in the previous row. The soil underneath is then improved. And so on. Double digging is the preferred way to prepare soil for high-use areas of the garden, though it is seldom practiced, for obvious reasons.

drainage *n* : the downward movement of water through a soil. Good drainage means that water percolates easily; with bad drainage, water remains stationary and the soil becomes soggy, a condition fatal to many plants. Adding organic amendments, gypsum or even sand separates soil particles and improves drainage; so does elevating the soil.

drift *n* : long irregular planting (as in a drift of daffodils).

elevate *v* : to raise a plant and its soil, in a raised bed or on mounded soil, so that the plant's sensitive crown is above the general soil level and does not stay wet for long. Also ensures that soil is full of air.

eye *n* : not-yet-active and barely visible bud.

fertilize *v 1* : to give a plant fertilizer or plant food, by scattering, spraying or otherwise distributing. Used interchangeably with feed, though some horticulturists object to the latter because fertilize is more specific, referring as it does to the act of improving the fertility of the soil, not of directly feeding a plant. 2 : to apply pollen to a flower's pistil in order to get fruit or seed.

fertilizer *n* : material that primarily provides nutrients to plants; refers to both organic fertilizers, made from natural materials, and manufactured chemical fertilizers.

flat *n* : shallow tray holding many young nursery plants.

foliar feeding *v* : applying to the leaves fertilizer that can be absorbed through the leaves; though the effect is quick, it is short-lived.

fungus *n* : lower form of plant lacking chlorophyll; includes mushrooms, molds, rusts and yeasts. Many are involved in plant diseases, such as powdery mildew, root rot or fusarium wilt on tomatoes.

genus *n* : first half of a Latin botanical name and a plant classification category between the very broad *family* and the very specific species. In text, genus name is capitalized and in italic, as in *Rosa californica*—*Rosa* being the genus—unless it is being used as a common name. When plants are in the same genus, they tend to be similar, which is not necessarily true of plants in the same family. Genus names often get changed when plants are scrutinized by botanists. A recent example was the moving of many *Chrysanthemum* into other genera, such as *Argyranthemum* and *Leucanthemum*, a frustrating event for gardeners already struggling with botanical names.

green manure *n* : plants grown, then tilled into the soil to add organic matter and nutrients.

harden off *v* : to acclimate a plant to a new environment, as in the gradual transfer of seedlings from indoors to out.

hardiness *n* : amount of frost a plant can survive in a given locale. For instance, a plant might be hardy in Seattle but not in Boston. In California, the term is often misused; it is of little relevance to gardeners here, except those in the high desert and mountains.

heirloom *n* : older, open-pollinated variety that is preserved and handed down.

hybrid *n* : cross between two varieties of the same plant. For a plant to be sold as an F1 hybrid (which stands for *first filial generation*), the parents must be known and the pollination process carefully controlled so that the resulting offspring are very similar. Although F1 hybrids are usually more vigorous, their seeds do not produce similar plants, so there is no point saving them.

lace *v* : to thin out a tree so that it retains its natural grace and admits more light.

liner *n* : young nursery plant being grown in its first container.

mulch *n* : material used to cover the ground around plants; prevents evaporation and weed growth.

native *n* : plant that historically grew or grows naturally in a specified region before humans altered the landscape.

naturalize *v 1* : to plant in a natural, random fashion. 2 : what certain plants do (unassisted by the gardener) when they are comfortably at home in a garden, reproducing and spreading by seed or offsets.

node *n* : joint in a stem where leaves sprout.

nutrient *n* : element required by plants. Nitrogen (N), phosphorus (P) and potassium (K) are the three most important and are listed on fertilizer packages as percentages (such as an N-P-K of 10-6-6). Micronutrients, such as magnesium and iron, are deficient or unavailable in many soils and are required by plants in lesser amounts.

open-pollinated *n* : varieties of plants that naturally cross and remain true to type; seed can be saved.

over pot *v* : to move a plant into too large a container, which often results in soil that stays soggy because there is too much wet soil and too few roots.

perennial *n* : plant that lasts more than a season but never quite becomes as woody as a shrub; herbaceous perennials are those that have foliage that dies down each winter.

pinch back *v* : to nip off the very end of a shoot, stimulating the growth of more branches below; plant become bushier and more floriferous.

pollenizer *n* : variety of plant that provides pollen for fertilization of the flowers (usually to produce fruit) or another variety, as in one kind of apple needing another nearby if it is to fruit.

pollinator *n* : insect or other creature that carries pollen from one plant to another.

potager [*French*] *n* : vegetable garden laid out in a formal pattern.

pot up *v :* see repot.

preplant *n* : fertilizer added to the bottom of a hole before planting; usually a good practice because many nutrients, later applied as fertilizer to the soil surface, do not move downward through the soil to the roots, where they are needed.

prick out *v* : to gently dig up a tiny seedling and move it to a larger container.

raised bed *n* : planting bed that is purposely mounded or elevated, usually to improve drainage.

remontant *n* : plant that flowers more than once a year, iris and rose, for example.

repot *v* : to move a plant up in pot size; the English use the term pot up.

root-bound *adj* : condition in which the roots of a plant left in a container too long are so numerous as to become tangled. Unless such roots are untangled at planting time, plants will have difficulty becoming established in the garden. It is also difficult to keep root-bound plants adequately watered.

rootstock *n* : roots of one kind of plant onto which another is grafted or budded; usually of a different variety, or even of another related genus. Rootstocks may be tougher, hardier or easier to propagate; gardeners must watch out that rootstock does not make suckers that compete with or overwhelm the poor plant on top.

scion *n* : short section of branch grafted onto another plant.

set out *v* : to plant annuals or vegetables from flats or packs into the garden.

side dress *v* : to add fertilizer in a band next to rows of plants.

slip *n* : cutting.

soil *n* : what gardeners call dirt.

species *n* : second half of a botanical name, which is very specific to that plant, such as the *californica* in *Rosa californica*. Often descriptive—in this case indicating that the plant is from California, though it may latinize a person's name or describe some part of the plant. In text, always in italics and usually lowercase.

spit *n* : wonderful English measurement equal to the depth of a spade.

stake *v* : to support a plant with bamboo poles, wooden stakes or metal supports.

standard *n* : shrub grown like a small tree, with a clearly defined trunk.

sucker *n* : sprout that arises from the roots; usually applies to roses when sprouts from the rootstock (below the bud union) grow. Remove them.

systemic *n* : chemical (such as an insecticide or herbicide) that is absorbed by the roots or leaves of a plant and distributed throughout the plant. Never use systemics on edibles.

thatch *n* : dead material at the base of grass.

top *v* : to cut back only the top of a tree; not recommended because it encourages weak and, therefore, dangerous growth.

trace elements *n* : minor nutrients essential to plant health. Plants often exhibit deficiency by becoming chlorotic, the condition characterized by green veins and yellowing leaves.

transplant *n* : plant that has been, or will be, moved to a larger container or garden bed.

variety *n* : additional subdivision of botanical name indicating a slightly different version of a plant that is found in the wild. In text, in italics and often proceeded by *var.*, as in *Rosa californica var. smausii* (thankfully there is no such plant). Many plants once listed as varieties become cultivars after pedigrees are scrutinized.

virus *n* : intracellular and generally incurable plant disease; viruses can be transmitted by sucking insects, such as aphids. Removal of diseased plants is the only remedy.

water sprout *n* : growth that shoots up from the tops of trees or shrubs (not from the roots; see **sucker**).

weed *n* : plant deemed to be in the wrong place.

whip *n* : young tree with only a skinny trunk and no side branches.

zone *n* : particular climatic area mapped for agriculture, determined by high and low temperatures, ocean or inland winds and other climatological data. USDA zones are broad; more specific zones originally mapped by the State of California for agriculture were adapted and popularized by *Sunset* magazine for gardeners as Zones 1-24. These are much more useful to California gardeners than the USDA zones frequently referred to in other publications.

Index

OTHER BOOKS FROM THE LOS ANGELES TIMES

CURBSIDE L.A.
An offbeat guide to the city of angels
by Cecilia Rasmussen

Enjoy a truly eclectic tour of Los Angeles. Explore the L.A. you've not seen with enticing excursions into the city's peerless history and diversity. $19.45

DAY HIKERS' GUIDE TO SOUTHERN CALIFORNIA
by John McKinney

Walks in Southern California, from the simply scenic to the challenging, as described by Los Angeles Times hiking columnist and author John McKinney. $16.45

52 WEEKS IN THE CALIFORNIA GARDEN
by Robert Smaus

How to make the most of your garden by the foremost authority on gardening in Southern California. $17.45

IMAGINING LOS ANGELES
Photographs of a 20th Century City
Foreword by Ray Bradbury

Collected here are some 175 photos from more than a dozen Southern California archives that tell the tale of men and women from all over the world who hoped and dared on a grand scale and who turned Los Angeles into the quintessential 20th century city. $28.95

SUNSET BOULEVARD
by Amy Dawes

There isn't a street in the world like Sunset Boulevard. Dazzling and decadent, disturbing and dangerous, it stretches all the way from downtown Los Angeles to the Pacific Ocean. This guide to the sights, sounds, experiences and lost legends of Sunset Boulevard proceeds geographically, from east to west, exploring neighborhoods and linking the present and the past. $28.45

THE SAN FERNANDO VALLEY
America's Suburb
by Kevin Roderick

Valley native Kevin Roderick recounts the area's vibrant past, from its Native American residents through the Spanish, Mexican and American settlers, spinning along the way the tales that give the Valley its unique history and culture. $26.45

LOW-FAT KITCHEN
by Donna Deane

From the pages of the *Los Angeles Times* Food Section come more than 110 recipes that use fresh food flavor, not fat, to satisfy your taste buds. $20.45

THE LOS ANGELES TIMES MODERN CALIFORNIA COOKING
Staff of The Times' Food Section

A sequel to the 1981 best seller, California Cookbook, the Modern California Cooking offers more than 300 recipes that reflect the cutting edge, international cuisine for which Southern California has become so famous in recent years. An ideal companion to the 1981 volume. $22.45

SOS RECIPES
30 years of requests
by Rose Dosti

This best-selling book offers hundreds of tried-and-true recipes for all-time favorite dishes that literally range from soup to nuts. $19.45

DEAR SOS / FAVORITE RESTAURANT RECIPES
by Rose Dosti

Rose Dosti has culled her perennially popular column in the Los Angeles Times food section to hand pick 225 of your all-time favorite recipes from restaurants throughout the country. $22.45

To order, call (800) 246-4042 or
visit our web site at
www.latimes.com/bookstore